Paper Lanterns

More Quotations from the Back Pages of
The Sun

EDITED BY SY SAFRANSKY
WITH TIM McKEE & ANDREW SNEE

THE SUN PUBLISHING COMPANY
DISTRIBUTED BY NORTH ATLANTIC BOOKS

Published by:
The Sun Publishing Company
107 North Roberson Street
Chapel Hill, NC 27516
(919) 942-5282

Distributed by:
North Atlantic Books
P.O. Box 12327
Berkeley, CA 94712

The Sun Publishing Company wishes to thank North Atlantic Books
and the nonprofit Society for the Study of Native Arts and Sciences
for the distribution of this book and for their work publishing and
distributing cutting-edge literature on the relationship of mind, body,
and nature.

Grateful acknowledgment to Daniel Ladinsky for his permission to
reprint his translations of Hafiz's poems "A One-Story House" and
"Buttering the Sky."

Thanks also to Tess Gallagher for permission to use "Late Fragment"
from All of Us: The Collected Poems, by Raymond Carver, copyright ©
1996 by Tess Gallagher. Reprinted by permission of Alfred A. Knopf,
a division of Random House, Inc.

Cover and book design: Robert Graham

The Sun Publishing Company's publications are available by visiting
www.thesunmagazine.org or by calling (515) 237-3698.

North Atlantic Books' publications are available through most
bookstores. For further information visit www.northatlanticbooks.com
or call (800)733-3000.

Library of Congress Cataloging-in-Publication Data

Paper lanterns : more quotations from the back pages of the Sun /
edited by Sy Safransky with Tim McKee and Andrew Snee.
     p. cm.
     ISBN 978-1-58394-246-8
     1. Quotations, English. I. Safransky, Sy. II. McKee, Tim. III. Snee,
Andrew. IV. Sun (Chapel Hill, N.C.)
PN6083.P37 2010
082—dc22
                                                       2010023470

10 9 8 7 6 5 4 3 2 1

Contents

Introduction

A recent visitor to our magazine office was surprised by the number of quotation books on my shelves. "There must be more than a hundred," he said. That sounded about right to me. "It's like a shrine," he went on, "a shrine to wisdom." Well, I said, I'd never thought of the books that way. I collect them, I explained, not to venerate the masters or to impress visitors but for the same reason a carpenter keeps his or her tools within reach.

For more than thirty years I've gathered quotations each month for the Sunbeams page in *The Sun*. Many come from those anthologies. Others are suggested by subscribers, or they're passages I've come across in my own reading, or, more recently, online. (It's too bad that so many Internet quotation sites are as unreliable as they are irresistible. It's a shame to have your head turned by a turn of phrase only to discover the next morning that the quotation was either inaccurate or misattributed. And you thought you were in love.)

Readers unfamiliar with *The Sun* might imagine that a feature called Sunbeams is unrelentingly positive, but the page is intended to challenge as well as comfort; to celebrate the ineffable beauty around us without ignoring the crushing injustices in our midst; to embrace all of life: the joys, the heartache, what Zorba in the film *Zorba the Greek* calls "the full catastrophe."

To come up with the right mix each month, we spend hours sorting through quotations from essays, fiction, poems, speeches, plays, films, newspaper articles, magazine interviews, and, if I can decipher my own handwriting, the note I hastily scribbled when a friend quoted her favorite author. We set the bar high: Nothing too platitudinous or flowery or stodgy or cynical or mean-spirited. No spiritual band-aids. No political bromides. No pompous aphorisms impatiently waiting to be carved into stone.

What a pleasure, then, to finally seat our honored guests around the dinner table: Henry Miller next to Mother Teresa, who is sitting beside Anaïs Nin, who is whispering something to Martin Luther King Jr. as he shakes hands with someone whose name I've only just learned. There's no caste system here; fame doesn't guarantee someone a seat at the table. Truthfulness gets them a seat. An arrow shot straight through my heart — pitch-perfect language, not a word wasted — gets them a seat. So does a shout from the rooftop, a kick in the ass. "Who can confidently say what ignites a certain combination of words, causing them to explode in the mind?" E.B. White asks. "Who knows why certain notes in music are capable of stirring the listener deeply? . . . These are high mysteries."

Paper Lanterns is our second compilation of Sunbeams. (The first, *Sunbeams: A Book of Quotations*, was published in 1991.) Unlike the earlier collection, there is an order to the quotations in *Paper Lanterns*, which takes us on a journey through innocence and experience, love and loss, disillusionment and awakening. This isn't a reference book organized by topic, however, but an anthology that, for better and for worse, reflects the sensibility of its editor. That's why some great thinkers appear again and again and others don't show up at all. (Full disclosure: As a college student I abandoned James Joyce's *Ulysses* midsentence — those were long sentences — and squandered the rest of the twentieth century ignoring the canon and reading whatever I damn well pleased.)

We've taken great pains to make sure that every quotation in *Paper Lanterns* is accurate and properly attributed. Sometimes, to provide necessary context, we list the novel, short story, play, or film from which the quotation comes. Although we've added a few punctuation marks to enhance readability, we generally took a hands-off approach. This includes allowing the occasional use of gender-exclusive language. Though we reject sexism, rewriting history is above our pay grade. If a nineteenth-century writer used only masculine pronouns, or made a sweeping statement about "mankind," we let it stand.

Putting this book together was a collective effort. Thanks go to editorial associates Erica Berkeley and Luc Saunders, who help me assemble the Sunbeams page each month; to Erika Simon and Elizabeth

Woodman for their assistance in shaping the text; to Seth Mirsky and Brent Winter for their careful proofreading; to Marianne Erhardt for her rigorous fact checking; to art director Robert Graham for making the book so handsome; to senior editor Andrew Snee for making the book more readable; and especially to managing editor Tim McKee, who made sure that a first draft of this anthology didn't continue to languish in a dusty corner of my office, and who shepherded the manuscript through every stage of production. My deepest gratitude goes to those we've quoted — men and women who labored long and hard to express in a few words a lifetime of experience; others who rarely wrote but paused in the middle of a busy life or a sleepless night with pen in hand, who wept and found a way to make of their suffering a gift, who laughed and found a way to make us laugh, too.

It's true, of course, that noble and thoughtful and lovely words haven't kept humans from killing each other and ravaging the planet. Nor have they necessarily rescued us from our self-created hells. Perhaps, as Hermann Hesse wrote in *Siddhartha*, "the wisdom which a wise man tries to communicate always sounds foolish. . . . Knowledge can be communicated, but not wisdom. One can find it, live it, be fortified by it, do wonders through it, but one cannot communicate and teach it." Perhaps I shy away from the notion of a shrine to wisdom because I know that one person's wisdom is another person's sacrilege, or worse: fighting words, a reason to go to war.

Still, Hesse kept writing book after book in an attempt to communicate *something*. I keep gathering quotations. For who's to say the world wouldn't be in an even worse fix had these voices not been raised in anger and praise? Who's to say that some well-worn but nonetheless powerful adage hasn't prevented one more blow from being struck or one more tree from being felled — or yanked someone up from the depths, gasping but still breathing?

May the words in this book deepen our empathy for our brilliant, bewildered, long-suffering human tribe. May they shine a little light when the darkness is upon us.

Sy Safransky
Editor and publisher, *The Sun*

PAPER LANTERNS

Flash, Flash, I Love You

Flash, Flash, I love you, but we only have fourteen hours left to save the earth.

Dale Arden, in the movie *Flash Gordon*

Millions and millions of years would still not give me half enough time to describe that tiny instant of eternity when you put your arms around me and I put my arms around you.

Jacques Prévert

Restore me with raisins, comfort me with apples, for I am sick with love.

Song of Solomon 2:5

I wasn't kissing her. I was whispering in her mouth.

Chico Marx

I never knew how to worship until I knew how to love.

Henry Ward Beecher

Music I heard with you was more than music, / And bread I broke with you was more than bread.

Conrad Aiken

There is only one big thing — desire. And before it, when it is big, all is little.

Willa Cather

. . . the first letter he received from her, and his feeling on seeing his own name in her handwriting.

Albert Camus

The crime of loving is forgetting.

Maurice Chevalier

Love is tremendously passionate and therefore it acts immediately. It has no time interval between the seeing and the doing. And when you have that love you can put away all your sacred books, all your gods.

J. Krishnamurti

Real love is a pilgrimage. It happens when there is no strategy, but it is very rare because most people are strategists.

Anita Brookner

Journeys end in lovers meeting.

William Shakespeare

Love is the final end of the world's history, the amen of the universe.

Novalis

Among those whom I like or admire, I can find no common denominator, but among those I love, I can: all of them make me laugh.

W.H. Auden

Love doesn't just sit there, like a stone; it has to be made, like bread; remade all the time, made new.

Ursula K. Le Guin

☙

There is something that happens between men and women in the dark that seems to make everything else unimportant.

Tennessee Williams,
A Streetcar Named Desire

A man falls in love through his eyes, a woman through her ears.

Woodrow Wyatt

Their bodies, like strangers meeting for the first time, introduced themselves to each other.

P.V. Narasimha Rao

To love one person with a private love is poor and miserable; to love all is glorious.

Thomas Traherne

The idea that nations should love one another, or that business concerns or marketing boards should love one another, or that a man in Portugal should love a man in Peru of whom he has never heard — it is absurd, unreal, dangerous. . . . The fact is we can only love what we know personally. And we cannot know much.

E.M. Forster

I am Tarzan of the Apes. I want you. I am yours. You are mine. We will live here together always in my house. I will bring you the best fruits, the tenderest deer, the finest meats that roam the jungle. I will hunt for you. I am the greatest of the jungle fighters. I will fight for you. I am the mightiest of the jungle fighters.

Edgar Rice Burroughs,
Tarzan of the Apes

I snore loudly, drink exuberantly, work excessively, and my future is drawing to a close. But I am tall and Jewish and I do love you.

David O. Selznick, proposing
marriage to Irene Mayer

She married a man who . . . became a myth; then the myth returned home and proved to be just a man after all.

Nelson Mandela, on the breakdown
of his marriage to Winnie Mandela

People come into your life for a reason, a season, or a lifetime. When you figure out which it is, you know exactly what to do.

Michelle Vestur

Visiting someone in a hospital recently, I watched an elderly couple. The man was in a wheelchair, the wife sitting next to him in the visitors' room. For the half-hour that I watched they never exchanged a word, just held hands and looked at each other, and once or twice the man patted his wife's face. The feeling of love was so thick in that room that I felt I was sharing in their communion and was shaken all day by their pain, their love, something sad and also joyful: the fullness of a human relationship.

Eda LeShan

He listened with the intense interest one feels in a stranger's life, the interest the young mistake for love.

Graham Greene,
The Heart of the Matter

Strangers become friends, become lovers, become husbands and wives, become ex-husbands and ex-wives, become strangers.

Brendan Gill

A simple enough pleasure, surely, to have breakfast alone with one's husband, but how seldom married people in the midst of life achieve it.

Anne Morrow Lindbergh

It was an unspoken pleasure that having . . . ruined so much and repaired little, we had endured.

Lillian Hellman

You know what getting married is? It's agreeing to taking this person who right now is at the top of his form, full of hopes and ideas, feeling good, looking good, wildly interested in you because you're the same way, and sticking by him while he slowly disintegrates. And he does the same for you. You're his responsibility now and he's yours. If no one else will take care of him, you will. If everyone else rejects you, he won't. What do you think love is? Going to bed all the time?

Jane Smiley, *At Paradise Gate*

That night, when the party was over, Howard went to our bedroom and lay in wait for me, wearing only his suit of tarnished flesh. I walked toward the bed through the pewter light, dressed in all the awful beauty of my years. We looked at one another.

Hilma Wolitzer

৩

Why is it better to love than be loved? It is surer.

Sacha Guitry

Maybe journey is not so much a journey ahead, or a journey into space, but a journey into presence. The farthest place on earth to journey is into the presence of the person nearest to you.

Nelle Morton

We live with one another on a rare life-sustaining planet as it makes a few dozen turns around its modest and finite star. The real news on this planet is love — why it exists, where it came from, and where it's going. How love fares against hate and indifference is the only reliable measure of historical progress that we have.

Gil Bailie

Say "I love you" to those you love. The eternal silence is long enough to be silent in, and that awaits us all.

George Eliot

Flash, Flash, I love you, but we only have fourteen hours left to save the earth.

Dale Arden, in the movie *Flash Gordon*

I carefully number the bricks of my heart for later reconstruction.

Jeff Silva

There were many ways of breaking a heart. Stories were full of hearts broken by love, but what really broke a heart was taking away its dream — whatever that dream might be.

Pearl S. Buck

Sorrows cannot all be explained away. . . . In a life truly lived, grief and loss accumulate like possessions.

Stefan Kanfer

It is only the happy who are hard, Gilles. I think perhaps it is better for the world if . . . one has a broken heart. One is then quick to recognize it elsewhere.

Helen Waddell, *Peter Abelard*

My life had got on the wrong track and my contact with men had become now a mere soliloquy. I had fallen so low that, if I had had to choose between falling in love with a woman and reading a book about love, I should have chosen the book.

> Nikos Kazantzakis,
> *Zorba the Greek*

I was made to suffer, oh yes, certainly I learned how to suffer. But is suffering so very serious? I have come to doubt it. It may be quite childish, a sort of undignified pastime. I'm referring to the kind of suffering a man inflicts on a woman or a woman on a man. It's extremely painful. I agree that it's hardly bearable. But I very much fear that this sort of pain deserves no consideration at all.

> Colette

Yes, I will go. I would rather grieve over your absence than over you.

> Antonio Porchia

When we cut flowers recklessly, carelessly, we are not paying attention to them.

> Dainin Katagiri

You out there, so secret. / What makes you think you're alone?

> Thomas McGrath

☾

One can live at a low flame. Most people do. For some, life is an exercise in moderation (best china saved for special occasions), but given something like death, what does it matter if one looks foolish now and then, or tries too hard, or cares too deeply?

> Diane Ackerman

There is a volume of love poetry in the prison library. I've memorized it page by page and can recite it word for word. Now I need someone who will listen.

> Jerome Washington

There is nothing safe about sex. There never will be.

> Norman Mailer

Sexual love is the most stupendous fact of the universe, and the most magical mystery our poor blind senses know.

> Amy Lowell

A man running after a hat is not half so ridiculous as a man running after a wife.

> G.K. Chesterton

It is something big and cosmic. What else do we have? There's only birth and death and the union of two people — and sex is the only one that happens to us more than once.

> Kathleen Winsor

I close your ears with kisses / And seal your nostrils; and round your neck you'll wear — / Nay, let me work — a delicate chain of kisses. / Like beads they go around, and not one misses / To touch its fellow on either side.

> D.H. Lawrence

That was a very racy remark for Gladys, whose idea of wild sex was Fred Astaire loosening his tie.

> Susan Isaacs,
> *Shining Through*

It's ill-becoming for an old broad to sing about how bad she wants it. But occasionally we do.

Lena Horne

There is one thing I would break up over, and that is if she caught me with another woman. I won't stand for that.

Steve Martin

If you wonder whether certain behavior constitutes infidelity, I recommend that you ask your spouse.

Frank Pittman

☾

Tamed as it may be, sexuality remains one of the demonic forces in human consciousness — pushing us at intervals close to taboo and dangerous desires, which range from the impulse to commit sudden arbitrary violence upon another person to the voluptuous yearning for the extinction of one's consciousness, for death itself. Even on the level of simple physical sensation and mood, making love surely resembles having an epileptic fit at least as much as, if not more than, it does eating a meal or conversing with someone.

Susan Sontag

We do not go to bed in single pairs; even if we choose not to refer to them, we still drag there with us the cultural impediments of our social class, our parents' lives, our bank balances, our sexual and emotional expectations, our whole biographies — all the bits and pieces of our unique existences.

Angela Carter

Everyone lies about sex, more or less, to themselves if not to others, to others if not to themselves, exaggerating its importance or minimizing its pull.

Daphne Merkin

Pornography is rather like trying to find out about a Beethoven symphony by having someone tell you about it and perhaps hum a few bars.

Robertson Davies

Condoms aren't completely safe. A friend of mine was wearing one and got hit by a bus.

Bob Rubin

If our sex life were determined by our first youthful experiments, most of the world would be doomed to celibacy. In no area of human experience are human beings more convinced that something better can be had if only they persevere.

P.D. James

I didn't want it like that. Not against the bricks or hunkering in somebody's car. I wanted it to come undone like gold thread, like a tent full of birds.

Sandra Cisneros, *One Holy Night*

It's all this cold-hearted fucking that is death and idiocy.

D.H. Lawrence

You can't remember sex. You can remember the fact of it, and recall the setting, and even the details, but the sex of the sex cannot be remembered, the substantive truth of it; it is by nature self-erasing; you can remember its anatomy and be left with a judgment as to the degree of your liking of it, but whatever it is as a splurge of being, as a loss, as a charge of the conviction of love stopping your heart like your execution, there is no memory of it in the brain, only the deduction that it happened and that time passed, leaving you with a silhouette that you want to fill in again.

E.L. Doctorow

You discover real true love at the moment when you are making love with your partner and realize that all your life together is a single continuous and ongoing act of lovemaking, in the course of which you happen to occasionally disengage bodies altogether for hours at a time. It is not something to which you return — it is something you suddenly find that you have never really left.

Spider and Jeanne Robinson

Sex is hardly ever just about sex.

Shirley MacLaine

I've looked on a lot of women with lust. I've committed adultery in my heart many times. This is something God recognizes I will do — and I have done it — and God forgives me for it.

Jimmy Carter

Guys would sleep with a bicycle if it had the right color lip gloss on. They have no shame. They're like bull elks in a field. It's a scent to them, a smell.

Tori Amos

Men look at women. Women watch themselves being looked at.

John Berger

In asking forgiveness of women for our mythologizing of their bodies, for being unreal about them, we can only appeal to their own sexuality, which is different but not basically different, perhaps, from our own. For women, too, there seems to be that tangle of supplication and possessiveness, that descent towards infantile undifferentiation, that omnipotent helplessness, that merger with the cosmic mother-warmth, that flushed pulse-quickened leap into overestimation, projection, general mix-up.

John Updike

If we forgive God for his crime against us, which is to have made us finite creatures, he will forgive our crime against him, which is that we are finite creatures.

Simone Weil

☽

The sex that is presented to us in everyday culture feels strange to me; its images are fragments, lifeless, removed from normal experience. Real sex, the sex in our cells and in the space between our neurons, leaks out and gets into things and stains our vision and colors our lives.

Sallie Tisdale

Luther, a former Augustinian friar who married, found the art of lovemaking not only delightful but sacred. In a letter to a friend, Luther is quoted as saying, "As you penetrate your wife, I'll penetrate mine, and we'll be united in Christ." Luther goes on to state that the best place to be at Christ's Second Coming is to be united in the act of making love.

Edward Hays

Nobody dies from lack of sex. It's lack of love we die from.

Margaret Atwood

Spirituality is rooted in desire. We long for something we can neither name nor describe, but which is no less real because of our inability to capture it with words.

Mary Jo Weaver

Sexuality poorly repressed unsettles some families; well repressed, it unsettles the whole world.

Karl Kraus

Sex is something I really don't understand too hot. . . . I keep making up these sex rules for myself, and then I break them right away.

J.D. Salinger,
The Catcher in the Rye

A kiss may ruin a human life.

Oscar Wilde

If kissing and being engaged were this inflammatory, marriage must burn clear to the bone. I wondered how flesh and blood could endure the ecstasy. How did married couples manage to look so calm and unexcited?

Jessamyn West

Once in my life I kissed a woman on the mouth romantically. The surprising thing about it was that she kissed in the same exact way she held a pencil and walked down the street in sandals and shook salt into a bowl of soup. Her gestures had a coherence that was utterly natural. I had expected a secret to be revealed when I kissed her, but discovered that she expressed her secret constantly, as we all do, night and day.

Bonnie Friedman

Love is not hasty to deliver us from temptation, for Love means that we be tried and purified.

Mary Baker Eddy

If the fire rages uncontrolled in a house, we call it a disastrous conflagration; if it burns in a smelting furnace, we call it a useful industrial force. In other words, our drives and impulses as they live within us are neither good nor bad, right nor wrong.

Gregory Zilboorg

To me heaven would be a big bull ring with me holding two *barrera* seats and a trout stream outside that no one else was allowed to fish in and two lovely houses in the town; one where I would have my wife and children and be monogamous and love them truly and well and the other where I would have my nine beautiful mistresses on nine different floors.

Ernest Hemingway

I think religion is the real deep entertainment — real profound and voluptuous and delicious entertainment. The real feast. . . . Nothing touches it — except if you're courting. If you're young, the hormonal thrust has its own excitement.

Leonard Cohen

When you know somebody that deeply, so many bodies lie in the bed alongside. We need a king-sized bed to contain them. Our bed is full of farmland, two hundred acres including the back pasture. And you know, that is where the best sex always is, despite the scent of cows. The Jungians say that in bed there are always at least four people, invisible man and dark surly woman. But in our bed there is a herd — siblings and offspring, his parents, my parents, and the church, full of incense and Latin. My temple, so old it's got the history of God engraved in the bedsheets. It isn't a bed. It's a text, a Russian novel.

Joan Logghe

It was an odd quandary for them. He needed sex in order to feel connected to her, and she needed to feel connected to him in order to enjoy sex.

Lisa Alther

The important thing in acting is to be able to laugh and cry. If I have to cry, I think of my sex life. If I have to laugh, I think of my sex life.

Glenda Jackson

An honorable human relationship — that is, one in which two people have the right to use the word "love" — is a process, delicate, violent, often terrifying to both persons involved, a process of refining the truths they can tell each other. It is important to do this because it breaks down human self-delusion and isolation. It is important to do this because in so doing we do justice to our own complexity. It is important to do this because we can count on so few people to go that hard way with us.

Adrienne Rich

To others we are not ourselves but a performer in their lives cast for a part we do not even know that we are playing.

Elizabeth Bibesco

Ideologies separate us. Dreams and anguish bring us together.

Eugene Ionesco

They have stopped deceiving you, not loving you. And it seems to you that they have stopped loving you.

Antonio Porchia

I wonder why love is so often equated with joy when it is everything else as well. Devastation, balm, obsession, granting and receiving excessive value, and losing it again. It is recognition, often of what you are not but might be. It sears and it heals. It is beyond pity and above law. It can seem like truth.

Florida Scott-Maxwell

On the relativity of distance: if in an all-but-empty restaurant somebody takes the table next to mine, he has come very close indeed — so close that a special reason must justify his choice. If the room is filled, the distance between two neighboring tables separates us sufficiently.

Rudolf Arnheim

When those closest to us respond to events differently than we do, when they seem to see the same scene as part of a different play, when they say things that we could not imagine saying in the same circumstances, the ground on which we stand seems to tremble and our footing is suddenly unsure.

Deborah Tannen

There are those who forget that death will come to all. For those who remember, quarrels come to an end.

The Dhammapada

The face of a lover is an unknown, precisely because it is invested with so much of oneself. It is a mystery, containing, like all mysteries, the possibility of torment.

James Baldwin

To fall in love is easy, even to remain in it is not difficult; our human loneliness is cause enough. But it is a hard quest worth making to find a comrade through whose steady presence one becomes steadily the person one desires to be.

Anna Louise Strong

A happy marriage is a long conversation which always seems too short.

Andre Maurois

Three things help me get through life successfully: an understanding husband, an extremely good analyst, and millions and millions of dollars.

Mary Tyler Moore

God is love, but get it in writing.

Gypsy Rose Lee

Never play cards with a man called Doc. Never eat at a place called Mom's. Never sleep with a woman whose troubles are worse than your own.

Nelson Algren

My grandfather ... drank ... and dated other women. Finally, my grandmother said, "Enough is enough," and she left him, which was pretty strange for the 1920s. She raised her six children herself. She did people's laundry by night and was a waitress at the Greyhound bus station in the day. The one poignant note: even though she'd thrown him out, she did his laundry for him until the day he died.

Polly Gardner

His wit was usually aggressive. Sometimes he chose the rapier. Lady Astor neither gave nor asked for quarter, and she got none from him. At a dinner party she told him, "Winston, if I were your wife, I'd poison your soup." He replied, "Nancy, if I were your husband, I'd drink it."

William Manchester

ꐂ

The music at a wedding procession always reminds me of the music of soldiers going into battle.

Heinrich Heine

The mind sees a magnificent pie in the sky; it dwells on it; it wants it; it yearns single-mindedly; the cry for more is endless.

Sai Baba

Commitment means we haven't left ourselves an escape hatch.

Charlotte Joko Beck

A young woman once said to an old woman, "What is life's heaviest burden?" And the old woman said, "To have nothing to carry."

Jewish proverb

Marriage is our last, best chance to grow up.

Joseph Barth

When he's late for dinner, I know he's either having an affair or is lying dead on the street. I always hope it's the street.

Jessica Tandy, on her husband, Hume Cronyn

Remember, you have come here having already understood the necessity of struggling with yourself — only with yourself. Therefore, thank everyone who gives you the opportunity.

G.I. Gurdjieff

Only a marriage with partners strong enough to risk divorce is strong enough to avoid it.

Carolyn Heilbrun

The state of marriage is one that requires more virtue and constancy than any other; it is a perpetual exercise of mortification.

Saint Francis de Sales

"When one of us dies, I'll move to the Riviera," said a woman to her husband when she saw the beautiful Mediterranean coast.

Richard Kehl

It has been said that the continuation of the species is due to humankind being forgiving.

The Mahabharata

What I cannot love, I overlook. Is that real friendship?

Anaïs Nin

If you were going to die soon and had only one phone call you could make, who would you call and what would you say? And why are you waiting?

Stephen Levine

☉

It takes a long time to be really married. One marries many times at many levels within a marriage. If you have more marriages than you have divorces within the marriage, you're lucky and you stick it out.

Ruby Dee

I had a rough marriage. Well, my wife was an immature woman, that's all I can say. See if this is not immature to you: I would be home in the bathroom taking a bath, and my wife would walk in whenever she felt like it and sink my boats.

Woody Allen

Thomas Edison lost much of his hearing at an early age. But . . . he and his wife attended stage plays. How did he hear the actor? His wife fingertipped key lines of dialogue in Morse code on his knee. Didn't I tell you he taught her Morse code? Then tapped out his mar-

riage proposal in her hand? She tapped
back her acceptance.

Richard Kehl

As I grew to adolescence, I imagined,
from closely observing the boredom
and vexations of matrimony, that the
act my parents committed and the one
I so longed to commit must be two different things.

Shirley Abbott

I am happy now that Charles calls on
my bedchamber less frequently than
of old. As it is, I endure but two calls a
week, and when I hear his steps outside
my door I lie down on my bed, close my
eyes, open my legs, and think of England.

Lady Alice Hillingdon

Women hope men will change after
marriage, but they don't; men hope
women won't change, but they do.

Bettina Arndt

After dinner, [Marcel] Duchamp would
take the bus to Nice to play at a chess
circle and return late with Lydie [his
first wife] lying awake waiting for him.
Even so, he did not go up to bed immediately, but set up the chess pieces to
study the position of a game he had been
playing. First thing in the morning when
he arose, he went to the chessboard to
make a move he had thought out during the night. But the piece could not
be moved. During the night Lydie had
arisen and glued down all the pieces. . . .
A few days later, Duchamp and Lydie
divorced, and he returned to the States.

Man Ray

Many who have spent a lifetime in it can
tell us less of love than the child that lost
a dog yesterday.

Thornton Wilder

Lovemaking is radical, while marriage
is conservative.

Eric Hoffer

And that heart which was a wild garden
was given to him who loved only trim
lawns. And the imbecile carried the
princess into slavery.

Antoine de Saint-Exupéry

We tend to think of the erotic as an
easy, tantalizing sexual arousal. I speak
of the erotic as the deepest life force, a
force which moves us toward living in a
fundamental way.

Audre Lorde

If my hands tremble with desire, they
tremble likewise when I reach for the
chalice on Sunday, and if lust makes me
run and caper, it is no stronger a force
than that which brings me to my knees
to say thanksgivings and litanies. What
can this capricious skin be but a blessing?

John Cheever

Love comes in at the eyes and subdues
the body. An army with banners.

Louise Bogan

What is erotic? The acrobatic play of
the imagination. The sea of memories
in which we bathe. The way we caress
and worship things with our eyes. Our

willingness to be stirred by the sight of the voluptuous. What is erotic is our passion for the liveliness of life.

Diane Ackerman

Sexual intercourse is kicking death in the ass while singing.

Charles Bukowski

The mattress, curved like a preacher's palm asking for witnesses in His name's sake, enclosed them each and every night and muffled their whispering, old-time love.

Toni Morrison, *Jazz*

We who were loved will never / unlive that crippling fever.

Adrienne Rich

However often marriage is dissolved, it remains indissoluble. Real divorce, the divorce of heart and nerve and fiber, does not exist, since there is no divorce from memory.

Virgilia Peterson

I begin to see what marriage is for. It's to keep people away from each other. Sometimes I think that two people who love each other can be saved from madness only by the things that come between them — children, duties, visits, bores, relations — the things that protect married people from each other.

Edith Wharton

Marriage is an extraordinary thing, and I doubt if any outsider — even a child of the marriage — has the right to judge.

Agatha Christie

One of the oddest features of Western Christianized culture is its ready acceptance of the myth of the stable family and the happy marriage. We have been taught to accept the myth not as a heroic ideal, something good, brave, and nearly impossible to fulfill, but as the very fiber of normal life. Given most families and most marriages, the belief seems admirable but foolhardy.

Jonathan Raban

The best marriages, like the best lives, were both happy and unhappy. There was even a kind of necessary tension, a certain tautness between the partners that gave the marriage strength, like the tautness of a full sail. You went forward on it.

Anne Morrow Lindbergh

☙

I'm not upset about my divorce. I'm only upset that I'm not a widow.

Roseanne Barr

The real killer was when you married the wrong person but had the right children.

Ann Beattie

Divorce is only less painful than the need for divorce.

Jane O'Reilly

Being married was like having a hippopotamus sitting on my face. . . . No matter how hard I pushed or which way I turned, I couldn't get up. I couldn't even breathe. . . . Hippopotamuses aren't all bad. They are what they are. But I wasn't meant to have one sitting on my face.

Faith Sullivan

I'm going to turn on the light and we'll be two people in a room looking at each other and wondering why on earth they were afraid of the dark.

Gale Wilhelm

After forty years of marriage, we still stood with broken swords in our hands.

Enid Bagnold

The goal of our life should not be to find joy in marriage, but to bring more love and truth into the world. We marry to assist each other in this task. The most selfish and hateful life of all is that of two beings who unite in order to enjoy life. The highest calling is that of the man who has dedicated his life to serving God and doing good, and who unites with a woman in order to further that purpose.

Leo Tolstoy

To love is to suffer. To avoid suffering one must not love. But then one suffers from not loving. Therefore, to love is to suffer. Not to love is to suffer. To suffer is to suffer. To be happy is to love. To be happy, then, is to suffer. But suffering makes one unhappy. Therefore, to be happy one must love, or love to suffer, or suffer from too much happiness. I hope you're getting this down.

Woody Allen

If you can't live without me, why aren't you dead yet?

Title of a book by Cynthia Heimel

I suspect that in every good marriage there are times when love seems to be over.

Madeleine L'Engle

Sighs are air, and go to the air, / Tears are water, and go to the sea. / Tell me, fair one, if you know: / When love is forgotten, where can it go?

Gustave Adolfo Bécquer

It is as absurd to say that a man can't love one woman all the time as it is to say that a violinist needs several violins to play the same piece of music.

Honoré de Balzac

Husbands are chiefly good as lovers when they are betraying their wives.

Marilyn Monroe

Many divorces are not really the result of irreparable injury but involve . . . a desire on the part of the man or woman to shatter the setup, start out from scratch alone, and make life work for them all over again. They want the risk of disaster, want to touch bottom, to see where bottom is, and, coming up, to breathe the air with relief and relish again.

Edward Hoagland

A bulging portfolio of spiritual experiences matters little if it does not have the power to sustain us through the inevitable moments of grief, loss, and change. Knowledge and achievements matter little if we do not yet know how to touch the heart of another and be touched.

Christina Feldman and Jack Kornfield

The night before their marriage, they held a ritual where they made their "shadow vows." The groom said, "I will give you an identity and make the world see you as an extension of myself." The bride replied, "I will be compliant and sweet, but underneath I will have the real control. If anything goes wrong, I will take your money and your house." They then drank champagne and laughed heartily at their foibles, knowing that in the course of the marriage, these shadow figures would inevitably come out. They were ahead of the game because they had recognized the shadow and unmasked it.

Robert A. Johnson

A successful marriage requires falling in love many times, always with the same person.

Mignon McLaughlin

❧

I don't think there's any difference between a crush and profound love. I think the experience is that you dissolve your sentries and your battalions for a moment and you really do see that there is this unfixed, free-flowing energy of emotion and thought between people. It's tangible and you can almost ride on it into another person's breast. Your heart opens and of course you're completely panicked because you're used to guarding this organ with your life. . . . I think all the spiritual training is just to allow you to be able to experience this from a slightly different perspective — one that's a little more stabilized.

Leonard Cohen

There are confessable agonies, sufferings of which one can positively be proud. Of bereavement, of parting, of the sense of sin and the fear of death the poets have eloquently spoken. They command the world's sympathy. But there are also discreditable anguishes, no less excruciating than the others, but of which the sufferer dare not, cannot speak. The anguish of thwarted desire, for example.

Aldous Huxley

The greatest love is a mother's; then comes a dog's; then comes a sweetheart's.

Polish proverb

Our desire must be like a slow and stately ship, sailing across endless oceans, never in search of safe anchorage. Then suddenly, unexpectedly, it will find mooring for a moment.

Etty Hillesum

How nicely the bitch Sensuality knows how to beg for a piece of the spirit when a piece of flesh is denied her.

Friedrich Nietzsche

Suddenly I wanted my loneliness back. Not the old loneliness where I wondered who or what the hell on this planet I could possibly be connected to, but a new loneliness, one in which I accepted the inevitable separateness of being that all of us must endure, the one where it was all right to be alone because there was no other alternative in the world — just yourself and the fair fact of who you were and then the rubbing against others who themselves knew their loneliness.

Charlie Smith

If you think nobody cares if you're alive, try missing a couple of car payments.

Earl Wilson

He threw everything over for a flawed and impossible passion, only to see the object of it turn against him, proving there is no reward for love except the experience of loving, and nothing to be learned by it except humility.

John le Carré,
The Secret Pilgrim

Break a vase, and the love that reassembles the fragments is stronger than that love which took its symmetry for granted when it was whole.

Derek Walcott

It seems to me we can never give up longing and wishing while we are thoroughly alive. There are certain things we feel to be beautiful and good, and we must hunger after them.

George Eliot

For the night was not impartial. No, the night loved some more than others, served some more than others.

Eudora Welty

We all have eyes for our own Dark Angel.

Arthur Rimbaud

Don't touch me! Don't question me! Don't speak to me! Stay with me!

Samuel Beckett, *Waiting for Godot*

If you marry, you will regret it. If you don't marry, you will also regret it.

Søren Kierkegaard

The saints are what they are, not because their sanctity makes them admirable to others, but because the gift of sainthood makes it possible for them to admire everybody else.

Thomas Merton

Love is or it ain't. Thin love ain't love at all.

Toni Morrison, *Beloved*

☉

A Daughter Is A Different Matter

A man can deceive his fiancée or his mistress as much as he likes, and in the eyes of the woman he loves, an ass may pass for a philosopher, but a daughter is a different matter.

Anton Chekhov

Families will not be broken. Curse and expel them, send their children wandering, drown them in floods and fires, and old women will make songs out of all these sorrows and sit in the porches and sing them on mild evenings.

Marilynne Robinson

To each other, we were as normal and nice as the smell of bread. We were just a family. In a family even exaggerations make perfect sense.

John Irving,
The Hotel New Hampshire

Happy or unhappy, families are all mysterious. We have only to imagine how differently we would be described — and will be described, after our deaths — by each of the family members who believe they know us.

Gloria Steinem

Everybody's always talking about people breaking into houses . . . but there are more people in the world who want to break out of houses.

Thornton Wilder

In the traditional family structure of Persia . . . one simply cannot discard close relatives just because one does not like them; rather one has to accommodate them, make allowances, and accept them, like misfortune.

Shusha Guppy

They fuck you up, your Mum and Dad, / They may not mean to, but they do.

Philip Larkin

The day the child realizes that all adults are imperfect, he becomes an adolescent; the day he forgives them, he becomes an adult; the day he forgives himself, he becomes wise.

Alden Nowlan

We are born into a family and, at the last, we rejoin its full extension when gathered to the ancestors.

James Hillman

Family jokes, of course, though rightly cursed by strangers, are the bond that keeps most families alive.

Stella Benson

. . . that best portion of a good man's life, / His little, nameless, unremembered acts / Of kindness and of love.

William Wordsworth

To feel the love of people whom we know is a fire that feeds our life. But to feel the affection that comes from those whom we do not know . . . — that is something still greater and more beautiful because it widens out the boundaries of our being and unites all living things.

Pablo Neruda

The tragedy in the lives of most of us is that we go through life walking down a high-walled lane with people of our own kind, the same economic station, the same national background and education and religious outlook. And beyond those walls, all humanity lies, unknown and unseen, and untouched by our restricted and impoverished lives.

Florence Luscomb

Our own pulse beats in every stranger's throat.

Barbara Deming

⊘

In the beginning there was my mother. A shape. A shape and a force, standing in the light. You could see her energy; it was visible in the air. Against any background she stood out.

Marilyn Krysl

She had risen and was walking about the room, her fat, worn face sharpening with a sort of animal alertness into power and protection. The claws that hide in every maternal creature slipped out of the fur of good manners.

Margaret Deland

My mother was my first jealous lover.

Barbara Grizzuti Harrison

Grown don't mean nothing to a mother. A child is a child. They get bigger, older, but grown? What's that supposed to mean? In my heart it don't mean a thing.

Toni Morrison, *Beloved*

At that moment, I missed my mother more than I had ever imagined possible and wanted only to live somewhere quiet and beautiful with her alone, but also at that moment I wanted only to see her lying dead, all withered and in a coffin at my feet.

Jamaica Kincaid, *Annie John*

There are two barriers that often prevent communication between the young and their elders. The first is middle-aged forgetfulness of the fact that they themselves are no longer young. The second is youthful ignorance of the fact that the middle-aged are still alive.

Jessamyn West

All that remains to the mother in modern consumer society is the role of scapegoat; psychoanalysis uses huge amounts of money and time to persuade analysands to foist their problems onto the absent mother, who has no opportunity to utter a word in her own defense. Hostility to the mother in our societies is an index of mental health.

Germaine Greer

Times are bad. Children no longer obey their parents, and everyone is writing a book.

Cicero

What mother and daughter understand each other, or even have sympathy for each other's lack of understanding?

Maya Angelou

A mother . . . is forever surprised and even faintly wronged that her sons and daughters are just people, for many mothers hope and half expect that their newborn child will make the world better, will somehow be a redeemer. Perhaps they are right, and they can believe that the rare quality they glimpsed in the child is active in the burdened adult.

Florida Scott-Maxwell

To love anything is to see it at once under the lowering clouds of danger.

G.K. Chesterton

I love my daughter. She and I have shared the same body. There is a part of her mind that is a part of mine. But when she was born, she sprang from me like a slippery fish, and has been swimming away ever since.

Amy Tan, *The Joy Luck Club*

My mother was dead for five years before I knew that I had loved her very much.

Lillian Hellman

When the strongest words for what I have to offer come out of me sounding like words I remember from my mother's mouth, then I either have to reassess the meaning of everything I have to say now, or re-examine the worth of her old words.

Audre Lorde

All women become like their mothers. That is their tragedy. No man does. That's his.

Oscar Wilde

I know her face by heart. Sometimes I think nothing will break her spell.

Daphne Merkin

Victoria's mother, the Duchess of Kent, totally dominated her daughter's upbringing and clearly had ambitions to be the power behind the throne once Victoria became queen. The princess slept in her mother's room and was never allowed to talk to anyone except in the presence of her German governess or the duchess. The very day that William IV died and Victoria ascended the throne, the Duchess of Kent came

to Victoria after the state dignitaries had departed and inquired if there was anything she could do for her. "I wish to be left alone," replied Victoria, and the same day she gave orders for her bed to be moved from the duchess's room.

The Little, Brown Book of Anecdotes

♲

All good qualities in a child are the result of environment, while all the bad ones are the result of poor heredity on the side of the other parent.

Elinor Goulding Smith

A man who has been the indisputable favorite of his mother keeps for life the feeling of a conqueror, that confidence of success that often induces real success.

Sigmund Freud

Few misfortunes can befall a boy which bring worse consequences than to have a really affectionate mother.

W. Somerset Maugham

Nothing would have satisfied Amelia but complete possession of her son, to all intents and purposes returning him to the dark slyness of her womb.

Marjorie Kinnan Rawlings,
The Sojourner

If a mother respects both herself and her child from his very first day onward, she will never need to teach him respect for others.

Alice Miller

The perjurer's mother told white lies.

Austin O'Malley

Out of the corner of one eye, I could see my mother. Out of the corner of the other eye, I could see her shadow on the wall, cast there by the lamplight. It was a big and solid shadow, and it looked so much like my mother that I became frightened. For I could not be sure whether for the rest of my life I would be able to tell when it was really my mother and when it was really her shadow standing between me and the rest of the world.

Jamaica Kincaid, *Annie John*

A mother's love for her child is like nothing else in the world. It knows no law, no pity; it dares all things and crushes down remorselessly all that stands in its path.

Agatha Christie

But the mother's yearning . . . feels the presence of the cherished child even in the debased, degraded man.

George Eliot

Over the years I have learned that motherhood is much like an austere religious order, the joining of which obligates one to relinquish all claims to personal possessions.

Nancy Stahl

Being asked to decide between your passion for work and your passion for children was like being asked by your doctor whether you preferred him to remove your brain or your heart.

Mary Kay Blakely

Why not have your first baby at sixty, when your husband is already dead and your career is over? Then you can really devote yourself to it.

Fran Lebowitz

I figure when my husband comes home from work, if the kids are still alive, then I've done my job.

Roseanne Barr

Certainly I can say that my own childhood was unhappy. This was due to a clash of wills between my mother and myself. My early life was a series of fierce battles, from which my mother invariably emerged the victor. If I could not be seen anywhere, she would say, "Go and find out what Bernard is doing and tell him to stop it."

Bernard Law Montgomery

No matter how old a mother is, she watches her middle-aged children for signs of improvement.

Florida Scott-Maxwell

If you bungle raising your children, I don't think whatever else you do well matters very much.

Jacqueline Kennedy

Whatever else is unsure in this stinking dunghill of a world, a mother's love is not.

James Joyce

Now that I am in my forties, she tells me I'm beautiful; now that I am in my forties, she sends me presents and we have the long, personal, and even remarkably honest phone calls I always wanted so intensely I forbade myself to imagine them. How strange. Perhaps Shaw was correct and if we lived to be several hundred years old, we would finally work it all out. I am deeply grateful. With my poems, I finally won even my mother. The longest wooing of my life.

Marge Piercy, *Braided Lives*

I don't like coming home. It keeps me from being nostalgic.

Stewart O'Nan, *Snow Angels*

My mother phones daily to ask, "Did you just try to reach me?" When I reply, "No," she adds, "So, if you're not too busy, call me while I'm still alive," and hangs up.

Erma Bombeck

Every man must define his identity against his mother. If he does not, he just falls back into her and is swallowed up.

Camille Paglia

Blaming mother is just a negative way of clinging to her still.

Nancy Friday

Do everything right, all of the time, and the child will prosper. It is as simple as that, except for fate, luck, heredity, chance, the astrological sign under which the child was born, his order of birth, his first encounter with evil, the girl who jilts him in spite of his excellent qualities, the war that is being fought when he is a young man, the drugs he may try once or too many times, the friends he makes, how he scores on tests, how well he endures kidding about his shortcomings, how ambitious he becomes, how far he falls behind, circumstantial evidence, danger when it is least expected, difficulty in triumphing over circumstance, people with hidden agendas, and animals with rabies.

Ann Beattie

∽

The fundamental defect of fathers in our competitive society is that they want their children to be a credit to them.

Bertrand Russell

Once an angry man dragged his father along the ground through his own orchard. "Stop!" cried the groaning old man at last. "Stop! I did not drag my father beyond this tree."

Gertrude Stein

Many people have asked, "Has writing this book made you feel closer to your father?" To which I could only answer: "My relationship with him has greatly improved since his death."

R.D. Laing

Had my father lived, he would have lain on me at full length and would have crushed me.

Jean-Paul Sartre

Providing for one's family as a good husband and father is a watertight excuse for making money hand over fist. Greed may be a sin. Exploitation of other people might, on the face of it, look rather nasty. But who can blame a man for "doing the best" for his children?

Eva Figes

He works so hard . . . I wish I could persuade him to take things a little more easily; but it would be like inducing a sledgehammer to loiter on the downward arc.

Margaret Halsey

When a father, absent during the day, returns home at six, his children receive only his temperament, not his teaching.

Robert Bly

I watched a small man with thick calluses on both hands work fifteen and sixteen hours a day. I saw him once literally bleed from the bottoms of his feet, a man who came here uneducated, alone, unable to speak the language, who taught me all I needed to know about faith and hard work by the simple eloquence of his example.

Mario Cuomo

It is much easier to become a father than to be one.

Kent Nerburn

My father never kept a diary, but he never threw away a canceled check, either. When he died a few years ago I came across thousands of them in perfect order in a series of shoe boxes. Amidst stacks of others that took the family from the children's milk through his own bifocals, I found the one that paid the doctor who delivered me. My father knew they didn't audit you for 1951 in 1980; he kept those checks for another reason.

Thomas Mallon

It's no good trying to fool yourself about love. You can't fall into it like a soft job without dirtying up your hands. It takes muscle and guts. And if you can't bear the thought of messing up your nice, clean soul, you'd better give up the whole idea of life and become a saint. Because you'll never make it as a human being. It's either this world or the next.

John Osborne

The pressures of being a parent are equal to any pressure on earth. To be a conscious parent, and really look to that little being's mental and physical health, is a responsibility which most of us, including me, avoid most of the time because it's too hard.

John Lennon

The words a father speaks to his children in the privacy of the home are not overheard at the time, but, as in whispering galleries, they will be clearly heard at the end and by posterity.

Jean Paul Richter

I had an amazing vision one time. I saw my whole male lineage behind my father lined up through a field and over a hill. It went back hundreds of generations. I had this tremendous sense that I was the outcome of all that work. The connection was very emotional and powerful. . . . Not only are you the outcome of everyone's previous work of all the lineages that came before you, but if you perfect yourself and . . . get rid of all the guilt and the suffering, then you get rid of it for all those who came before you, too. As you free yourself, you free the whole horde. I felt that I was one with all this love for all these men before me.

Richard Gere

William Haddad was an associate of President John F. Kennedy. After Kennedy was assassinated, his young son, John, asked Mr. Haddad, "Are you a daddy?" Haddad told him he was. Said little John, "Then will you throw me up in the air?"

Bartlett's Book of Anecdotes

His father watched him across the gulf of years and pathos which always must divide a father from his son.

John P. Marquand,
The Late George Apley

When a father gives to his son, both laugh; when a son gives to his father, both cry.

Yiddish proverb

☺

I grew up to have my father's looks, my father's speech patterns, my father's posture, my father's opinions, and my mother's contempt for my father.

Jules Feiffer, *Hold Me!*

When one has not had a good father, one must create one.

Friedrich Nietzsche

When one makes children unhappy, one is a criminal and runs the risk of killing them. When one makes them happy, one does right, but one runs the risk of making them silly, presumptuous, and insolent.

Charles Péguy

Always take out your watch when a child asks you the time.

J.A. Spender

Love in action is a harsh and dreadful thing compared to love in dreams.

Fyodor Dostoyevsky

Most American children suffer too much mother and too little father.

Gloria Steinem

Fear was my father, Father Fear. / His look drained the stones.

Theodore Roethke

Father's birthday. He would have been ninety-six, ninety-six, yes, today; and could have been ninety-six, like other people one has known: but mercifully was not. His life would have entirely ended mine.

Virginia Woolf

A man can deceive his fiancée or his mistress as much as he likes, and in the eyes of the woman he loves, an ass may pass for a philosopher, but a daughter is a different matter.

Anton Chekhov

What was it, this being "a good father"? To love one's sons and daughters was not enough; to carry in one's bone and blood a pride in them, a longing for their growth and development — this was not enough. One had to be a ready companion to games and jokes and outings to earn from the world this accolade. The devil with it.

Laura Z. Hobson

I could not point to any need in childhood as strong as that for a father's protection.

Sigmund Freud

Some people are your relatives but others are your ancestors, and you choose
the ones you want to have as ancestors.
You create yourself out of those values.

Ralph Ellison

Her father was waiting. When she saw
him, she felt the usual shift in her feelings. A lift, a jump, a tug. Pleasure, but
not totally. Love, but not completely.
Dependence. Fear, familiarity, identification. That's part of me there, walking
along. Tree from which I sprang. His
spasm produced me. Shake of his body
and here I am.

Shirley Ann Grau

You teach your daughters the diameters
of the planets, and wonder when you
have done that why they do not delight
in your company.

Samuel Johnson

The thing to remember about fathers is,
they're men.

Phyllis McGinley

⟨

PAPER LANTERNS

To Teach A Boy Nothing

We do not know an edible root in the woods. We cannot tell our course by the stars, nor the hour of the day by the sun. It is well if we can swim and skate. We are afraid of a horse, of a cow, of a dog, of a cat, of a spider. Far better was the Roman rule to teach a boy nothing that he could not learn standing.

Ralph Waldo Emerson

My schooling did me a great deal of harm and no good whatever; it was simply dragging a child's soul through the dirt.

George Bernard Shaw

You must adjust. . . . This is the legend imprinted in every schoolbook, the invisible message on every blackboard. Our schools have become vast factories for the manufacture of robots.

Robert Lindner

School is about two parts ABCs to fifty parts Where Do I Stand in the Great Pecking Order of Humankind.

Barbara Kingsolver

Can we accept this extreme statement that amounts to saying that human life is shattered by education? . . . Education directs all our attention towards knowledge and attaches no importance to understanding. Exposing children to this kind of influence means that they reach adult life having lost themselves, being entirely dependent upon external things — possessions, the opinions of other people, appearances, and so on.

John G. Bennett

What does education often do? It makes a straight-cut ditch of a free, meandering brook.

Henry David Thoreau

All intellectuals complain about their school days. This is ridiculous.

Lord Clark

I owe everything to a system that made me learn by heart till I wept. As a result, I have thousands of lines of poetry by heart. I owe everything to this.

George Steiner

I took a course in speed-reading and was able to read *War and Peace* in twenty minutes. It's about Russia.

Woody Allen

I think of the story about the trainee who came to Anna Freud and said, "What do you do if you evaluate a child you don't like?" "Arrange to evaluate a second time," said Anna Freud. "But what if after the second session you still don't like him?" "I see the child a third time," she said. "But if it's still there, the dislike, after the third session," asked the student. "What do you do then?" "I don't know," said Anna Freud. "It's never happened to me."

Jean Goodwin

A teacher affects eternity; he can never tell where his influence stops.

Henry Adams

One mother can achieve more than a hundred teachers.

Jewish saying

There is this idea now in this country that all people who succeed, succeed on their own, and all people who fail, fail on their own, whereas neither is true. The vast majority of people in this country stay where they're born. Very few people move too far from home. Rich people rarely become poor, and poor people rarely become rich. But we live in a society ruled by anecdote, so that we have no sense at all of what actually happens to most people.

Fran Lebowitz

Soon the child's clear eye is clouded over by ideas and opinions, preconceptions and abstractions. Simple free being becomes encrusted with the burdensome armor of the ego. Not until years later does an instinct come that a vital sense of mystery has been withdrawn. The sun glints through the pines, and the heart is pierced in a moment of beauty and strange pain, like a memory of paradise. After that day . . . we become seekers.

Peter Matthiessen

As a child, I reacted to stress by developing this compulsion: I would draw an ugly house on a piece of paper, and then erase the house line by line and turn it into a beautiful one.

Sylvia Stone

If your everyday practice is to open to all your emotions, to all the people you meet, to all the situations you encounter, without closing down, trusting that you can do that — then that will take you as far as you can go. And then you'll understand all the teachings that anyone has ever taught.

Pema Chödrön

Even a minor event in the life of a child is an event of that child's world and thus a world event.

Gaston Bachelard

When I was a child, a volcano erupted unexpectedly in Iceland, burying a small town at the foot of its cone. All the children in the town were in school at the time, and they all perished. The parents sent their sons and daughters out the door that morning, same as they always did, and never saw them again. I remember my mother being profoundly moved by that tragedy. She always made sure that the last words we had in the morning were loving ones. That cannot always have been easy, but my memory is that she usually succeeded.

Barbara Cawthorne Crafton

Nothing you do for children is ever wasted. They seem not to notice us, hovering, averting our eyes, and they seldom offer thanks, but what we do for them is never wasted.

Garrison Keillor

The teenagers aren't all bad. I love 'em if nobody else does. There ain't nothing wrong with young people. Jus' quit lyin' to 'em.

Jackie "Moms" Mabley

Children have never been good at listening to their elders, but they have never failed to imitate them.

James Baldwin

☙

Esalen's Law: (1) You always teach others what you most need to learn yourself. (2) You are your own worst student.

Richard Price

School was a worry to her. She was not glib or quick in a world where glibness and quickness were easily confused with ability to learn.

Tillie Olsen

Moholy was a friend of mine. As a matter of fact, I met him in 1938 in Chicago, and he is the guy who got me on the trail of reading. He said to me, "Do you read?" Just out of the blue. And I said, "No." And he said, "Pity." That's all he said. Unlike me. I sound like a guy trying to get everybody to join every library in the country. But he just said, "Pity," and that was enough.

Paul Rand

We think work with the brain is more worthy than work with the hands. Nobody who thinks with his hands could ever fall for this.

E.F. Schumacher

If the aborigine drafted an IQ test, all of Western civilization presumably would flunk it.

Stanley Marion Garn

Miss Manners refuses to allow society to seek its own level. Having peered through her lorgnette into the abyss, she can guess how low that level will be.

Judith Martin, aka Miss Manners

School is an institution built on the axiom that learning is the result of teaching. And institutional wisdom continues to accept this axiom, despite overwhelming evidence to the contrary.

Ivan Illich

The first step is to measure whatever can be easily measured. That is OK as far as it goes. The second step is to disregard that which can't be measured or give it an arbitrary quantitative value. This is artificial and misleading. The third step is to presume that what can't be easily measured really isn't very important. This is blindness. The fourth step is to say that what can't be easily measured doesn't exist. This is suicide.

Daniel Yankelovich

Facts call us to reflect, even as the tossings of a capsizing vessel cause the crew to rush on deck and to climb the masts.

Albert Schweitzer

Technological progress is like an axe in the hands of a pathological criminal.

Albert Einstein

When science finally locates the center of the universe, some people will be surprised to learn they're not it.

Bernard Bailey

Our imagination is stretched to the utmost, not, as in fiction, to imagine things which are not really there, but just to comprehend those things which are there.

Richard Feynman

The true definition of science is this: the study of the beauty of the world.

Simone Weil

I love the story of the rabbi who sent his disciple to learn from a fellow rabbi. When the disciple asked what he should learn, what parts of Torah, the teacher answered: "I am sending you to learn from him — not words of Torah, but how he ties his shoelaces!" It's the details, the small daily things which we learn from our role models, not necessarily book knowledge, which we can glean for our own lives.

Dov Peretz Elkins

The classical tradition of striptease . . . offers a valid metaphor for the activity of reading. The dancer teases the audience, as the text teases its readers, with the promise of an ultimate revelation that is indefinitely postponed.

David Lodge

To embrace the child may threaten the adult who values information above wonder, entertainment above play, and intelligence above ignorance. If we were really to care for the child, we would have to face our own lower natures — our indomitable emotions, our insane desires, and the vast range of our incapacity.

Thomas Moore

As a father taking his very well-brought-up young daughter to the opera for the first time, [Peter] Ustinov was unwise enough to choose the Baths of Caracalla in Rome. The opera was *Aida*: during one particular scene the whole stage seemed to be covered with animals — camels, elephants, horses, unwanted cats, and so on. At a climactic point, almost all the animals relieved themselves simultaneously. As he stared aghast at this incredible sight, Ustinov felt a light

tapping on his shoulder and heard his daughter's earnest voice: "Daddy, is it all right if I laugh?"

The Little, Brown Book of Anecdotes

⌒

I remember a medicine man in Africa who said to me almost with tears in his eyes: "We have no dreams anymore since the British are in the country." When I asked him why, he answered, "The District Commissioner knows everything."

Carl Jung

We would be a lot safer if the government would take its money out of science and put it into astrology and the reading of palms. . . . Only in superstition is there hope. If you want to become a friend of civilization, then become an enemy of the truth and a fanatic for harmless balderdash.

Kurt Vonnegut

Life is extinct on other planets because their scientists were more advanced than ours.

John F. Kennedy

Researchers . . . estimate that there is more information in a weekly edition of the *New York Times* than a person in the sixteenth century processed in a lifetime.

Lawrence Shainberg

Truth, poor child, was nobody's daughter. She took off her clothes and jumped in the water.

Dorothy L. Sayers

The attitude that I take is that everyday life is more interesting than forms of celebration, when we become aware of it. That *when* is when our intentions go down to zero. Then suddenly you notice that the world is magical.

John Cage

During Einstein's stay in Zurich, Paulette Brupbacher asked the whereabouts of his laboratory. With a smile, he took a fountain pen out of his breast pocket and said, "Here."

Carl Seelig

What is a television apparatus to man, who has only to shut his eyes to see the most inaccessible regions of the seen and the never seen, who has only to imagine in order to pierce through walls and cause all the planetary Baghdads of his dreams to rise from the dust?

Salvador Dali

The only thing God didn't do to Job was give him a computer.

I.F. Stone

May we remember, as we log on, that half the world's people have never used a telephone, and recall, as we chatter, that most of those around us have no chance to speak or move as they choose. May we recall that more than half a million beings live without food, and that as many children live amidst poverty and war.

Pico Iyer

Few people have the imagination for reality.

Johann Wolfgang von Goethe

It is well to remember that by the time scale of the universe, the shapes of all things and systems are as fugitive and evanescent as those clouds driven before a gale, which coalesce and dissolve as they go.

David Pye

Technology is not in itself opposed to spirituality and religion. But it presents a great temptation.

Thomas Merton

We have grasped the mystery of the atom and rejected the Sermon on the Mount.

Omar Bradley

Spaceships and time machines are no escape from the human condition. Let Othello subject Desdemona to a lie-detector test; his jealousy will still blind him to the evidence. Let Oedipus triumph over gravity; he won't triumph over his fate.

Arthur Koestler

Well, I'll tell you what a phone is for. It's not for looking someone in the eyeball and saying, I love you.

Louise Mattlage

Call a thing immoral or ugly, soul-destroying or a degradation of man, a peril to the peace of the world or to the well-being of future generations; as long as you have not shown it to be "uneconomic" you have not really questioned its right to exist, grow, and prosper.

E.F. Schumacher

One way of getting an idea of our fellow countrymen's miseries is to go and look at their pleasures.

George Eliot

At the end of his life, Ezra Pound observed to a friend: "Nothing really matters, does it?" Today I understand this. At the end, or close to the end, or closer to the end than the beginning, the value of what we once thought mattered is lost to us. Even survival, once so important, money, food, family, country, accomplishment, recognition, fame, even: Pound was right. He once said to Allen Ginsberg: "At seventy I realized that instead of being a lunatic, I was a moron."

Doris Grumbach

A discussion between Haldane and a friend began to take a predictable turn. The friend said with a sigh, "It's no use going on. I know what you will say next, and I know what you will do next." The distinguished scientist promptly sat down on the floor, turned two back somersaults, and returned to his seat. "There," he said with a smile. "That's to prove that you're not always right."

Bartlett's Book of Anecdotes

Life and love are life and love, a bunch of violets is a bunch of violets, and to drag in the idea of a point is to ruin everything.

D.H. Lawrence

We are shut up in schools and college recitation rooms for ten or fifteen years, and come out at last with a bellyful of words and do not know a thing. We cannot use our hands, or our legs, or our eyes, or our arms. We do not know an edible root in the woods. We cannot tell our course by the stars, nor the hour of the day by the sun. It is well if we can swim and skate. We are afraid of a horse, of a cow, of a dog, of a cat, of a spider. Far better was the Roman rule to teach a boy nothing that he could not learn standing.

Ralph Waldo Emerson

We should take care not to make the intellect our god; it has, of course, powerful muscles, but no personality.

Albert Einstein

A scholar was bragging to a boatman about all the knowledge he had acquired. "Can you swim?" the boatman asked. "No," the scholar replied. . . . "Then all of your knowledge is wasted," replied the boatman, "because the boat is sinking."

Zen story

Why three hundred thousand varieties of beetles? The great English geneticist J.B.S. Haldane was once cornered by a distinguished theologian who asked him what inferences one could draw, from a study of the created world, as to the nature of its Creator. Haldane answered, "An inordinate fondness for beetles."

David Quammen

Knowledge is one. Its division into subjects is a concession to human weakness.

Sir Halford John Mackinder

Do not be a magician, be magic.

Leonard Cohen

No object is mysterious. The mystery is in your eye.

Elizabeth Bowen

Five senses; an incurably abstract intellect; a haphazardly selective memory; a set of preconceptions and assumptions so numerous that I can never examine more than a minority of them — never become even conscious of them all. How much of total reality can such an apparatus let through?

C.S. Lewis

I knew of a physicist at the University of Chicago who was rather crazy like some scientists, and the idea of the insolidity, the instability of the physical world, impressed him so much that he used to go around in enormous padded slippers for fear he should fall through the floor.

Alan Watts

Do exactly what you would do if you felt most secure.

Meister Eckhart

If I could learn the word for yes it could teach me questions.

W.S. Merwin

I was going to buy a copy of *The Power of Positive Thinking*, and then I thought: What the hell good would that do?

Ronnie Shakes

I noticed in New York, where the traffic is so bad and the air is so bad, everything, and the food, and the coffee, everything, and the streets are falling to pieces, you get into a taxi and very frequently the poor taxi driver is just beside himself with irritation. And one day I got into one and the driver began talking a blue streak, accusing absolutely everyone of being wrong. You know, he was full of irritation about everything, and I simply remained quiet. I did not answer his questions, I did not enter into a conversation, and very shortly the driver began changing his ideas, and simply through my being silent he began, before I got out of the car, saying rather nice things about the world around him.

John Cage

Our alphabet's first sound is but the lengthening of a sigh.

Joseph Brodsky

২

Do you suppose I consider your miserable fiddle when the spirit seizes me?

Ludwig van Beethoven, in response to complaints about the difficulty of playing his Grosse Fugue

Idle dreamers have given real visionaries a bad name.

Robert Fritz

The thing is to stalk your calling in a certain skilled and supple way, to locate the most tender and live spot and plug into that pulse. This is yielding, not fighting. . . . I think it would be well, and proper, and obedient, and pure, to grasp your one necessity and not let it go, to dangle from it limp wherever it takes you.

Annie Dillard

A little boy came home and told his mother he had gotten first prize in an examination. The question had been "How many legs does a horse have?" He had answered, "Three." When his mother asked how he had gotten the first prize, he replied that all the other children had said, "Two."

Richard Kehl

Realism is a corruption of reality.

Wallace Stevens

During his years of poverty, Balzac lived in an unheated and almost unfurnished garret. On one of the bare walls the writer inscribed the words, "Rosewood paneling with commode"; on another, "Gobelin tapestry with Venetian mirror"; and in the place of honor over the empty fireplace, "Picture by Raphael."

E. Fuller

Imagination is the voice of daring. If there is anything godlike about God it is that. He dared to imagine everything.

Henry Miller

Whatever our point of view or frame of reference, the world is richer and more amazing than we realize. All frames of reference are limited. All points of view can be supplemented by further experience under new and various conditions.

Donald Granger

The first rule of intelligent tinkering is to save all the parts.

Paul Ehrlich

That's the way things come clear. All of a sudden. And then you realize how obvious they've been all along.

Madeleine L'Engle

We need to give ourselves permission to act out our dreams and visions, not look for more sensations, more phenomena, but live our strongest dreams — even if it takes a lifetime.

Vijali Hamilton

They will say you are on the wrong road, if it is your own.

Antonio Porchia

A man is original when he speaks the truth that has always been known to all good men.

Patrick Kavanagh

The epitaph that I would write for history would say: "I conceal nothing." It is not enough not to lie. One should strive not to lie in a negative sense by remaining silent.

Leo Tolstoy

In the late 1600s the finest instruments originated from three rival families whose workshops were side by side in the Italian village of Cremona. First were the Amatis, and outside their shop hung a sign: "The best violins in all Italy." Not to be outdone, their next-door neighbors, the family Guarnerius, hung a bolder sign proclaiming: "The Best Violins In All The World!" At the end

of the street was the workshop of Anton Stradivarius, and on its front door
was a simple notice which read: "The
best violins on the block."

Freda Bright

The man who is too old to learn was
probably always too old to learn.

Henry S. Haskins

There are some things which cannot be
learned quickly, and time, which is all
we have, must be paid heavily for their
acquiring. They are the very simplest
things and, because it takes a man's life
to know them, the little new that each
man gets from life is very costly and the
only heritage he has to leave.

Ernest Hemingway

In this country we encourage "creativity"
among the mediocre, but real bursting
creativity appalls us. We put it down as
undisciplined, as somehow "too much."

Pauline Kael

Creative minds always have been known
to survive any kind of bad training.

Anna Freud

ↄ

It Is Not Down In Any Map

It is not down in any map; true places never are.

Herman Melville, *Moby-Dick*

Man made the city, God made the country, but the devil made the small town.

Source unknown

To be rooted is perhaps the most important and least recognized need of the human soul.

Simone Weil

Your next-door neighbor . . . is not a man; he is an environment. He is the barking of a dog; he is the noise of a pianola; he is a dispute about a party wall; he is drains that are worse than yours, or roses that are better than yours.

G.K. Chesterton

In little towns, lives roll along so close to one another; loves and hates beat about, their wings almost touching.

Willa Cather

It is in the shelter of each other that the people live.

Irish proverb

You make what seems a simple choice: choose a man or a job or a neighborhood — and what you have chosen is not a man or a job or a neighborhood, but a life.

Jessamyn West

It is one of the few consolations of this planet that houses cannot move.

Robert Kelly

Home, as far as I'm concerned, is the place you have to leave. And then, if you're like me, spend the rest of your life mourning.

Paulette Bates Alden

I am not much an advocate for traveling; and I observe that men run away to other countries because they are not good in their own, and run back to their own because they pass for nothing in the new places. For the most part, only the light characters travel. Who are you that you have no task to keep you at home?

Ralph Waldo Emerson

One never reaches home, but wherever friendly paths intersect, the whole world looks like home for a time.

Hermann Hesse

There are things you just can't do in life. You can't beat the phone company, you can't make a waiter see you until he's ready to see you, and you can't go home again.

Bill Bryson

People had changed — or rather fridges had changed them. Mrs. Munde felt that being able to store food for longer periods had broken down the community spirit. There was no need to share now, no need to meet every day, gathering your veg or killing a few rabbits.

Jeanette Winterson,
Boating for Beginners

How can you say you have fulfilled the law and prophets, when it is written in the law that you should love your neighbor as yourself? Look, many of your brothers, sons of Abraham, are covered with filth and dying of hunger. Meanwhile your own house is filled with goods, and not a thing goes out of it to them.

Origen

The weakness of pure individualism is that there are no pure individuals.

Kenneth Boulding

What may be wealth to an individual may not be wealth to a community.

Henry George

But there were years when, in search of what I thought were better, nobler things, I denied these, my people, and my family. I forgot the songs they sang — and most of those songs are now dead; I erased their dialect from my tongue; I was ashamed of them and their ways of life. But now, yes, I love them; they are a part of my blood; they, with all their virtues and their faults, played a great part in forming my way of looking at life.

Agnes Smedley

Christ didn't say, "Love humanity as thyself," but, "Love thy neighbor as thyself," and do you know why? Because your neighbor, by definition, is the person nearby, the man sitting next to you in the underground who smells, perhaps; the man next to you in the queue who maybe tries to barge ahead of you; in short, your neighbor is the person who threatens your own liberty.

Luciano De Crescenzo

One man's ceiling is another man's floor.

Paul Simon

Years ago I recognized my kinship with all living things, and I made up my mind that I was not one bit better than the meanest on the earth. I said then, and I say now, that while there is a lower class, I am in it; while there is a criminal element, I am of it; while there is a soul in prison, I am not free.

Eugene V. Debs

A thing is right when it tends to preserve the integrity, stability, and beauty of the biotic community.

Aldo Leopold

Few are the giants of the soul who actually feel that the human race is their family circle.

Freya Stark

The fact that we are human beings is infinitely more important than all the peculiarities that distinguish human beings from one another.

Simone de Beauvoir

During my second year of nursing school, our professor gave us a quiz. I . . . breezed through the questions until I read the last one: "What is the first name of the woman who cleans the school?" Surely this was some kind of joke. I had seen the cleaning woman several times . . . but how would I know her name? I handed in my paper, leaving the last question blank. Before the class ended, one student asked if the last question would count toward our quiz grade. "Absolutely," the professor said. "In your careers, you will meet many people. All are significant. They deserve your attention and care, even if all you do is smile and say hello." I've never forgotten that lesson. I also learned her name was Dorothy.

JoAnn C. Jones

We have all known the long loneliness, and we have learned that the only solution is love and that love comes with community.

Dorothy Day

Owning your own home is America's unique recipe for avoiding revolution and promoting pseudoequality at the same time. To keep citizens puttering in their yards instead of sputtering on the barricades, the government has gladly deprived itself of billions in tax revenues by letting home "owners" deduct mortgage-interest payments.

Florence King

What's the use of a fine house if you haven't got a tolerable planet to put it on?

Henry David Thoreau

I think nobody owns land until their dead are in it.

Joan Didion

If one considered life as a simple loan, one would perhaps be less exacting. We possess actually nothing; everything goes through us.

Eugène Delacroix

One should keep old roads and old friends.

German proverb

Sixty years ago, you could simply take your children out into the barn; even if you lived in the cities, there were working men all around you. Chances are your son would learn to use his body. But more and more now the children are going to the Internet . . . and the danger is that it will simply cause deeper isolation among many young males than they already have. It is a lie to say that there is communication going on. It is just a form of chatter. True communication takes place when two people are standing close to each other — maybe a foot away — so that you can feel when the other person is lying, through his body.

Robert Bly

We really are fifteen countries, and it's remarkable that each of us thinks we represent the real America. The Midwesterner in Kansas, the black American in Durham — both are certain they are the real American.

Maya Angelou

It is grossly selfish to require of one's neighbor that he should think in the same way, and hold the same opinions. Why should he? If he can think, he will probably think differently. If he cannot think, it is monstrous to require thought of any kind from him.

Oscar Wilde

There is little lonelier than small-town life when small talk is the principal means of peace.

Carol Bly

All that a city will ever allow you is an angle on it — an oblique, indirect sample of what it contains, or what passes through it; a point of view.

Peter Conrad

In living in the world by his own will and skill, the stupidest peasant or tribesman is more competent than the most intelligent worker or technician or intellectual in a society of specialists.

Wendell Berry

Forget the damned motor car and build the cities for lovers and friends.

Lewis Mumford

Sometimes a neighbor whom we have disliked a lifetime for his arrogance and conceit lets fall a single commonplace remark that shows us another side, another man, really; a man uncertain, and puzzled, and in the dark like ourselves.

Willa Cather

An old man sat outside the walls of a great city. When travelers approached they would ask the old man, "What kind of people live in this city?" And the old man would answer, "What kind of people lived in the place where you came from?" If the travelers answered, "Only bad people lived in the place where we came from," then the old man would reply, "Continue on; you will find only bad people here." But if the travelers answered, "Only good people lived in the place where we have come from," then the old man would say, "Enter, for here, too, you will find only good people."

Yiddish folk tale

We often visited Ellen's homeland, where our children had no trouble becoming attached to the Danish scene. When I asked our son how he could communicate with the Danish children

with whom he played, he said, "We can't talk together, but we can laugh together."

Victor Weisskopf

To feel at home, stay at home.

Clifton Fadiman

I live in my house as I live inside my skin: I know more beautiful, more ample, more sturdy, and more picturesque skins, but it would seem to me unnatural to exchange them for mine.

Primo Levi

People wish to be settled. Only as far as they are unsettled is there any hope for them.

Ralph Waldo Emerson

Right now I am a passenger on space vehicle Earth zooming about the sun at sixty thousand miles per hour somewhere in the solar system.

R. Buckminster Fuller

Whither goest thou, America, in thy shiny car at night?

Jack Kerouac

There is a third dimension to traveling: the longing for what is beyond.

Jan Myrdal

And in the morning, rising up a great while before day, he went out, and departed into a solitary place, and there prayed.

Mark 1:35

People commonly travel the world over to see rivers and mountains, new stars, garish birds, freak fish, grotesque breeds of human; they fall into an animal stupor that gapes at existence, and they think they have seen something.

Søren Kierkegaard

It is not down in any map; true places never are.

Herman Melville, *Moby-Dick*

What is more intriguing than a spot on the bathroom floor which, as you sit emptying your bowels, assumes a hundred different forms, figures, shapes? Often I found myself on my knees studying a stain on the floor — studying it to detect all that was hidden at first sight.

Henry Miller

A striking building stands before us as an individual every bit as soulful as we are.

Thomas Moore

When I was very young and the urge to be someplace was on me, I was assured by mature people that maturity would cure this itch. When years described me as mature, the remedy prescribed was middle age. In middle age, I was assured that greater age would calm my fever, and now that I am fifty-eight perhaps senility will do the job. Nothing has worked. . . . In other words, I don't improve. In further words, once a bum always a bum. I fear the disease is incurable.

John Steinbeck

I think that to get under the surface and really appreciate the beauty of any country, one has to go there poor.

Grace Moore

Well, I learned a lot. . . . You'd be surprised. They're all individual countries.

Ronald Reagan, on his tour of South America

I never get lost because I don't know where I'm going.

Ikkyu

I will take with me the emptiness of my hands / What you do not have you find everywhere.

W.S. Merwin

Hold the map close to your face. Breathe into it, and you will hear a river start. Open the map.

Greg Kuzma

When the Nandi men are away on a foray, nobody at home may pronounce the names of the absent warriors; they must be referred to as birds.

Sir James George Frazer

In the palm of one hand now the rain falls. From the other the grass grows. What can I tell you?

Vasko Popa

It is easier to sail many thousand miles through cold and storm and cannibals . . . with five hundred men and boys to assist one, than it is to explore the private sea, the Atlantic and Pacific Ocean of one's being, alone.

Henry David Thoreau

A part, a large part, of traveling is an engagement of the ego vs. the world. . . . The world is hydra-headed, as old as the rocks and as changing as the sea, enmeshed inextricably in its ways. The ego wants to arrive at places safely and on time.

Sybille Bedford

Don't think, but look.

Ludwig Wittgenstein

I have been a stranger in a strange land.

Exodus 2:22

Life is a foreign language. All men mispronounce it.

Christopher Morley

The journey to happiness involves finding the courage to go down into ourselves and take responsibility for what's there. All of it.

Richard Rohr

We are infinitely more complicated than our ideas about ourselves.

C.K. Williams

It's a contention of Heat-Moon's — believing, as he does, any traveler who misses the journey misses about all he's going to get — that a man becomes his attentions. His observations and curiosity, they make and remake him.

William Least Heat-Moon

Good news: but if you ask me what it is, I know not; / It is a track of feet in the snow, / It is a lantern showing a path, / It is a door set open.

G.K. Chesterton

In orbiting the sun, the earth departs from a straight line by one-ninth of an inch every eighteen miles — a very straight line in human terms. If the orbit changed by one-tenth of an inch every eighteen miles, our orbit would be vastly larger and we would all freeze to death. One-eighth of an inch? We would all be incinerated.

Science Digest

The day in the woods I took a compass was the day I got lost for sure.

John Cage

We keep our distance. It is all we have.

Richard Shelton

Whenever I prepare for a journey, I prepare as though for death. Should I never return, all is in order. This is what life has taught me.

Katherine Mansfield

Sometimes the things we want most are impossible for us. You may long to come home, yet wander forever.

Nadine Gordimer

One's destination is never a place but rather a new way of looking at things.

Henry Miller

☉

PAPER LANTERNS

So What The Hell, Leap

When in doubt, make a fool of yourself. There is a microscopically thin line between being brilliantly creative and acting like the most gigantic idiot on earth. So what the hell, leap.

Cynthia Heimel

I walk out; I see something, some event that would otherwise have been utterly missed and lost; or something sees me, some enormous power brushes me with its clean wing, and I resound like a beaten bell.

Annie Dillard

How much shall I be changed, / Before I am changed!

John Donne

There can be no love in one who does not love himself, and one can only love himself if he has the compassion that grows out of the terrifying confrontation with one's own self. . . . If you hate yourself with a fierce loathing, you may try to run from your own shadow in a campaign to do good, not for love, but to rescue your ego and convince yourself you are not evil. In the eyes of how many world-transforming activists do we see dissonance, anxiety, fear, and self-loathing? They would reform the world, but they cannot even reform themselves, much less quit smoking.

William Irwin Thompson

Just yesterday, I was looking at the catalog of a nearby college. I couldn't believe the courses they are offering. How to use a computer. How to make a good investment. How to get a good job. How to, how to. There was hardly one course to make the inner man grow. If you suggest that a course in ancient history may play a role in a person's growth, they laugh at you.

Sophia Mumford

Question: Though I have labored long and hard in the service of the Lord, I have received no improvement; I am still an ordinary and ignorant man.
Answer: You have gained the realization that you are ordinary and ignorant, and this in itself is a worthy accomplishment.

Baal Shem Tov

The psychic task which a person can and must set for himself is not to feel secure, but to be able to tolerate insecurity.

Erich Fromm

Do not think of your faults, still less of others' faults; in every person who comes near you look for what is good and strong; honor that; rejoice in it; and, as you can, try to imitate it. Your faults will drop off, like dead leaves, when their time comes.

John Ruskin

What is our innocence, / what is our guilt? All are / naked, none is safe.

Marianne Moore

It's what Kierkegaard called a leap of faith, of just taking the risk to go for love and truth, throw ourselves into the abyss. . . . The leap of faith is that the abyss is perfect freedom, that it doesn't lead to self-annihilation or destruction, but the exact opposite. I mean, one's self is just an illusion, just a hallucination. It's a source of all one's unhappiness and suffering and attachments and needs. Don't you want to get rid of yourself?

R.D. Laing

It is a great grace of God to practice self-examination; but too much is as bad as too little. . . . Believe me, by God's help we shall advance more by contemplating the Divinity than by keeping our eyes fixed on ourselves.

Saint Teresa of Avila

The outward work will never be puny if the inward work is great.

Meister Eckhart

Fortunately, psychoanalysis is not the only way to resolve inner conflicts. Life itself still remains a very effective therapist.

Karen Horney

That summer that I was ten — / Can it be there was only one / summer that I was ten?

May Swenson

Things do not change; we change.

Henry David Thoreau

Do not believe that he who seeks to comfort you lives untroubled among the simple and quiet words that sometimes do you good. His life has much difficulty and sadness and remains far behind yours. Were it otherwise, he would never have been able to find those words.

Rainer Maria Rilke

This is my last message to you: in sorrow, seek happiness.

Fyodor Dostoyevsky

Happiness is a mystery, like religion, and should never be rationalized.

G.K. Chesterton

To be happy even without happiness — that is happiness.

Marie von Ebner-Eschenbach

Even if your house is flooded or burned to the ground, whatever the danger that threatens it, let it concern only the house. If there's a flood, don't let it flood your mind. If there's a fire, don't let it burn your heart. Let it be merely the house . . . that is flooded and burned. Allow the mind to let go of its attachments. The time is ripe.

Ajahn Chah

When all becomes silent around you, and you recoil in terror — see that your work has become a flight from suffering and responsibility, your unselfishness a thinly disguised masochism; hear, throbbing within you, the spiteful, cruel heart of the steppe wolf — do not then anesthetize yourself by once again calling up the shouts and horns of the hunt, but gaze steadfastly at the vision until you have plumbed its depths.

Dag Hammarskjöld

The minute you begin to do what you want to do, it's really a different kind of life.

R. Buckminster Fuller

When you say yes, you get thirty blows of my staff; when you say no, you get thirty blows of my staff just the same.

Tokusan

Notice the difference between what happens when a man says to himself, "I failed three times," and what happens when he says, "I am a failure."

S.I. Hayakawa

Once in a while it really hits people that they don't have to experience the world in the way they have been told to.

Alan Keightley

The only thing that changed was my mind.

Laurie Nedvin

Once I was beautiful, now I am myself.

Anne Sexton

In a dark time, the eye begins to see.

Theodore Roethke

Is it really so difficult to tell a good action from a bad one? I think one usually knows right away or a moment afterward, in a horrid flash of regret.

Mary McCarthy

There can be no love if one does not remain oneself with all one's strength.

Italo Calvino

౭

True genius without heart is a thing of naught — for not great understanding alone, nor imagination alone, nor both together make genius. Love, love, love, that is the soul of genius.

Wolfgang Amadeus Mozart

Nothing will ever be attempted if all possible objections must be first overcome.

Samuel Johnson

Everyone has talent. What is rare is the courage to follow the talent to the dark place where it leads.

Erica Jong

Venus favors the bold.

Ovid

Among the many legends that surround the Nepalese Gurkhas of the British Army is the story of a paratroop regiment in the Second World War. The leader of the regiment asked for volunteers for a particularly dangerous drop behind enemy lines. About half the Gurkhas promptly stepped forward. The leader then went through what the volunteers would be asked to do. Halfway into his explanation, a surprised voice piped up from the back: "Oh, you mean we can use parachutes?" Every remaining Gurkha joined the volunteers.

Radio Times

To a brave man, good and bad luck are like his right and left hands. He uses both.

Saint Catherine of Siena

A guidance counselor who has made a fetish of security . . . may steer a youth away from his dream of becoming a poet, an artist, a musician, or any other of thousands of things, because . . . it does not pay well, there are no vacancies, it has no "future."

Henry M. Wriston

The reward for conformity was that everyone liked you except yourself.

Rita Mae Brown

Every man has the right to risk his own life in order to preserve it. Has it ever been said that a man who throws himself out the window to escape from a fire is guilty of suicide?

Jean-Jacques Rousseau

Don't just do something, Buddha said. Stand there!

Daniel Berrigan

Men are afraid to rock the boat in which they hope to drift safely through life's currents, when, actually, the boat is stuck on a sandbar. They would be better off to rock the boat and try to shake it loose, or, better still, jump in the water and swim for the shore.

Thomas Szasz

When in doubt, make a fool of yourself. There is a microscopically thin line between being brilliantly creative and acting like the most gigantic idiot on earth. So what the hell, leap.

Cynthia Heimel

A ship in harbor is safe — but that is not what ships are built for.

John A. Shedd

We are asleep with compasses in our hands.

W.S. Merwin

If you once turn on your side after the hour at which you ought to rise, it is all over. Bolt up at once.

Sir Walter Scott

Take risks: if you win, you will be happy; if you lose, you will be wise.

Source unknown

Whenever you fall, pick something up.

Oswald Avery

Risk! Risk anything! Care no more for the opinion of others, for those voices. Do the hardest thing on earth for you. Act for yourself. Face the truth.

Katherine Mansfield

There are no easy methods of learning difficult things; the method is to close your door, give out that you are not at home, and work.

Joseph de Maistre

When I was young, I observed that nine out of ten things I did were failures. So I did ten times more work.

George Bernard Shaw

Courage doesn't always roar. Sometimes courage is the little voice at the end of the day that says, I'll try again tomorrow.

Mary Anne Radmacher

I have not failed. I have found ten thousand ways that won't work.

Thomas Edison

If you think you're boring your audience, go slower not faster.

Gustav Mahler

Envy is a con man, a tugger at your sleeve, a knocker at your door. Let me in for just a moment, it says, for just one moment of your time. . . . The antidote to envy is one's own work. Not the thinking about it. Not the assessing of it. But the doing of it. The answers you want can come only from the work itself. It drives the spooks away.

Bonita Friedman

The person who is waiting for something to turn up might start with their shirt sleeves.

Garth Henrichs

☉

We act as though comfort and luxury were the chief requirements of life, when all that we need to make us really happy is something to be enthusiastic about.

Charles Kingsley

The last time I saw him [British sculptor Henry Moore] . . . he talked about his new grandson and showed us drawings in a studio he had just built to extend his workday. . . . I asked him, "Now that you're eighty, you must know the secret of life. What is the secret of life?" With anyone else the answer would have begun with an ironic laugh, but Henry Moore answered me straight: "The secret of life is to have a task, something you devote your entire life to, something you bring everything to every minute of the day for your whole life. And the most important thing is — it must be something you cannot possibly do!"

Donald Hall

We can learn to work and speak when we are afraid in the same way we have learned to work and speak when we are tired.

Audre Lorde

Appealing workplaces are to be avoided. One wants a room with no view, so imagination can meet memory in the dark.

Annie Dillard

How do I work? I grope.

Albert Einstein

Monotony is the law of nature. Look at the monotonous manner in which the sun rises. . . . The monotony of necessary occupations is exhilarating and life-giving.

Mohandas K. Gandhi

Opportunity is missed by most people because it is dressed in overalls and looks like work.

Thomas Edison

What never vary are the necessities of being in the world, of having to labor and to die there.

Jean-Paul Sartre

The pitcher cries for water to carry / and a person for work that is real.

Marge Piercy

It is not hard work which is dreary; it is superficial work.

Edith Hamilton

It is the best work that He wants, not the dregs of our exhaustion. . . . I think He must prefer quality to quantity.

George MacDonald

Every day I shall put my papers in order and every day I shall say farewell. And the real farewell, when it comes, will only be a small outward confirmation of what has been accomplished within me from day to day.

Etty Hillesum

In 1954, Professor [Philipp] Frank retired from Harvard, and I helped him clean out his office. It was unbelievable chaos. He had, as I remember, a roll-top desk, and from it he extracted letters, some of which he had never opened and which dated from the 1930s. He opened a few and observed, "You see, they were not so important anyway."

Jeremy Bernstein

No group or class should be freed from doing the toil of the culture. One of our current problems is that there are too many people who simply have no idea how much unpleasant, tedious, and repetitive work is required to support their "high-level" activities, and how ineffective they would be without the effort of those they all too often disdain.

Robert Theobold

All labor that uplifts humanity has dignity and importance and should be undertaken with painstaking excellence.

Martin Luther King Jr.

❧

One cannot be deeply responsive to the world without being saddened very often.

Erich Fromm

All men should strive to learn before they die what they are running from, and to, and why.

James Thurber

You know what happens to scar tissue. It's the strongest part of your skin.

Michael R. Mantell

When weaving a blanket, an Indian woman leaves a flaw . . . to let the soul out.

Martha Graham

The monsters of our childhood do not fade away, neither are they ever wholly monstrous. But neither, in my experience, do we ever reach a plane of detachment regarding our parents, however wise and old we may become. To pretend otherwise is to cheat.

John le Carré

In the office there was an old, soft, and worn blue velvet couch, above which a hundred thousand dissected dreams floated in the peaceful, still air.

Anne Roiphe

"You seem to be reacting to your boyfriend as if he were your father," your shrink may say stonily (unless she is a strict Freudian, in which case she'll shut up and wait until you think of it yourself, a process that usually takes ten years. This is why strict Freudians have such lovely summer houses).

Cynthia Heimel

Psychoanalysis is confession without absolution.

G.K. Chesterton

It is slow, painful, and difficult for an adult to reconstruct a radically different way of seeing life, however needlessly miserable his preconceptions make him.

Peter Marris

The greatest and most important problems of life are all fundamentally insoluble. . . . They can never be solved but only outgrown.

Carl Jung

There are only two ways to live your life. One is as though nothing is a miracle. The other is as though everything is a miracle.

Albert Einstein

The reasonable man adapts himself to the world; the unreasonable one persists in trying to adapt the world to himself. Therefore, all progress depends on the unreasonable man.

George Bernard Shaw

To be nobody but yourself, in a world which is doing its best, night and day, to make you everybody else, means to fight the hardest battle which any human being can fight, and never stop fighting.

e.e. cummings

One day, someone showed me a glass of water that was half full. And he said, "Is it half full or half empty?" So I drank the water. No more problem.

Alexander Jodorowsky

Reality is not what it is. It consists of the many realities which it can be made into.

Wallace Stevens

Reality is not always probable, or likely.

Jorge Luis Borges

If you want to know who you are, watch your feet. Because where your feet take you, that is who you are.

Frederick Buechner

People often say that this or that person has not yet found himself. But the self is not something that one finds. It is something that one creates.

Thomas Szasz

What I most want / is to spring out of this personality, / then to sit apart from that leaping. / I've lived too long where I can be reached.

Rumi

When we came in she had her chair sideways, by the window, looking out at the snow, and she said, without even looking up to know that it was us, that the doctors had said that sitting and staring at the snow was a waste of time. She should get involved in something. She laughed and told us it wasn't a waste of time. It would be a waste of time just to stare at snowflakes, but she was counting, and even that might be a waste of time, but she was only counting the ones that were just alike.

Ann Beattie,
Chilly Scenes of Winter

Rosiness is not a worse windowpane than gloomy gray when viewing the world.

Grace Paley

There is a great difference between taking a thing seriously and taking it literally.

Source unknown

Have you ever seen an inchworm crawl up a leaf or twig, and then clinging to the very end, revolve in the air, feeling for something to reach? That's like me. I am trying to find something out there beyond the place on which I have a footing.

Albert Pinkham Ryder

Inventing a story with grass, / I find a young horse deep inside it.

James Dickey

To see truth, contemplate all phenomena as a lie.

Thaganapa

Our intellect and other gifts have been given to be used for God's greater glory, but sometimes they become the very god for us. That is the saddest part: we are losing our balance when this happens. We must free ourselves to be filled by God. Even God cannot fill what is full.

Mother Teresa

A little girl, after hearing Beethoven's Ninth Symphony for the first time, asked, "What do we do now?"

Richard Kehl

All know that the drop merges into the ocean but few know that the ocean merges into the drop.

Kabir

The difficulty is not how to understand beauty, but how to be able to stand it.

Hanns Sachs

She lived in capital letters.

**Al Carmine, in a eulogy
for Marion Tanner**

No; we have been as usual asking the wrong question. It does not matter a hoot what the mockingbird on the chimney is singing. . . . The real and proper question is: why is it beautiful?

Annie Dillard

May I ask you a highly personal question? It's what life does all the time.

Kurt Vonnegut

It is only possible to succeed at second-rate pursuits — like becoming a millionaire or a prime minister, winning a war, seducing beautiful women, flying through the stratosphere, or landing on the moon. First-rate pursuits — involving, as they must, trying to understand what life is about and trying to convey that understanding — inevitably result in a sense of failure. A Napoleon, a Churchill, a Roosevelt can feel himself to be successful, but never a Socrates, a Pascal, a Blake. Understanding is forever unattainable.

Malcolm Muggeridge

Q: Why does a Jew always answer a question with a question?
A: And why should a Jew *not* answer a question with a question?

Erica Jong

The American artist Chester Harding, painting Daniel Boone's portrait, asked the old frontiersman, then in his eighties, if he had ever been lost. Boone replied, "No, I can't say I was ever lost, but I was bewildered once for three days."

Richard Kehl

I learned to make my mind large, as the universe is large, so that there is room for paradoxes.

Maxine Hong Kingston

The world of science lives fairly comfortably with paradox. We know that light is a wave, and also that light is a particle. The discoveries made in the infinitely small world of particle physics indicate randomness and chance, and I do not find it any more difficult to live with the paradox of a universe of randomness and chance and a universe of pattern and purpose than I do with light as a wave and light as a particle. Living with contradiction is nothing new to the human being.

Madeleine L'Engle

I arise in the morning torn between a desire to improve the world and a desire to enjoy the world. This makes it hard to plan the day.

E.B. White

And this is the simple truth — that to live is to feel oneself lost. He who accepts it has already begun to find himself to be on firm ground.

José Ortega y Gasset

As for conforming outwardly, and living your own life inwardly, I don't think much of that.

Henry David Thoreau

In a world of fugitives, the person taking the opposite direction will appear to run away.

T.S. Eliot

I'll tell you about a dream I had recently. When I was a schoolboy in Bucharest, my father used to come into my room in the evening and check my homework. He would open my drawers and find nothing but bits of poetry, drawings, and papers. He would get very angry and say that I was a lazybones, a good-for-nothing. In my dream, he comes into my room and says, "I hear you have done great things in the world. You have written books. Show me what you have done." And I open my drawers and I find only singed papers, dust, and ashes. He gets very angry and I try to appease him, saying, "You are right, Daddy. I've done nothing, nothing."

Eugene Ionesco

Wouldn't this be a great world if insecurity and desperation made us more attractive?

James L. Brooks

The human heart dares not stay away too long from that which hurt it most. There is a return journey to anguish that few of us are released from making.

Lillian Smith

For a long time it had seemed to me that life was about to begin — real life. But there was always some obstacle in the way, something to be gotten through first, some unfinished business, time still to be served, or a debt to be paid. Then life would begin. At last it dawned on me that these obstacles were my life.

Alfred D'Souza

Many a man who has known himself at ten forgets himself utterly between ten and thirty.

Catherine Drinker Bowen

I don't think there are any sins; I think there are things you don't admit, look into, or confront, so confrontation is my response.

Robert Duncan

To rise into love you must descend into your wounds.

Robert Bly

We learn, as the thread plays out, that we belong / Less to what flatters us than to what scars.

Stanley Kunitz

I think in people's hearts they understand that the heart is cooking like shish kebab in your breast, and no matter what you do the passions come and go and they sear you, they burn you. If it's not your lover, it's your children; if it's not your children, it's your job; if it's not your job, it's growing old; if it's not growing old, it's getting sick. This predicament cannot be resolved. That is the wound that does not heal, and rather than approach it from the point of view of stitching or cauterizing it, there is a kind of wisdom of living with the wound.

Leonard Cohen

During the past thirty years, people from all the civilized countries of the earth have consulted me. Among all my patients in the second half of life — that is to say, over thirty-five — there has not been one whose problem in the last resort was not that of finding a religious outlook on life. It is safe to say that every one of them fell ill because they had lost that which the living religions of every age have given to their followers; and none of them has been really healed who did not regain his religious outlook.

Carl Jung

People travel to wonder at the height of mountains, at the huge waves of the sea, at the long courses of rivers, at the vast compass of the ocean, at the circular motion of the stars; and they pass themselves by without wondering.

Saint Augustine

Nothing we have intensely sensed, while awake or while asleep, is ever lost, no matter how much we would later reject it as irrational or hallucinatory; the very act of its burial in the memory makes it more firmly part of whatever it is we are, and it will assert itself unexpectedly, when we are fatigued or unwary.

James McConkey

Imagine you are dead. After many years in exile, you are permitted to cast a single glance earthward. You see a lamppost and an old dog lifting his leg against it. You are so moved that you cannot help sobbing.

Paul Klee

Art Is Prayer

Art is prayer — not the vulgarized notations handed down to us in the scriptures, but a fresh vital discovery of one's own special presence in the world. Marc Chagall was once asked if he attended a synagogue; he answered that his work is prayer.

Joseph Zinker

What am I in the eyes of most people? A good-for-nothing, an eccentric and disagreeable man, somebody who has no position in society and never will have. Very well, even if that were true, I should want to show by my work what there is in the heart of such an eccentric man, of such a nobody.

Vincent van Gogh

The aim of an artist is not to solve a problem irrefutably, but to make people love life in all its countless, inexhaustible manifestations. If I were told that I could write a novel whereby I might irrefutably establish what seemed to me the correct point of view on all social problems, I would not even devote two hours to such a novel; but if I were to be told that what I should write would be read in about twenty years' time by those who are now children and that they would laugh and cry over it and love life, I would devote all my own life and all my energies to it.

Leo Tolstoy

Discontent is at the root of the creative process: the most gifted members of the human species are at their creative best when they cannot have their way.

Eric Hoffer

I think one's art goes as far and as deep as one's love goes.

Andrew Wyeth

Once, many years ago in Berkeley at a concert, while a Brahms symphony was being played, I happened to sit next to the composer Darius Milhaud. In the

midst of it, he said to me, "They think because it is long it is deep."

Rudolf Arnheim

There is no immaculate conception in art.

Walter Kuhn

The essence of all beautiful art, all great art, is gratitude.

Friedrich Nietzsche

Where the spirit does not work with the hand there is no art.

Leonardo da Vinci

Andrés Segovia once said his interest in the guitar began when he was eight years old. "One day a man walked by me in the street playing a guitar. He put my fingers on the strings and I played, not as if I were learning but as if I were remembering."

Richard Kehl

Every creator painfully experiences the chasm between his inner vision and its ultimate expression.

Isaac Bashevis Singer

By the time I was three, I was spending every waking moment at the keyboard; standing, placing my hands on the keyboard, and pushing notes. And I would choose very carefully what tones I would play because I knew that when I would play a note I would become that note.

Lorin Hollander

What do we know of his [Mozart's] inner mechanisms? Only one thing is certain: depression or psychic suffering does not diminish his productivity, unlike other creative people, but increases it qualitatively and quantitatively.

Wolfgang Hildesheimer

No one should drive a hard bargain with an artist.

Ludwig van Beethoven

I found the answer [to how and what to paint] when I joined a school of painters in Paris after the war who called themselves neomeditationists. . . . They believed an artist had to wait for inspiration, very quietly, and they did most of their waiting at the Café du Dôme or the Rotonde with brandy. It was then that I realized that all the really good ideas I'd ever had came to me while I was milking a cow. So I went back to Iowa.

Grant Wood

What you have to do now is work. There's no right way to start.

Anna Held Audette

One of the great joys of being a painter is the pleasure of being so intimately connected with the [tradition of art]. . . . I mean, the longer you work, the more you appreciate what those marvelous painters did, and how damned good they are. And it's a little bit of a paradox. You think, *I think I'll give up right now — I've seen the Vermeer show.* But he's a human being like us, and, by God, you can just keep going!

Wayne Thiebaud

It's very possible that your life in art — your successful life in art — might be a struggle from start to finish.

Sally Warner

If you don't live it, it won't come out your horn.

Charlie Parker

Artists don't talk about art. Artists talk about work. If I have anything to say to young writers, it's stop thinking of writing as art. Think of it as work.

Paddy Chayefsky

I've painted for a very long time, but I don't get tired or bored by it; I love to do it. If I don't paint one day, I don't feel well physically or mentally. My eyes bother me when I don't paint. But when I paint a full day, I feel satisfied and everything seems to be OK. I would never stop, never retire. I don't see how people can retire; I don't understand that. My brother Moses died while he was painting. He was actually working on a painting, and the last words he said were to the model: "Phoebe, don't frown." Then he died. He worked to the very last minute.

Ralph Soyer

☺

There really is no such thing as Art. There are only artists.

E.H. Gombrich

Could *Hamlet* have been written by a committee, or the *Mona Lisa* painted by a club? Could the New Testament have been composed as a conference report? Creative ideas do not spring from groups. They spring from individuals. The divine spark leaps from the finger of God to the finger of Adam, whether it takes ultimate shape in a law of physics or a law of the land, a poem or a policy, a sonata or a mechanical computer.

A. Whitney Griswold

I played with the idea of becoming a writer and later of becoming a painter, but my father discouraged the idea of either writing or painting as a career. "Do not treat the muses as cows to be milked," he said.

Franz Heider

Art interests me very much, but the truth interests me infinitely more.

Alberto Giacometti

One can't judge Wagner's opera *Lohengrin* after a first hearing, and I certainly don't intend hearing it a second time.

Gioachino Rossini

A man's work is nothing but this slow trek to rediscover, through the detours of art, those two or three great and simple images in whose presence his heart first opened.

Albert Camus

Art is prayer — not the vulgarized notations handed down to us in the scriptures, but a fresh vital discovery of one's own special presence in the world. Marc Chagall was once asked if he attended a synagogue; he answered that his work is prayer.

Joseph Zinker

The notes I handle no better than many pianists. But the pauses between the notes — ah, that is where the art resides.

Artur Schnabel

Max Ernst used to describe how, as a child, he would watch his father painting in the back garden. One day Ernst Senior was stymied by a tree that he could not paint satisfactorily, so, to the outrage of his son the budding surrealist, he fetched an axe and chopped it down, editing it from both life and art.

Robert Hughes

Art does not like to lie down on the bed that is made for it; it runs away as soon as one says its name; it loves to be incognito. Its best moments are when it forgets what it is called.

Jean Dubuffet

The artist Leon Kroll was having trouble with a seascape. "My boy," said Winslow Homer, "if you want to make a great sea, use only two waves."

Richard Kehl

A Japanese artist was commissioned by an American to do a painting. The completed work had, in a lower corner, the branch of a cherry tree with a few blossoms and a bird perched upon it. The entire upper half of the painting was white. Unhappy, the American asked the artist to put something else in the painting because it looked, well, so bare. The Japanese refused the request. When pressed for an explanation, the artist said that if he did fill up the painting, there would be no space for the bird to fly.

Robert A. Rosenstone

Man stands for long time with mouth open before roast duck flies in.

Chinese saying

The best work is done with the heart breaking, or overflowing.

Mignon McLaughlin

I merely took the energy it takes to pout and wrote some blues.

Duke Ellington

What was any art but . . . a mold in which to imprison for a moment the shining elusive element which is life itself — life hurrying past us and running away, too strong to stop, too sweet to lose.

Willa Cather

One of Vladimir de Pachmann's favorite tricks before a recital was to play about with the piano stool, adjusting and re-adjusting it, until the audience became desperate. Then he would rush into the wings to fetch a large book, place it on the seat, and try that. He would indicate that all was still not satisfactory and would tear one page from the book and try again.

Little, Brown Book of Anecdotes

Art is spirituality in drag.

Jennifer Yane

Art is not necessary at all. All that is necessary to make this world a better place to live in is to love — to love as Christ loved, as Buddha loved.

Isadora Duncan

I tell you, the more I think, the more I feel that there is nothing more truly artistic than to love people.

Vincent van Gogh

Writing and travel broaden your ass if not your mind and I like to write standing up.

Ernest Hemingway

I write because, exacting as it may be to do so, it is still more difficult to refrain, and because — however conscious of one's limitations one may be — there is always at the back of one's mind an irrational hope that this next book will be different: it will be the rounded achievement, the complete fulfillment. It never has been: yet I am still writing.

Iris Origo

Delay is natural to a writer. He is like a surfer — he bides his time, waits for the perfect wave on which to ride in. Delay is instinctive with him. He waits for the surge (of emotion? of strength? of courage?) that will carry him along. . . . I am apt to let something simmer for a while in my mind before trying to put it into words. I walk around, straightening pictures on the wall, rugs on the floor — as though not until everything in the world was lined up and perfectly true could anybody reasonably expect me to set a word down on paper.

E.B. White

There is a difference between a book of two hundred pages from the very beginning, and a book of two hundred pages which is the result of an original eight hundred pages. The six hundred are there. Only you don't see them.

Elie Wiesel

I asked Ring Lardner the other day how he writes his short stories, and he said he wrote a few widely separated words or phrases on a piece of paper and then went back and filled in the spaces.

Harold Ross

Everywhere I go I'm asked if I think the university stifles writers. My opinion is that they don't stifle enough of them. There's many a bestseller that could have been prevented by a good teacher.

Flannery O'Connor

A cow does not know how much milk it has until the milkman starts working on it. Then it looks round in surprise and sees the pail full to the brim. In the same way a writer has no idea how much he has to say till his pen draws it out of him. Thoughts will then appear on the paper that he is amazed to find that he has possessed.

Gerald Branan

Writing is the only profession where no one considers you ridiculous if you earn no money.

Jules Renard

I believe in miracles in every area of life except writing. Experience has shown me that there are no miracles in writing. The only thing that produces good writing is hard work.

Isaac Bashevis Singer

The business of the poet and novelist is to show the sorriness underlying the grandest things, and the grandeur underlying the sorriest things.

Thomas Hardy

Writing is simply the writer and the reader on opposite ends of a pencil; they should be as close together as that.

Jay R. Gould

Though I'd been taught at our dining-room table about the solar system, and knew the earth revolved around the sun, and our moon around us, I never found out the moon didn't come up in the west until I was a writer and Herschel Brickell, the literary critic, told me after I misplaced it in a story. He said valuable words to me about my new profession: "Always be sure you get your moon in the right part of the sky."

Eudora Welty

Contrary to what many of you might imagine, a career in letters is not without its drawbacks — chief among them the unpleasant fact that one is frequently called upon to sit down and write.

Fran Lebowitz

Lucky accidents seldom happen to writers who don't work. You will find that you rewrite a poem and it never seems quite right. Then a much better poem may come rather fast and you wonder why you bothered with all that work on the earlier poem. Actually, the hard work you do on one poem is put in on all poems. The hard work on the first poem is responsible for the sudden ease of the second. If you just sit around waiting for the easy ones, nothing will come. Get to work.

Richard Hugo

[Novelist Sinclair Lewis] doted on names; he believed people became their names. He had a stack of telephone books from all over the world, so he could find an odd but apt name for a character. . . . When he had to name a new character, he would make a list of a dozen possibilities and . . . day after day he would pick up the list and cross off a name or two, until he had made his final choice by elimination. I would sometimes hear him at his desk calling out names, as if summoning lost souls.

John Hersey

The ideal view for daily writing, hour on hour, is the blank brick wall of a cold-storage warehouse. Failing this, a stretch of sky will do, cloudless if possible.

Edna Ferber

I am not a writer except when I write.

Juan Carlos Onetti

I was working on the proof of one of my poems all the morning, and took out a comma. In the afternoon, I put it back in again.

Oscar Wilde

I have asked a lot of my emotions — 120 stories. The price was high . . . because there was one little drop of something, not blood, not a tear, not my seed, but me more intimately than these, in every

story; it was the extra I had. Now it is gone.

F. Scott Fitzgerald

❧

Poetry is what comes up behind us and whispers the singing name of home in our ears.

John Ciardi

A writer is a person for whom writing is more difficult than it is for other people.

Thomas Mann

It's like driving a car at night. You never see further than your headlights, but you can make the whole trip that way.

E.L. Doctorow

It's a nervous work. The state that you need to be in to write is the state that others are paying large sums to get rid of.

Shirley Hazzard

There are three rules for writing the novel. Unfortunately, no one knows what they are.

W. Somerset Maugham

I know some very great writers, writers you love who write beautifully and have made a great deal of money, and not one of them sits down routinely feeling wildly enthusiastic and confident. Not one of them writes elegant first drafts. All right, one of them does, but we do not like her very much. We do not think that she has a rich inner life or that God likes her or can even stand her.

Anne Lamott

I didn't have to think up so much as a comma or a semicolon; it was all given, straight from the celestial recording room. Weary, I would beg for a break, an intermission, time enough, let's say, to go to the toilet or take a breath of fresh air on the balcony. Nothing doing!

Henry Miller

A true poet does not bother to be poetical. Nor does a nursery gardener scent his roses.

Jean Cocteau

An exclamation mark is like laughing at your own joke.

F. Scott Fitzgerald

Concentrate, don't embroider.

Spencer Tracy

When I was a little boy, they called me a liar, but now that I am a grown-up, they call me a writer.

Isaac Bashevis Singer

A word is not the same with one writer as with another. One tears it from his guts. The other pulls it out of his overcoat pocket.

Charles Péguy

Poetry is not an expression of the party line. It's that time of night, lying in bed, thinking what you really think, making the private world public; that's what the poet does.

Allen Ginsberg

Poetry is nobody's business except the poet's, and everybody else can fuck off.

Philip Larkin

Writer's block is what you get if you're too full of yourself and trying to be García Márquez. You sit and stare at the wall and nothing happens for you. It's like imagining you're a tree and trying to sprout leaves. Once you come to your senses and accept who you are, then there's no problem. I'm not García Márquez. I'm a late-middle-aged midlist fair-to-middling writer with a comfortable midriff, and it gives me quite a bit of pleasure.

Garrison Keillor

How vain it is to sit down to write when you have not stood up to live.

Henry David Thoreau

I love metaphor. It provides two loaves where there seems to be one. Sometimes it throws in a load of fish.

Bernard Malamud

Successful writers are not the ones who write the best sentences. They are the ones who keep writing.

Bonnie Friedman

If you wish to be a writer, write.

Epictetus

I write when I'm inspired, and I see to it that I'm inspired at nine o'clock every morning.

Peter De Vries

Just as appetite comes by eating, so work brings inspiration.

Igor Stravinsky

Q: We write essays and stories all the time in school. It doesn't seem like a very difficult thing to do. Is it?

A: Not at all. All you need is a perfect ear, absolute pitch, the devotion to your work that a priest of God has for his, the guts of a burglar, no conscience except to writing, and you're in. It's easy. Never give it a thought.

Ernest Hemingway

What words say does not last. / The words last. / Because words are always the same / and what they say is never the same.

Antonio Porchia

You sit in front of the typewriter and the first thing you have to deal with is the government of the mind, the superego, sitting up there on top of your head.

Bruce Robinson

A fly alighting on the sheet of white paper was excuse enough for him to give himself the right to idle. He did not write, for fear of disturbing the fly.

Jules Renard

When Alexander the Great visited Diogenes and asked whether he could do anything for the famed teacher, Diogenes replied: "Only stand out of my light." Perhaps someday we shall know how to heighten creativity. Until then, one of the best things we can do for creative men and women is to stand out of their light.

John W. Gardner

Whenever I saw a rich person I would ask where his or her money was from, and invariably, or should I say inevitably, the answer was a natural resource, or else an unnatural resource. Oil was a common answer, or real estate, or steel — this was before computers. The answer was never the answer you wanted to hear. The answer was never "Poetry — their money's from poetry, Fran." Or "That's one of the great essay fortunes in this country."

Fran Lebowitz

As I look back on what I have written, I can see that the very persons who have taken away my time are those who have given me something to say.

Katherine Paterson

Mostly, we authors must repeat ourselves — that's the truth. We have two or three great moving experiences in our lives — experiences so great and moving that it doesn't seem at the time that anyone else has been caught up and pounded and dazzled and astonished and beaten and broken and rescued and illuminated and rewarded and humbled in just that way before.

F. Scott Fitzgerald

When a poet's mind is perfectly equipped for its work, it is constantly amalgamating disparate experiences; the ordinary man's experience is chaotic, irregular, fragmentary. The latter falls in love, or reads Spinoza, and these two experiences have nothing to do with each other, or with the noise of the typewriter or the smell of cooking; in the mind of the poet these experiences are always forming new wholes.

T.S. Eliot

I personally think we developed language because of our deep inner need to complain.

Jane Wagner

It reminds me of a string of wet sponges; it reminds me of tattered washing on the line; it reminds me of stale bean soup, of college yells, of dogs barking idiotically through endless nights. It is so bad that a sort of grandeur creeps into it. It drags itself up out of the dark abysm of pish and crawls insanely up the topmost pinnacle of posh. It is rumble and bumble. It is flap and doodle. It is balder and dash.

H.L. Mencken, on Warren
G. Harding's inaugural address

Omit needless words. Vigorous writing is concise. A sentence should contain no unnecessary words, a paragraph no unnecessary sentences, for the same reason that a drawing should have no unnecessary lines and a machine no unnecessary parts.

William Strunk Jr.

We defend ourselves by descriptions and tame the world by generalizing.

Iris Murdoch

Since the concepts people live by are derived only from perceptions and from language, and since the perceptions are received and interpreted only in light of earlier concepts, man comes pretty close to living in a house that language built.

Russell F.W. Smith

Today the discredit of words is very great. Most of the time the media transmit lies. In the face of an intolerable world, words appear to change very little. State power has become congenitally deaf, which is why — but the editorialists forget it — terrorists are reduced to bombs and hijacking.

John Berger

Once when I was in Elaine de Kooning's studio [on Broadway], at a time when the metal sculptor Herbert Ferber occupied the studio immediately above, there came through the floor a most horrible crashing and banging. "What in the world is that?" I asked, and Elaine said, "Oh, that's Herbert thinking."

Donald Barthelme

In order to swim one takes off all one's clothes. In order to aspire to the truth one must undress in a far more inward sense, divest oneself of all one's inward clothes — of thoughts, conceptions, selfishness — before one is sufficiently naked.

Søren Kierkegaard

Language is a tailor's shop where nothing fits.

Rumi

I always wanted to write a book that ended with the word mayonnaise.

Richard Brautigan

Truthful words are not beautiful; beautiful words are not truthful. Good words are not persuasive; persuasive words are not good.

Lao Tzu

I am so wise I had my mouth sewn
shut.

John Berryman

The writer does not learn to write so
that he can "write," but because without
the necessary tools he cannot dig his
way out of prison.

Alan Comfort

Magazines all too frequently lead to
books and should be regarded by the
prudent as the heavy petting of literature.

Fran Lebowitz

For Christ sake write and don't worry
about what the boys will say nor whether it will be a masterpiece nor what. I
write one page of masterpiece to ninety-
one pages of shit.

Ernest Hemingway

❧

The End Of Safety

Any real change implies the breakup of the world as one has always known it, the loss of all that gave one an identity, the end of safety.

James Baldwin

There comes a time in a man's life when to get where he has to go — if there are no doors or windows — he walks through a wall.

Bernard Malamud

Damaged people are dangerous. They know they can survive.

Josephine Hart

Character is what you do when nobody is looking.

Henry Huffman

He who knows he is infirm, and would yet climb, does not think of the summit which he believes to be beyond his reach but climbs slowly onwards, taking very short steps, looking below as often as he likes but not above him, never trying his powers, but seldom stopping, and then, sometimes, behold! He is on the top.

Samuel Butler

Better to strengthen your back than lighten your burden.

Source unknown

Steep and craggy is the path of the gods.

Porphyry

Anything can happen to anybody. In the last movie I did, *Above Suspicion*, I played a paraplegic. I went to a rehab center and I worked with the people there so I could simulate being a paraplegic. And every day I would get into my car and drive away and go, "Thank God that's not me." I remember the smugness of that, as if I was privileged in a way. And seven months later, I was

in this condition. The point is we are all one great big family and any one of us can get hurt at any moment. . . . We should never walk by somebody who's in a wheelchair and be afraid of them or think of them as a stranger. It could be us — in fact, it is us.

Christopher Reeve

In the Dalebura tribe a woman, a cripple from birth, was carried about by the tribespeople, each in turn, until her death at the age of sixty-six. . . . They never desert the sick.

Irving King

Anyone who regards love as a deal made on the basis of "needs" is in danger of falling into a purely quantitative ethic. If love is a deal, then who is to say that you should not make as many deals as possible?

Thomas Merton

The people you have to lie to, own you. The things you have to lie about, own you. When your children see you owned . . . then they are not your children anymore, they are the children of what owns you. If money owns you, they are the children of money. If your need for pretense and illusion owns you, they are the children of pretense and illusion. If your fear of loneliness owns you, they are the children of the fear of loneliness. If your fear of the truth owns you, they are the children of the fear of truth.

Michael Ventura

The power of movement lies in the fact that it can indeed change the habits of people. This change is not the result of force but of dedication, of moral persuasion.

Steve Biko

Character is what emerges from all the little things you were too busy to do yesterday, but did anyway.

Mignon McLaughlin

I've had occasions when I wondered seriously how anyone could feel as bad as this and live. The answer came back that I was still alive, that's all.

William S. Burroughs

The meaning of life must be conceived in terms of the specific meaning of a personal life in a given situation.

Viktor Frankl

I remember talking with a friend who has worked for many years at the Catholic Worker, a ministry to the poor in New York City. Daily she tries to respond to waves of human misery that are as ceaseless as surf in that community. Out of my deep not-knowing, I asked how she could keep doing a work that never showed any results, a work in which the problems keep getting worse instead of better. I will never forget her enigmatic answer: "The thing you don't understand, Parker, is that just because something is impossible doesn't mean you shouldn't do it."

Parker J. Palmer

ↄ

You possess only whatever will not be lost in a shipwreck.

al-Ghazali

There is no such thing as security. There never has been.

Germaine Greer

There will be a rain dance on Friday, weather permitting.

George Carlin

Buddha's doctrine: Man suffers because of his craving to possess and keep forever things which are essentially impermanent. Chief among these things is his own person, for this is his means of isolating himself from the rest of life, his castle into which he can retreat and from which he can assert himself against external forces. He believes that his fortified and isolated position is the best means of obtaining happiness; it enables him to fight against change, to strive to keep pleasing things for himself, to shut out suffering and shape circumstance as he wills. In short, it is his means of resisting life. The Buddha taught that all things, including his castle, are essentially impermanent, and that as soon as man tries to possess them they slip away; the frustration of the desire to possess is the immediate cause of suffering.

Alan Watts

It is as if I were attempting to trace with the point of a pencil the shadow of the tracing pencil.

Nathanael West

It's in the darkness of men's eyes that they get lost.

Black Elk

Money is only money, beans tonight and steak tomorrow. So long as you can look yourself in the eye.

Meridel Le Sueur

Man is condemned to be free.

Jean-Paul Sartre

The only person who is really free is the one who can turn down an invitation to dinner without any excuse.

Jules Renard

A rabbi entered a room in his home and saw his son deep in prayer. In the corner stood a cradle with a crying baby. "Son, can't you hear?" the rabbi said. "The baby is crying." The son said, "Oh, Father, I was lost in God." And the rabbi said, "One who is lost in God can see the very fly crawling up the wall."

Abel Herzberg

We wake, if we ever wake at all, to mystery, rumors of death, beauty, violence.

Annie Dillard

For six years now, I have gone around by myself and built up my science. And now I am a master. Son, I can love anything. No longer do I have to think about it even. I see a street full of people and a beautiful light comes in me. I watch a bird in the sky. Or I meet a traveler on the road. Everything, son. And anybody. All strangers and all loved! Do you realize what a science like mine can mean?

Carson McCullers,
A Tree, A Rock, A Cloud

If I had been asked in the first years of my spiritual life endeavor what I wanted people to say in appreciation of me, I would have answered, "Let them say he is a holy man." Years later I would have answered, "Let them say he is a loving man." And now I would like people to say of me, "He is a free man."

Anthony de Mello

We all have to rise in the end, not just one or two who were smart enough, had will enough for their own salvation, but all the halt, the maimed, and the blind of us, which is most of us.

Maureen Duffy

☯

The Chinese say that when you have too much trouble, you write poetry. There are two kinds of poetry: in one you jump in; in the other you jump out. If you jump out, you become a philosopher. If you jump in, you die with the poem.

Richard Kehl

Have the courage to live. Anyone can die.

Robert Cody

It's true that heroes are inspiring, but mustn't they also do some rescuing if they are to be worthy of their name? Would Wonder Woman matter if she only sent commiserating telegrams to the distressed?

Jeanette Winterson

It was involuntary. They sank my boat.

John F. Kennedy, when asked how
he became a war hero

An individual who breaks a law that conscience tells him is unjust, and who willingly accepts the penalty of imprisonment in order to arouse the conscience of the community over its injustice, is in reality expressing the highest respect for the law.

Martin Luther King Jr.

When you go to court, you are putting your fate into the hands of twelve people who weren't smart enough to get out of jury duty.

Norm Crosby

Perfect courage is to do without witnesses what one would be capable of doing with the world looking on.

François de La Rochefoucauld

A great part of courage is the courage of having done the thing before.

Ralph Waldo Emerson

You hear them at the grocery store deliberating the balsamic vinegar and olive oils, the cold-pressed virgin olive oil, the warm-pressed olive oil, and you think: These people probably subscribe to an olive-oil magazine. . . . These are people with too much money and very little character, people who are all sensibility and no sense, all nostalgia and no history, the people my Aunt Eleanor used to call "a ten-dollar haircut on a fifty-nine-cent head."

Garrison Keillor

The course of a river is almost always disapproved of by the source.

Jean Cocteau

The more characteristic American hero in the earlier day, and the more beloved type at all times, was not the hustler but the whittler.

Mark Sullivan

It was chilling to realize that the sentimental qualities most valued between people, like loyalty, constancy, and affection, are the ones most likely to impede change.

Ted Simon

History never looks like history when you are living through it. It always looks confusing and messy, and it always feels uncomfortable.

John W. Gardner

In our world of big names, curiously, our true heroes tend to be anonymous: . . . the teacher, the nurse, the mother, the honest cop, the hard workers at lonely, underpaid, unglamorous, unpublicized jobs.

Daniel J. Boorstin

There is plenty of courage among us for the abstract but not for the concrete.

Helen Keller

That is at bottom the only courage that is demanded of us: to have courage for the most strange, the most singular, and the most inexplicable that we may encounter. That mankind has in this sense been cowardly has done life endless harm; the experiences that are called "visions," the whole so-called spirit world, death, all those things that are so closely akin to us, have by daily parrying been so crowded out of life that the senses with which we could have grasped them are atrophied. To say nothing of God.

Rainer Maria Rilke

While we are watching a sunset or listening to a piece of good music or having a good meal, if, for some reason, we have the immanence of the Christ break in upon our consciousness and we feel a sense of oceanic love and oneness . . . it is easy to come up with all sorts of excuses about why we shouldn't be feeling it. It is easy to deny it or, on the other hand, to think that since we are feeling this, therefore we must be a great realized master. Instead, we could be feeling that this is an experience of the most ordinary and natural state for a human being.

David Spangler

My mistake was what Pascal, if I remember rightly, calls "error of stoicism": thinking we can do always what we can do sometimes.

C.S. Lewis

"I'm very brave generally," he went on in a low voice, "only today I happen to have a headache."

Tweedledum, in Lewis Carroll's
Through the Looking Glass

☉

Progress is not an illusion. It happens, but it is slow and invariably disappointing.

George Orwell

It's not the same to talk of bulls as to be in the bullring.

Spanish proverb

I do not love strife, because I have always found that in the end each remains of the same opinion.

Catherine the Great

It was completely fruitless to quarrel with the world, whereas the quarrel with oneself was occasionally fruitful, and always, she had to admit, interesting.

May Sarton

If a man like Malcolm X could change and repudiate racism, if I myself and other former Muslims can change, if young whites can change, then there is hope for America.

Eldridge Cleaver

Our enemy is by tradition our savior, in preventing us from superficiality.

Joyce Carol Oates

To die for the revolution is a one-shot deal; to live for the revolution means taking on the more difficult commitment of changing our day-to-day life patterns.

Frances M. Beal

Those of us who have the situation in Lebanon in perspective and know exactly how to plot a gay-rights campaign are usually morons. We snap at our children when they have innocent homework questions. We don't notice when our lover has a deadline. We forget to call our best friend back when she's just had root canal. Homework, root canal, and deadlines are the important things in life, and only when we have these major dramas taken care of can we presume to look at the larger questions.

Cynthia Heimel

Why must you always try to be omnipotent, and shove things about? Tragic things happen sometimes that we just have to submit to.

Rebecca West

Do you not see how necessary a world of pains and troubles is to school an intelligence and make it a soul?

John Keats

The reverse side also has a reverse side.

Japanese proverb

We are changing, we have got to change, and we can no more help it than leaves can help going yellow and coming loose in autumn.

D.H. Lawrence

The need for change bulldozed a road down the center of my mind.

Maya Angelou

One of these days I'm going to put Band-Aids across my mouth so that smiling will become less of a reflex in uncomfortable situations.

Ingrid Bengis

Even a purely moral act that has no hope of immediate and visible political effect can gradually and indirectly, over time, gain in political significance.

Václav Havel

The status quo sits on society like fat on cold chicken soup and it's quite content to be what it is. Unless someone comes along to stir things up there just won't be change.

Abbie Hoffman

Ideologies . . . have no heart of their own. They're the whores and angels of our striving selves.

John le Carré

Real generosity toward the future lies in giving all to the present.

Albert Camus

"Realistic" people who pursue "practical" aims are rarely as realistic or practical in the long run of life as the dreamers who pursue their dreams.

Hans Selye

When your dreams tire, they go underground / and out of kindness that's where they stay.

Libby Houston

Every daring attempt to make a great change in existing conditions, every lofty vision of new possibilities for the human race, has been labeled utopian.

Emma Goldman

If you have built castles in the air, your work need not be lost; that is where they should be. Now put the foundations under them.

Henry David Thoreau

No nation, no social institution, ever acquired coherence without some sort of a fight. Out of the fight come its myths and its heroes.

Thurman Arnold

It isn't necessary to imagine the world ending in fire or ice. There are two other possibilities: one is paperwork, and the other is nostalgia.

Frank Zappa

The most radical revolutionary will become a conservative on the day after the revolution.

Hannah Arendt

Freedom lies beyond conformity or rebellion.

Sam Keen

It will be necessary to realize that there is nothing in the world which is not holy. At the same time, we will find out that all our conceptions of what is holy and secular will be as nothing in the light of high holiness, the infinite source.

Rav Kook

The dragon we must slay is no more than the monster of everyday expectations.

Sheldon Kopp

If you cry, "Forward!" you must be sure to make clear the direction in which to go. Don't you see that if you fail to do that and simply call out the word to a monk and a revolutionary, they will go in precisely opposite directions?

Anton Chekhov

There is a time for departure even when there's no certain place to go.

Tennessee Williams

Many of the commonest assumptions, it seems to me, are arbitrary ones: that the new is better than the old, the untried superior to the tried, the complex more advantageous than the simple, the fast quicker than the slow, the big greater than the small, and the world as remodeled by Man the Architect functionally sounder and more agreeable than the world as it was before he changed everything to suit his vogues and his conniptions.

E.B. White

Sometimes small things are the ones one is grateful for all through life. At a faculty reception . . . a British lady taught me how to tie my shoes with a double knot so that they keep tied more securely and still come apart in a jiffy. Kneeling on the floor in the midst of the chattering sherry-sippers she tied my shoes. I've rememberd her twice a day ever since.

Rudolf Arnheim

The line separating good and evil passes not through states, nor between classes, nor between political parties either — but right through every human heart. . . . This line shifts. Inside us, it oscillates with the years. And even within hearts overwhelmed by evil, one small bridgehead of good is retained. And even in the best of hearts, there remains . . . an un-uprooted small corner of evil.

Aleksandr Solzhenitsyn

If you look at history, even recent history, you see that there is indeed progress. . . . Over time, the cycle is clearly, generally upwards. And it doesn't happen by laws of nature. And it doesn't happen by social laws. . . . It happens as a result of hard work by dedicated people who are willing to look at problems honestly, to look at them without illusions, and to go to work chipping away at them, with no guarantee of success — in fact, with a need for a rather high tolerance for failure along the way, and plenty of disappointments.

Noam Chomsky

We have entered a new Middle Ages . . . a time when it is terribly important, and often dangerous, to preserve values and knowledge — to stand up for visions that most of this crazed world can't comprehend or tolerate. . . . The future lives in our individual, often lonely, and certainly unprofitable acts of integrity, or it doesn't live at all.

Michael Ventura

Justice without love is not justice. Love without justice is not love.

Mother Teresa

❦

Those are my principles. If you don't like them, I have others.

Groucho Marx

No matter how cynical you get, it's almost impossible to keep up.

Lily Tomlin

. . . and down they forgot as up they grew.

e.e. cummings

My conscience aches, but it's going to lose the fight.

Allanah Myles

If there existed no external means for dimming their consciences, one-half of the men would at once shoot themselves, because to live contrary to one's reason is a most intolerable state, and all men of our time are in such a state.

Leo Tolstoy

You can really learn something about a person when he's put into circumstances in which civilized values place his own identity, even his very being, in jeopardy. . . . I often think: How would a friend with whom you've drunk a lot of vodka and had a lot of fun respond when one morning you plant yourself on his doorstep and say, "Hide me. I'm being chased by the Nazis."

Roman Polanski

One must think like a hero to behave like a merely decent human being.

May Sarton

God will not look you over for medals, degrees, or diplomas, but for scars.

Elbert Hubbard

A commentary on the times is that the word honesty is now preceded by old-fashioned.

Larry Wolters

I would rather be the man who bought the Brooklyn Bridge than the man who sold it.

Will Rogers

We may argue eloquently that "honesty is the best policy." Unfortunately, the moment honesty is adopted for the sake of policy it mysteriously ceases to be honesty.

Dorothy L. Sayers

I never had a policy; I have simply tried to do what seemed best as each day came.

Abraham Lincoln

The naked truth is always better than the best-dressed lie.

Ann Landers

Only threats are frightening; one soon comes to terms with facts.

Oswald Spengler

Excuse me, sir; I cannot consent to receive pay for services I do not render.

Robert E. Lee, explaining his rejection of a ten-thousand-dollar-a-year salary to act as titular head of an insurance company after the Civil War

There are few things more disturbing than to find, in somebody we detest, a moral quality which seems to us demonstrably superior to anything we ourselves possess. It augurs not merely an unfairness on the part of creation, but a lack of artistic judgment. Sainthood is acceptable only in saints.

Pamela Hansford Johnson

My goal in life is to be as good a person as my dog already thinks I am.

Source unknown

Do every act of your life as if it were your last.

Marcus Aurelius

I hope you have not been leading a double life, pretending to be wicked and really being good all the time. That would be hypocrisy.

Oscar Wilde

If we had done as the kings told us five hundred years ago, we would all have been slaves. If we had done as the priest told us, we would all have been idiots. If we had done as the doctors told us, we would all have been dead. We have been saved by disobedience. We have been saved by the splendid thing called independence, and I want to see more of it, day after day, and I want to see children raised so that they will have it.

Robert Ingersoll

A lot of people are waiting for Martin Luther King Jr. or Mahatma Gandhi to come back, but they are gone. We are it. It is up to us. It is up to you.

Marian Wright Edelman

Put your ear down close to your soul and listen hard.

Anne Sexton

The mountain remains unmoved at its seeming defeat by the mist.

Rabindranath Tagore

☽

To know oneself, one should assert oneself. Psychology is action, not thinking about oneself. We continue to shape our personality all our life. If we knew ourselves perfectly, we should die.

Albert Camus

The self-confidence of the warrior is not the self-confidence of the average man. The average man seeks certainty in the eyes of the onlooker and calls that self-confidence. The warrior seeks impeccability in his own eyes and calls that humbleness. The average man is hooked to his fellow men, while the warrior is hooked only to himself.

Carlos Castaneda

You've been somebody long enough. You spent the first half of your life becoming somebody. Now you can work on becoming nobody, which is really somebody. For when you become nobody there is no tension, no pretense, no one trying to be anyone or anything. The natural state of the mind shines through unobstructed — and the natural state of the mind is pure love.

Ram Dass and Stephen Levine

When a man has boils or scabies, he isn't disgusted with himself; he puts his infected hand in his dish and he licks his fingers without any repugnance. But if he sees a small sore on someone else's hand, he can't swallow his food. It's the same with moral blemishes: when you see defects such as indifference, pride, and lust in yourself, they don't bother you; but as soon as you notice them in others, you feel hurt and resentful.

Rumi

We are the hurdles we leap to be ourselves.

Michael McClure

One can fool life for a long time, but in the end it always makes us what we were intended to be.

André Malraux

I stand on the terrible threshold, and I see / The end and the beginning in each other's arms.

Stanley Kunitz

One may understand the cosmos, but never the ego; the self is more distant than any star.

G.K. Chesterton

It was the rhythm of all living, apparently, and for most people. Happiness, and then pain. Perhaps then happiness again, but now, with it, the awareness of its own mortality.

Laura Z. Hobson

If you're able to be yourself, then you have no competition.

Barbara Cook

Life has no other discipline to impose, if we would but realize it, than to accept life unquestioningly. Everything we shut our eyes to, everything we run away from, everything we deny, denigrate, or despise, serves to defeat us in the end. What seems nasty, painful, evil, can become a source of beauty, joy, and strength, if faced with an open mind. Every moment is a golden one for him who has the vision to recognize it as such.

Henry Miller

The only thing that one really knows about human nature is that it changes. Change is the one quality we can predicate of it. The systems that fail are those that rely on the permanency of human nature, and not on its growth and development. The error of Louis XIV was that he thought human nature would always be the same. The result of his error was the French Revolution. It was an admirable result.

Oscar Wilde

As long as you are trying to be something other than what you actually are, your mind merely wears itself out. But if you say, "This is what I am, it is a fact, and I am going to investigate, understand it," then you can go beyond.

J. Krishnamurti

The unconscious wants truth. It ceases to speak to those who want something else more than truth.

Adrienne Rich

It is better to conquer yourself than to win a thousand battles. Then the victory is yours. It cannot be taken from you, not by angels or by demons, heaven or hell.

The Buddha

Character — the willingness to accept responsibility for one's own life — is the source from which self-respect springs.

Joan Didion

Without self-respect you are a criminal in hiding, living in a prison you have built around yourself, and even if the prison is comfortable and luxurious, it is still a prison.

Maxwell Maltz

After the Easter Rebellion of 1916 [in Ireland, Eamon] De Valera was sentenced to penal servitude. En route to his prison, he took out his pipe and was about to light it when he stopped suddenly and said, "I will not let them deprive me of this pleasure in jail!" He immediately threw away the pipe and from that day never smoked again.

Bartlett's Book of Anecdotes

Any real change implies the breakup of the world as one has always known it, the loss of all that gave one an identity, the end of safety.

James Baldwin

You desire to know the art of living, my friend? It is contained in one phrase: make use of suffering.

Henri Frédéric Amiel

This work is about transformation — from the person we are to the person we really are. In the end, we can't be anyone else.

Marion Rosen

The thing you are ripening toward is the fruit of your life. It will make you bright inside, no matter what you are outside. It is a shining thing.

Stewart Edward White

☺

Tell me what is it that you plan to do / with your one wild and precious life?

Mary Oliver

I tried for years to live according to everyone else's morality. I tried to live like everyone else, to be like everyone else. I said the right things even when I felt and thought quite differently. And the result is a catastrophe.

Albert Camus

Ecstasy is what everyone craves — not love or sex, but a hot-blooded, soaring intensity, in which being alive is a joy and a thrill. That enravishment doesn't give meaning to life, and yet without it life seems meaningless.

Diane Ackerman

God is not indifferent to your need. / You have a thousand prayers, / but God has one.

Anne Sexton

You never see animals going through the absurd and often horrible fooleries of magic and religion. . . . Only man behaves with such gratuitous folly. It is the price he has to pay for being intelligent but not, as yet, intelligent enough.

Aldous Huxley

[Emperor Menelik II of Ethiopia] had one eccentricity. If he felt unwell, he was convinced that he had only to eat a few pages of the Bible in order to feel better. This odd behavior did him little harm, as long as his testamentary intake was modest. However, in December 1913 he was recovering from a stroke when he suddenly felt extremely ill. On his in-

structions, the complete Book of Kings was torn from the Bible and fed to him, page by page. He died before he had consumed the entire book.

Bartlett's Book of Anecdotes

I was thrown out of NYU my freshman year for cheating on my metaphysics final, you know. I looked within the soul of the boy sitting next to me.

Woody Allen

The lights of an all-night diner were irresistible. I entered the steamy, greasy warmth, felt the meat smell cling to my clothing. I sat down at the counter and picked up a matchbox. On it was printed, "Ace 24-hour cafe — where nice people meet." And tears came to my eyes for the hopefulness, the sweetness, the enduring promise of plain human love. And I understood the incarnation for, I believe, the first time: Christ took on flesh for love, because the flesh is lovable.

Mary Gordon

If Christ had been put on television to preach the Sermon on the Mount, viewers would either have switched to another channel, or contented themselves with remarking that the speaker had an interesting face. Christ might have become a television personality, but there would have been no Christianity.

Malcolm Muggeridge

The instinct of nearly all societies is to lock up anybody who is truly free. First, society begins by trying to beat you up. If this fails, they try to poison you. If this fails, too, they finish by loading honors on your head.

Jean Cocteau

There are two tragedies in life. One is not to get your heart's desire. The other is to get it.

George Bernard Shaw

Within your own house dwells the treasure of joy; so why do you go begging from door to door?

Sufi saying

Intent is not a thought, or an object, or a wish. Intent is what can make a man succeed when his thoughts tell him that he is defeated. It operates in spite of the warrior's indulgence. Intent is what makes him invulnerable. Intent is what sends a shaman through a wall, through space, to infinity.

Carlos Castaneda

I learned long ago that the world could neither deprive me of something nor give me anything, and I now have one ambition and one joy.

Mary Baker Eddy

If you want to identify me ask me not where I live, or what I like to eat, or how I comb my hair, but ask me what I think I am living for, in detail, and ask me what I think is keeping me from living fully for the thing I want to live for. Between these two answers you can determine the identity of any person. The better the answer he has, the more of a person he is.

Thomas Merton

A joyful heart is the normal result of a heart burning with love.

Mother Teresa

If there has to be a god can she be a committee of women dedicated to wiping out earthly oppression?

Hattie Gossett

Look at everything as though you were seeing it for the first or last time. Then your time on earth will be filled with glory.

Betty Smith

Every time I see something terrible, it's like I see it at age nineteen. I keep a freshness that way.

Ralph Nader

We're in the midst of a flood of biblical proportions. . . . I see everybody holding on in their individual way to an orange crate, to a piece of wood, and we're passing each other in this swollen river that has pretty well taken down all the landmarks and overturned everything we've got. And people insist, under the circumstances, on describing themselves as "liberal" or "conservative." It seems to me completely mad.

Leonard Cohen

The world dies over and over again, but the skeleton always gets up and walks.

Henry Miller

☉

It is impossible to persuade a man who does not disagree, but smiles.

Muriel Spark

Given a child falling into a river, an old person in a burning building, and a woman fainting in the street, a band of convicts would risk their lives to give aid as quickly at least as a band of millionaires.

Clarence Darrow

The saints may derive holiness from being alone but they can only express it in their relationship with other human beings. Similarly, the insights man gains in solitude can only find expression in his relationship with others, in a growing awareness of their needs, in sharing their joys and sorrows, in trying to comfort those who are desperate, to make life more tolerable for those who suffer.

G. Peter Fleck

Sometime in your life, hope that you might see one starved man, the look on his face when the bread finally arrives. Hope that you might have baked it or bought it or even kneaded it yourself. For that look on his face, for your meeting his eyes across a piece of bread, you might be willing to lose a lot, or suffer a lot, or die a little, even.

Daniel Berrigan

You save your soul by saving someone else's body.

Arthur Hertzberg

People talk about the courage of condemned men walking to the place of execution. Sometimes it needs as much courage to walk with any kind of bearing toward another person's habitual misery.

Graham Greene

Our horizons should broaden from the narrow circle of those known to us to include all those in need or suffering, whole nations as well as individuals. When I quiet my words and let myself simply be open, I find myself praying for the people who are dying right now, the babies who are being born right now, the frail old woman lying sleepless in a nursing home right now, the prisoners who are being tortured right now.

Margaret Guenther

Call the world, if you please, "The Vale of Soul Making." Then you will find out the use of the world.

John Keats

Beatniks were conventional anyway. I mean they thought they were getting away from it, which is pretty corny. You never do. You just change one thing for another.

Charlotte Bingham

Those who cling to life die, and those who defy death live.

Uyesugi Kenshin

Master Shaku Soen liked to take an evening stroll through a nearby village. One day he heard loud lamentations from a house and, on entering quietly, realized that the householder had died and the family and neighbors were crying. He sat down and cried with them. An old man noticed him and remarked, rather shaken on seeing the famous master crying with them, "I would have thought that you at least were beyond such things." "But it is this which puts me beyond it," replied the master with a sob.

Irmgard Schloegl

There is hunger for ordinary bread, and there is hunger for love, for kindness, for thoughtfulness; and this is the great poverty that makes people suffer so much.

Mother Teresa

When we are not physically starving, we have the luxury to realize psychic and emotional starvation.

Cherríe Moraga

Fear less, hope more; eat less, chew more; whine less, breathe more; talk less, say more; hate less, love more; and all good things are yours.

Swedish proverb

What a miserable thing life is: you're living in clover, only the clover isn't good enough.

Bertolt Brecht

The Uruguayan political prisoners may not talk without permission or whistle, smile, sing, walk fast, or greet other prisoners; nor may they make or receive drawings of pregnant women, couples, butterflies, stars, or birds.

One Sunday, Didasko Pérez, school teacher, tortured and jailed "for having ideological ideas," is visited by his daughter Milay, age five. She brings him a drawing of birds. The guards destroy it at the entrance of the jail.

On the following Sunday, Milay brings him a drawing of trees. Trees are not forbidden, and the drawing gets through. Didasko praises her work and asks about the colored circles scattered in the treetops, many small circles half hidden among the branches: "Are they

oranges? What fruit is it?" The child puts her finger to her mouth: "Shh."

And she whispers in his ear: "Silly, don't you see they're eyes? They're the eyes of the birds that I've smuggled in for you."

Eduardo Galeano

Do not avoid contact with suffering or close your eyes before suffering. Do not lose awareness of the existence of suffering in the life of the world. Find ways to be with those who are suffering by all means, including personal contact and visits, images, sound. By such means, awaken yourself and others to the reality of suffering in the world.

Thich Nhat Hanh

Suffering . . . no matter how multiplied . . . is always individual.

Anne Morrow Lindbergh

The study of crime begins with the knowledge of oneself.

Henry Miller

Every sorrow suggests a thousand songs, and every song recalls a thousand sorrows, and so they are infinite in number, and all the same.

Marilynne Robinson

There is a wisdom that is woe, a woe that is madness.

Herman Melville

You can go only halfway into the darkest forest; then you are coming out the other side.

Chinese proverb

Just because you've stopped sinking doesn't mean you're not still underwater.

Amy Hempel

During Mary's absence, I have taken over the duty of watering the plants in the apartment, and I find that the dislike I had for one of them because it depressed me with its ailing appearance is changing to affection. I move it to a location favorable to its need for shade, I water it carefully and trim off the dead leaves, and I am reminded of my lifelong conviction that a powerful means of arousing love for someone or something is to do things for that person or object. . . . I would even be willing to believe that self-love is so strong because the self is the person for whom one does the most.

Rudolf Arnheim

A flower falls, even though we love it, and a weed grows, even though we do not love it.

Dōgen

As soon as you have made a thought, laugh at it.

Lao Tzu

Ninety percent of this game is half mental.

Yogi Berra

It is not enough to have a good mind. The main thing is to use it well.

René Descartes

She enjoyed sucking her thumb. He said it was immature. So she stopped, and then there was nothing left that she could enjoy. So she became an alcoholic instead. He didn't mind that nearly so much; at least that seemed mature.

Alberto Königsberg

A child's trust has the stubbornest roots: it takes far more digging than you would expect to pull out every little piece.

Deborah Moggach

Most of us are about as eager to be changed as we were to be born, and go through our changes in a similar state of shock.

James Baldwin

All birth is unwilling.

Pearl S. Buck

Consider how hard it is to change yourself and you'll understand what little chance you have of trying to change others.

Jacob M. Braude

You must do the thing you think you cannot do.

Eleanor Roosevelt

There often seems to be a playfulness to wise people, as if either their equanimity has as its source this playfulness or the playfulness flows from the equanimity; and they can persuade other people who are in a state of agitation to calm down and manage a smile.

Edward Hoagland

Comparison is degrading. It perverts one's outlook. And on comparison one is brought up. All our education is based on it and so is our culture. So there is everlasting struggle to be something other than what one is. The understanding of what one is uncovers creativeness, but comparison breeds competitiveness, ruthlessness, ambition, which we think brings about progress. Progress has only led so far to more ruthless wars and misery than the world has ever known.

J. Krishnamurti

Whole sight; or all the rest is desolation.

John Fowles

We are two mirrors crossing their swords.

Octavio Paz

It goes without saying that as soon as one cherishes the thought of winning the contest or displaying one's skill in technique, swordsmanship is doomed.

Takano Shigeyoshi

I am trying to be unfamiliar with what I am doing.

John Cage

Every time we say, "Thy will be done," we should have in mind all possible misfortunes added together.

Simone Weil

Then it was as if I suddenly saw the secret beauty of their hearts, the depths of their hearts where neither sin nor desire nor self-knowledge can reach, the core of their reality, the person that each one is in God's eyes. If only they could see themselves as they really are. If only we could see each other that way all the time, there would be no more war, no more hatred, no more cruelty, no more greed. . . . I suppose the big problem is that we would fall down and worship each other.

Thomas Merton

I got up on my feet and went over to the bowl in the corner and threw cold water on my face. After a while I felt a little better, but very little. I needed a drink, I needed a lot of life insurance, I needed a vacation, I needed a home in the country. What I had was a coat, a hat, and a gun. I put them on and went out of the room.

Raymond Chandler,
Farewell My Lovely

How frequently in the course of our lives the evil which in itself we seek most to shun, and which when we are fallen into is the most dreadful to us, is oftentimes the very means or door of our deliverance.

Daniel Dafoe

The only tyrant I accept in this world is the "still small voice" within me.

Mohandas K. Gandhi

There is no poetry where there are no mistakes.

Joy Harjo

How strange to use "You only live once" as an excuse to throw away a life.

Source unknown

Failure is an event, never a person.

William D. Brown

Sometimes I lie awake at night, and I ask, "Where have I gone wrong?" Then a voice says to me, "This is going to take more than one night."

Charlie Brown, in
Charles Schulz's *Peanuts*

Through error you come to the truth. I am a man because I err. You never reach any truth without making 14 mistakes, and very likely 114.

Fyodor Dostoyevsky

I don't like people who have never fallen or stumbled. Their virtue is lifeless and it isn't of much value. Life hasn't revealed its beauty to them.

Boris Pasternak

If you're going through hell, keep going.

Winston Churchill

Sometimes it proves the highest understanding not to understand.

Baltasar Gracian y Morales

When the Japanese mend broken objects, they aggrandize the damage by filling the cracks with gold. They believe that when something's suffered damage and has a history it becomes more beautiful.

Barbara Bloom

We have no right to ask, when sorrow comes, "Why did this happen to me?" unless we ask the same question for every moment of happiness that comes our way.

Source unknown

The unendurable is the beginning of the curve of joy.

Djuna Barnes

"Sometimes," he said, "I believe we're given the same lessons to learn, over and over, exactly the same experiences, till we get them right. Things keep circling past us."

Anne Tyler,
Earthly Possessions

I am caught again in those revolving doors of childhood.

Lillian Smith

I have woven a parachute out of everything broken.

William Stafford

Life is a shipwreck, but we must not forget to sing in the lifeboats.

Voltaire

Like a plant that starts up in showers and sunshine and does not know which has best helped it to grow, it is difficult to say whether the hard things or the pleasant things did me most good.

Lucy Larcom

Finish every day and be done with it. . . . You have done what you could; some blunders and absurdities no doubt crept in; forget them as soon as you can. Tomorrow is a new day. You shall begin it serenely and with too high a spirit to be encumbered with your old nonsense.

Ralph Waldo Emerson

When you're stuck in a spiral, to change all aspects of the spin you need only to change one thing.

Christina Baldwin

Do everything. One thing may turn out right.

Humphrey Bogart

My contemplation of life and human nature in that secluded place [prison] had taught me that he who cannot change the very fabric of his thought will never be able to change reality, and will never, therefore, make any progress. . . . I discovered my real self in Cell 54.

Anwar Sadat

Faced with the choice between changing one's mind and proving that there is no need to do so, almost everyone gets busy on the proof.

John Kenneth Galbraith

The birds are molting. If only man could molt also — his mind once a year its errors, his heart once a year its useless passions.

James Allen

Adversity has the same effect on a man that severe training has on the pugilist: it reduces him to his fighting weight.

Josh Billings

If we would only give, just once, the same amount of reflection to what we want to get out of life that we give to the question of what to do with a two-week vacation, we would be startled at our false standards and the aimless procession of our busy days.

Dorothy Canfield Fisher

Our entire life, with our fine moral code and our precious freedom, consists ultimately in accepting ourselves as we are.

Jean Anouilh

To change one's life: Start immediately. Do it flamboyantly. No exceptions.

William James

☉

He's not the finest character that ever lived. But he's a human being, and a terrible thing is happening to him. So attention must be paid. He's not to be allowed to fall into his grave like an old dog. Attention, attention must be finally paid to such a person.

Arthur Miller,
Death of a Salesman

Who has not sat before his own heart's curtain? It lifts, and the scenery is falling apart.

Rainer Maria Rilke

His fear was like a large cardboard box inside his head, empty but bulky, leaving room for little else.

Jane Smiley,
The Blinding Light of the Mind

She did not talk to people as if they were strange, hard shells she had to crack open to get inside. She talked as if she were already in the shell. In their very shell.

Marita Bonner, *Frye Street*

Life is pain. Anyone who says different is trying to sell you something.

William Goldman

Sorrow was like the wind. It came in gusts, shaking the woman. She braced herself.

Marjorie Kinnan Rawlings,
South Moon Under

All religion begins with the cry "Help."

William James

You come to see . . . that suffering is required; and you no more want to avoid it than you want to avoid putting your next foot on the ground when you are walking. In the spiritual path, joy and suffering follow one another like two feet, and you come to a point of not minding which "foot" is on the ground. You realize, on the contrary, that it is extremely uncomfortable hopping all the time on the joy foot.

John G. Bennett

The hardest thing we are asked to do in this world is to remain aware of suffering, suffering about which we can do nothing.

May Sarton

What is the source of our first suffering? It lies in the fact that we hesitated to speak. It was born in the moment when we accumulated silent things within us.

Gaston Bachelard

Don't let what you cannot do interfere with what you can do.

John Wooden

The spiritual life does not remove us from the world, but leads us deeper into it.

Henri J.M. Nouwen

I don't consider myself a pessimist at all. I think of a pessimist as someone who is waiting for it to rain. And I feel soaked to the skin.

Leonard Cohen

Why is life speeded up so? Why are things so terribly, unbearably precious that you can't enjoy them, but can only wait breathless in dread of their going?

Anne Morrow Lindbergh

Once you fully apprehend the vacuity of a life without struggle, you are equipped with the basic means of salvation.

Tennessee Williams

We must travel in the direction of our fear.

John Berryman

When the pain of loneliness comes upon you, confront it, look at it without any thought of running away. If you run away you will never understand it, and it will always be there waiting for you around the corner.

J. Krishnamurti

In lunatic asylums it is a well-known fact that patients are far more dangerous when suffering from fear than when moved by rage or hatred.

Carl Jung

Fear grows out of the things we think; it lives in our minds. Compassion grows out of the things we are, and lives in our hearts.

Barbara Garrison

Fear tastes like a rusty knife and do not let her into your house.

John Cheever

I admire the serene assurance of those who have religious faith. It is wonderful to observe the calm confidence of a Christian with four aces.

Mark Twain

There is no such thing as inner peace. There is only nervousness or death.

Fran Lebowitz

In the absence of a natural disaster, we are left again to our own uneasy devices.

Joan Didion

A man's worst enemies can't wish on him what he can think up himself.

Yiddish proverb

Both speech and silence transgress.

Zen saying

There are times when we must sink to the bottom of our misery to understand truth, just as we must descend to the bottom of a well to see the stars in broad daylight.

Václav Havel

And yet his grief is a great guide through this world. Even, perhaps, the surest of guides. As long as guides are needed.

W.S. Merwin

To view your life as blessed does not require you to deny your pain. It simply demands a more complicated vision, one in which a condition or event is not either good or bad but is, rather, both good and bad, not sequentially but simultaneously. In my experience, the more such ambivalences you can hold in your head, the better off you are, intellectually and emotionally.

Nancy Mairs

The tears . . . streamed down, and I let them flow as freely as they would, making of them a pillow for my heart. On them it rested.

Saint Augustine

The unending paradox is that we do learn through pain.

Madeleine L'Engle

The harder we look at our aches and ailments, the more we will be startled by the painful truths they are trying to convey about our dangerously disembodied way of life.

Marion Woodman

Let us remember that sorrow alone is the creator of great things.

Ernest Renan

In the autumn I gathered all my sorrows and buried them in my garden. And when April returned and spring came to wed the earth, there grew in my garden beautiful flowers unlike all other flowers. And my neighbors came to behold them, and they all said to me, "When autumn comes again, at seeding time, will you not give us of the seeds of these flowers that we may have them in our gardens?"

Khalil Gibran

If there is a meaning in life at all, then there must be a meaning in suffering.

Viktor Frankl

We must become alone, so utterly alone, that we withdraw into our innermost self. It is a way of bitter suffering. But then our solitude is overcome and we are no longer alone, for we find that our innermost self is the spirit, that it is God, the indivisible. And suddenly we find ourselves in the midst of the world, yet undisturbed by its multiplicity, for in our innermost soul we know ourselves to be one with all being.

Hermann Hesse

Since my house burned down, / I now own a better view / of the rising moon.

Masahide

I do not believe that sheer suffering teaches. If suffering alone taught, then all the world would be wise, since everyone suffers. To suffering must be added mourning, understanding, patience, love, openness, and the willingness to remain vulnerable.

Anne Morrow Lindbergh

Consciously or unconsciously, we are all utterly selfish, and so long as we get what we want, we consider that everything is all right. But the moment an event takes place to shatter all this, we cry out in despair, hoping to find other comforts which, of course, will again be shattered. So this process goes on, and if you want to be caught in it, knowing full well the implications of it, then go ahead. But if you see the absurdity of it

all, then you will naturally stop crying and live with a smile on your face.

J. Krishnamurti

When you look back at the anguish, suffering, and traumas in your life, you'll see that these are the periods of biggest growth. After a loss that brings you dreadfully painful months, you are a different man, a different woman. Many years later, you will be able to look back and see the positive things — togetherness in family, faith, or whatever — that came out of your pain.

Elisabeth Kübler-Ross

Those who have suffered understand suffering and thereby extend their hand.

Patti Smith

Years ago I used to commiserate with all people who suffered. Now I commiserate only with those who suffer in ignorance, who do not understand the purpose and ultimate utility of pain.

Bill Wilson

Do not run toward pain, but do not run from it, either. Pain is your guide. Pain is what guides a person in every serious undertaking. Unless an aching longing and passion arises in someone to get or achieve something, he will never get or achieve it.

Andrew Harvey

We are here on earth to do good to others. What the others are here for, I don't know.

W.H. Auden

A difficult life is better for someone who truly wants to learn. Comfortable lives always end in bitterness.

Rumi

God has . . . ordered things that we may learn to bear one another's burdens; for there is no man without his faults, none without his burden. None is sufficient in himself; none is wise in himself; therefore, we must support one another, comfort, help, teach, and advise one another.

Thomas à Kempis

So long as one is able to pose, one still has much to learn about suffering.

Ellen Glasgow

People should worry about each other. Because worry is just love in its worst form. But it's still love.

Simon Gray

God gave burdens, also shoulders.

Yiddish proverb

Human beings are so made that the ones who do the crushing feel nothing; it is the person crushed who feels what is happening. Unless one has placed oneself on the side of the oppressed, to feel with them, one cannot understand.

Simone Weil

Compassion is not a relationship between the healer and the wounded. It's a relationship between equals. Only when we know our own darkness well can we be present with the darkness of others. Compassion becomes real when we recognize our shared humanity.

Pema Chödrön

It is impossible to get out of your skin into somebody else's. . . . Somebody else's tragedy is not the same as your own.

Diane Arbus

I know what the cure is: it is to give up, to relinquish, to surrender, so that our little hearts may beat in unison with the great heart of the world.

Henry Miller

Compassion has nothing to do with achievement at all. It is spacious, and very generous. When a person develops compassion, he is uncertain whether he is being generous to others or to himself, because compassion is environmental generosity. . . . We could say compassion is the ultimate attitude of wealth: an antipoverty attitude, a war on want.

Chögyam Trungpa Rinpoche

What wisdom can you find that is greater than kindness?

Jean-Jacques Rousseau

Say yes when nobody asked.

Lao proverb

☉

This Sad And Tender Heart

Tenderness contains an element of sadness. It is not the sadness of feeling sorry for yourself or feeling deprived, but it is a natural situation of fullness. You feel so full and rich, as if you were about to shed tears. Your eyes are full of tears, and the moment you blink, the tears will spill out of your eyes and roll down your cheeks. In order to be a good warrior, one has to feel this sad and tender heart.

Chögyam Trungpa Rinpoche

If we could read the secret history of our enemies we should find in each man's life sorrow and suffering enough to disarm all hostility.

Henry Wadsworth Longfellow

There are many things in your heart that you can never tell to another person. They are you, your private joys and sorrows, and you can never tell them. You cheapen yourself, the inside of yourself, when you tell them.

Greta Garbo

The most radical thing you can do is introduce people to each other.

Glenn Hilke

"Listen," F. Jasmine said. "What I've been trying to say is this. Doesn't it strike you as strange that I am I, and you are you? I am F. Jasmine Addams. And you are Berenice Sadie Brown. And we can look at each other, and touch each other, and stay together year in and year out in the same room. Yet always I am I, and you are you. And I can't ever be anything else but me, and you can't ever be anything else but you. Have you ever thought of that? And does it seem to you strange?"

Carson McCullers,
The Member of the Wedding

I wonder whether you realize a deep, great fact. That souls — all human souls — are interconnected. That we can not only pray for each other but suffer for each other. Nothing is more real than this interconnection — this precious power put by God into the very heart of our infirmities.

Baron von Hügel

The person and society are yoked, like mind and body. Arguing which is more important is like debating whether oxygen or hydrogen is the more essential property of water.

Marilyn Ferguson

Self-importance is our greatest enemy. Think about it. What weakens us is feeling offended by the deeds and misdeeds of our fellow men. Our self-importance requires that we spend most of our lives offended by someone.

Carlos Castaneda

Thinking about the people in this floating world far into the night — my sleeve is wet with tears.

Ryōkan

If the world can only be healed by those whose hearts have healed, then the healing of hearts will have to take place in a broken world.

Gil Bailie

I never ask a wounded person how he feels; I myself become the wounded person.

Walt Whitman

The worst sin toward our fellow creatures is not to hate them, but to be indifferent to them.

George Bernard Shaw

Compassion is not at all weak. It is the strength that arises out of seeing the true nature of suffering in the world. Compassion allows us to bear witness to that suffering, whether it is in ourselves or others, without fear; it allows us to name injustice without hesitation, and to act strongly, with all the skill at our disposal. To develop this mind state of compassion . . . is to learn to live, as the Buddha put it, with sympathy for all living beings, without exception.

Sharon Salzberg

When we quit thinking primarily about ourselves and our own self-preservation, we undergo a truly heroic transformation of consciousness.

Joseph Campbell

He who wants to do good knocks at the gate; he who loves finds the gate open.

Rabindranath Tagore

If I want to build big biceps, I need to use every opportunity to practice lifting weights. If I want to live in a way that is loving and generous and fearless, then I need to practice overcoming any tendency to be angry or greedy or confused. Life is a terrific gym. Every situation is an opportunity to practice.

Sylvia Boorstein

The more we take the welfare of others to heart and work for their benefit, the more benefit we derive for ourselves. This is a fact we can see. And the more selfish we remain and self-centered, the more selfish our way of life is, the lonelier we feel and the more miserable. This is also a fact we can see.

The Dalai Lama

The situation of the soul in contemplation is something like the situation of Adam and Eve in paradise. Everything is yours, but on one infinitely impor-

tant condition: that it is all given. There is nothing that you can claim, nothing that you can demand, nothing that you can take. And as soon as you try to take something as if it were your own — you lose your Eden.

Thomas Merton

What is sacred about all of our lives, even those of us who would never dream of using such a word for it, is that God speaks to us through what happens to us — even through such unpromising events as walking up the road to get the mail out of the mailbox, maybe, or seeing something in the TV news that brings you up short, or laughing yourself silly with a friend. If skeptics ask to be shown an instance of God speaking to them in their lives, I suggest that they pay closer attention to the next time when, for unaccountable reasons, they find tears in their eyes.

Frederick Buechner

I owe much to my friends, but . . . even more to my enemies. The real person springs to life under a sting even better than under a caress.

André Gide

Let there be such oneness between us that when one cries, the other tastes salt.

Hebrew saying

A man who possesses a veneration of life will not simply say his prayers. He will throw himself into the battle to preserve life, if for no other reason than that he himself is an extension of life around him.

Albert Schweitzer

The love of our neighbor in all its fullness simply means being able to say to him, "What are you going through?"

Simone Weil

☟

In the range of my character at any given moment, I have acted in the only way it seemed to me I could have acted. This in no way means that I have done what was right; only what was possible for me. Sometimes I have done what I knew was wrong, and have rationalized. But rationalization is a form of desperation. It takes kindness to forgive oneself for one's life.

Anne Truitt

I was taught when I was young that if people would only love one another, all would be well with the world. This seemed simple and very nice; but I found when I tried to put it into practice not only that other people were seldom lovable, but that I was not very lovable myself.

George Bernard Shaw

Christianity teaches that we should love our enemies, but fails to outline the steps required to evolve that capacity; it forgets that loving our enemies is the end point, not the beginning point, of spiritual practice.

Lauren Artress

Did you ever see little dogs caressing and playing with one another? So that you might say there is nothing more friendly? But, that you may know what friendship is, throw a bit of flesh among them, and you will learn.

Epictetus

Everyone says forgiveness is a lovely idea, until they have something to forgive.

C.S. Lewis

To forgive oneself? No, that doesn't work: we have to be forgiven. But we can only believe this is possible if we ourselves can forgive.

Dag Hammarskjöld

Forgiveness is giving up all hope of having had a better past.

Anne Lamott

One of the most time-consuming things is to have an enemy.

E.B. White

You will not become a saint through other people's sins.

Anton Chekhov

It does not do you good to leave a dragon out of your calculations, if you live near him.

J.R.R. Tolkien

Anger stirs and wakes in her; it opens its mouth, and like a hot-mouthed puppy, laps up the dredges of her shame. Anger is better.

Toni Morrison, *The Bluest Eye*

I have learned through bitter experience the one supreme lesson to conserve my anger, and, as heat conserved is transmitted into energy, even so our anger controlled can be transmitted into a power which can move the world.

Mohandas K. Gandhi

Think, when you are enraged at any-one, what would probably become your sentiments should he die during the dispute.

William Shenstone

Anger makes us all stupid.

Johanna Spyri

Quoting the Psalms: "Be angry, but do not sin." Jesus was angry more than 50 percent of the time, and it's very dangerous theology to try to improve on Jesus. The anger needs to be focused, but anger is what maintains your sanity. Anger keeps you from tolerating the intolerable.

William Sloane Coffin Jr.

Could a greater miracle take place than for us to look through each other's eyes for an instant?

Henry David Thoreau

The world is divided into people who think they are right.

Source unknown

If you understand something, you don't forgive it, you are the thing itself: forgiveness is for what you don't understand.

Doris Lessing

How should man, a being created in the likeness of God, live? What way of living is compatible with the grandeur and mystery of living?

Abraham Joshua Heschel

Many promising reconciliations have broken down because, while both parties came prepared to forgive, neither party came prepared to be forgiven.

Charles Williams

Once a woman has forgiven her man, she must not reheat his sins for breakfast.

Marlene Dietrich

Man in the Cook County Jail being strapped into the electric chair: "This will certainly teach me a lesson."

Source unknown

Be in the world as though you were a stranger or a wayfarer, and consider yourself one of the inhabitants of the graves.

Mohammed

I thought that I had arrived at the very throne of God, and I said to it, "O throne, they tell us that God rests upon thee." "O Bayazid," replied the throne, "we are told here that God dwells in a humble heart."

Bayazid Bistami

Wife and daughter are driving and rejoicing together, another car careens into their lane, and mother and daughter are killed. The other driver is thoroughly drunk in celebration of the birth of his first child. At home, in trauma and desolation, the bereaved husband, after some days, becomes aware of the one person who is suffering more than he is. He drives to the young man's house, knocks on the door, and confronts the surprised man. He speaks two quiet sentences. "Do not be afraid. I have come to forgive you."

Stephen Covey and Truman Madsen

☙

We have not learned anything, we don't know anything, we don't have anything, we don't give anything, we can't do anything, we don't sell anything, we don't help, we don't understand, we don't betray. And we will not forget.

Sign posted in Czechoslovakia after the Soviet invasion, 1968

Forgiveness is not simply the absolving of an enemy, or one who has done us wrong. Forgiveness must encompass all those things which disturb the tranquility of our soul: the barking dog that robs you of sleep, the heat of summer, the cold of winter. Forgive the ingrown toenail, the flea that bites; forgive the cranky child, wrinkles, a forgotten birthday.

Barbara Wood

Forgive your enemies, but never forget their names.

John F. Kennedy

There's no point in burying a hatchet if you're going to put up a marker on the site.

Sydney Harris

Love is an act of endless forgiveness, a tender look which becomes a habit.

Peter Ustinov

I respect kindness to human beings first of all, and kindness to animals. I don't respect the law; I have a total irreverence for anything connected with society, except that which makes the roads safer, the beer stronger, the food cheaper, and old men and old women warmer in the winter and happier in the summer.

Brendan Behan

The Sufis advise us to speak only after our words have managed to pass through three gates. At the first gate, we ask ourselves, "Are these words true?" If so, we let them pass on; if not, back they go. At the second gate we ask, "Are they necessary?" At the last gate, we ask, "Are they kind?"

Eknath Easwaran

The sun, each second, transforms 4 million tons of itself into light. . . . Human generosity is possible only because at the center of the solar system a magnificent stellar generosity pours forth free energy day and night without stop and without complaint and without the slightest hesitation.

Brian Swimme

Three things in human life are important. The first is to be kind. The second is to be kind. And the third is to be kind.

Henry James

All cruel people describe themselves as paragons of frankness.

Tennessee Williams

The compulsion to do good is an innate American trait. Only North Americans seem to believe that they always should, may, and actually can choose somebody with whom to share their blessings. Ultimately this attitude leads to bombing people into the acceptance of gifts.

Ivan Illich

You can easily judge the character of a man by how he treats those who can do nothing for him or to him.

James D. Miles

hatred bounces.

e.e. cummings

Even the rich are hungry for love, for being cared for, for being wanted, for having someone to call their own.

Mother Teresa

Kindness is in our power, even when fondness is not.

Samuel Johnson

He says that when he arrived with sheriff's deputies there in the cane field to identify his son, he knelt by his boy . . . and prayed the Our Father. And when he came to the words "Forgive us our trespasses as we forgive those who trespass against us," he did not halt or equivocate, and he said, "Whoever did this, I forgive him." But he acknowledges that it's a struggle to overcome the feelings of bitterness and revenge that well up, especially as he remembers David's birthday year after year and loses him all over again. . . . Forgiveness is never going to be easy. Each day it must be prayed for and struggled for and won.

Helen Prejean

God may forgive you, but I never will.

Queen Elizabeth I

I hold myself to be incapable of hating any being on earth. By a long course of prayerful discipline, I have ceased for over forty years to hate anybody. I know this is a big claim. Nevertheless, I make it in all humility.

Mohandas K. Gandhi

There is no way under the sun to make a man worthy of love except by loving him.

Thomas Merton

I forgive everyone and I ask for everyone's forgiveness. OK? Don't gossip too much.

Cesare Pavese, suicide note

Mabel Pettigrew thought: *I can read him like a book.* She had not read a book for over forty years, could never concentrate on reading, but this nevertheless was her thought.

Muriel Spark, *Memento Mori*

Whatever people in general do not understand, they are always prepared to dislike; the incomprehensible is always the obnoxious.

L.E. Landon

We didn't have a relationship; we had a personality clash.

Alice Molloy

My God! The English language is a form of communication! Conversation isn't just crossfire where you shoot and get shot at! Where you've got to duck for your life and aim to kill! Words aren't only bombs and bullets — no, they're little gifts, containing meanings!

Philip Roth

Good communication is as stimulating as black coffee, and just as hard to sleep after.

Anne Morrow Lindbergh

Why can we remember the tiniest detail that has happened to us and not remember how many times we have told it to the same person?

François de La Rochefoucauld

When people talk, listen completely. Don't be thinking what you're going to say. Most people never listen.

Ernest Hemingway

We want people to feel with us more than to act for us.

George Eliot

The only reason that we don't open our hearts and minds to other people is that they trigger confusion in us that we don't feel brave enough or sane enough to deal with. To the degree that we look clearly and compassionately at ourselves, we feel confident and fearless about looking into someone else's eyes.

Pema Chödrön

Love involves a peculiar, unfathomable combination of understanding and mis-understanding.

Diane Arbus

The world was wide, and I would not waste my life in friction when it could be turned into momentum.

Frances Willard

What value has compassion that does not take its object in its arms?

Antoine de Saint-Exupéry

Ordinary compassion and love give rise to a very close feeling, but it is essentially attachment. As long as the other person appears to you as beautiful or good, love remains, but as soon as he or she appears to you as less beautiful or good, your love completely changes. . . . Instead of love, you now feel hostility. With genuine love and compassion, another person's appearance or behavior has no effect on your attitude. Real compassion comes from seeing the other's suffering. You feel a sense of responsibility, and you want to do something for him or her.

The Dalai Lama

No man should judge unless he asks himself in absolute honesty whether in a similar situation he might not have done the same.

Viktor Frankl

We are called to play the good Samaritan on life's roadside; but that will be only an initial act. One day . . . the whole Jericho road must be transformed so that men and women will not be constantly beaten and robbed as they make their journey on life's highway. True compassion is more than flinging a coin to a beggar; it is not haphazard and superficial. It understands that an edifice which produces beggars needs restructuring.

Martin Luther King Jr.

There are plenty of good reasons for fighting . . . but no good reason ever to hate without reservation, to imagine that God Almighty Himself hates with you, too. Where's evil? It's that large part of every man that wants to hate without limit, that wants to hate with God on its side.

Kurt Vonnegut

It is easy enough to be friendly to one's friends. But to befriend the one who regards himself as your enemy is the quintessence of true religion. The other is mere business.

Mohandas K. Gandhi

In this world, you must be a bit too kind to be kind enough.

Pierre Carlet de Chamblain de Marivaux

There was once a rabbi who was revered by the people as a man of God. Not a day went by when a crowd of people wasn't standing at his door seeking advice or healing or the holy man's blessing. . . . There was, however, in the audience a disagreeable fellow who never missed a chance to contradict the master. He would observe the rabbi's weaknesses and make fun of his defects to the dismay of the disciples, who began to look

on him as the devil incarnate. Well, one day the "devil" took ill and died. Everyone heaved a sigh of relief. Outwardly, they looked appropriately solemn, but in their hearts they were glad. . . . So the people were surprised to see the master plunged in genuine grief at the funeral. When asked by a disciple later if he was mourning over the eternal fate of the dead man, he said, "No, no. Why should I mourn over our friend, who is now in heaven? It was for myself I was grieving. That man was the only friend I had. Here I am surrounded by people who revere me. He was the only one who challenged me. I fear that with him gone, I shall stop growing." And, as he said those words, the master burst into tears.

Anthony de Mello

☙

Rabbi Irving Greenberg: "You just learned one of the secrets of Jewish survival. We disagree with each other all the time."
Rabbi Lawrence Kushner: "No we don't."

Reported in the *New York Times*

An association of men who will not quarrel with one another is a thing which has never yet existed, from the greatest confederacy of nations down to a town meeting or a vestry.

Thomas Jefferson

Is an intelligent human being likely to be much more than a large-scale manufacturer of misunderstanding?

Philip Roth

Nobody knows the age of the human race, but everybody agrees that it is old enough to know better.

Source unknown

Rarely an hour passed that they didn't argue about something. They had lived together for so many years that they mistook their arguments for conversations.

Marjorie Kellogg,
Tell Me That You Love Me, Junie Moon

If other people are going to talk, conversation becomes impossible.

James McNeill Whistler

What we've got here is a failure to communicate.

The Captain, in the movie
Cool Hand Luke

Don't introduce me to him. I want to go on hating him, and I can't do that to a man I know.

Charles Lamb

It is in deep solitude that I find the gentleness with which I can truly love my brothers. The more solitary I am, the more affection I have for them. . . . Solitude and silence teach me to love my brothers for what they are, not for what they say.

Thomas Merton

One of the lessons of history is that nothing is often a good thing to do and always a clever thing to say.

Will Durant

In a quarrel, each side is right.

Yiddish folk saying

Too often we underestimate the power of a touch, a smile, a kind word, a listening ear, an honest compliment, or the smallest act of caring, all of which have the potential to turn a life around.

Leo Buscaglia

When a friend is in trouble, don't annoy him by asking if there is anything you can do. Think up something appropriate and do it.

Edgar Watson Howe

The kindest word in the world is the unkind word, unsaid.

Source unknown

We have a long, long way to go. So let us hasten along the road, the road of human tenderness and generosity. Groping, we may find one another's hands in the dark.

Emily Greene Balch

We have become terribly vulnerable, not because we suffer but because we have separated ourselves from each other. A patient once told me that he had tried to ignore his own suffering and the suffering of other people because he had wanted to be happy. Yet becoming numb to suffering will not make us happy. The part in us that feels suffering is the same as the part that feels joy.

Rachel Naomi Remen

Human beings cling to their delicious tyrannies and to their exquisite nonsense, like a drunkard to his bottle, and go on till death stares them in the face.

Sydney Smith

The older I grow, the more I listen to people who don't talk much.

Germain G. Glien

It could be that there's only one word / and it's all we need / it's here in this pencil / every pencil in the world / is like this.

W.S. Merwin

Tenderness contains an element of sadness. It is not the sadness of feeling sorry for yourself or feeling deprived, but it is a natural situation of fullness. You feel so full and rich, as if you were about to shed tears. Your eyes are full of tears, and the moment you blink, the tears will spill out of your eyes and roll down your cheeks. In order to be a good warrior, one has to feel this sad and tender heart.

Chögyam Trungpa Rinpoche

The violets in the mountains have broken the rocks.

Tennessee Williams

Another plan I have is World Peace through Formal Introductions. The idea is that everyone in the world would be required to meet everyone else in the world, formally, at least once. You'd have to look the person in the eye, shake hands, repeat their name, and try to remember one outstanding physical characteristic. My theory is, if you knew everyone in the

world personally, you'd be less inclined to fight them in a war: "Who? The Malaysians? Are you kidding? I know those people!"

George Carlin

You are in prison. All you can wish for, if you are a sensible man, is to escape. But how escape? It is necessary to tunnel under a wall. One man can do nothing. But let us suppose there are ten or twenty men. If they work in turn and if one covers another they can complete the tunnel and escape. . . . No one can escape from prison without the help of those who have escaped before.

G.I. Gurdjieff

❧

PAPER LANTERNS

Until Justice Rolls Down

No, no, we are not satisfied, and we will not be satisfied until justice rolls down like waters and righteousness like a mighty stream.

Martin Luther King Jr.

How wonderful it is that nobody need wait a single moment before starting to improve the world.

Anne Frank

Occupy the space you occupy.

Adrienne Rich

It isn't enough for your heart to break, because everybody's heart is broken now.

Allen Ginsberg

No cause is left but the most ancient of all, the one, in fact, that from the beginning of our history has determined the very existence of politics: the cause of freedom versus tyranny.

Hannah Arendt

I do not believe in political movements. I believe in personal movement, that movement of the soul when a man who looks at himself is so ashamed that he tries to make some sort of change — within himself, not on the outside.

Joseph Brodsky

As you come to know the seriousness of our situation — the war, the racism, the poverty in the world — you come to realize that it is not going to be changed just by words or demonstrations. It's a question of risking your life. It's a question of living your life in drastically different ways.

Dorothy Day

Never doubt that a group of thoughtful, committed citizens can change the world; indeed, it's the only thing that ever has.

Margaret Mead

The true meaning of life is to plant trees under whose shade you do not expect to sit.

Nelson Henderson

A young man eagerly described what he dreamed of doing for the poor. Said the master, "When do you propose to make your dream come true?" The young man answered, "As soon as opportunity arrives." "Opportunity never arrives," said the master. "It's here."

Anthony de Mello

There is a haphazard sort of doing good which is nothing but temperamental pleasure-seeking.

Fanny Lewald

The Gospel is not made to dominate the world. It's the grain of sand that upsets the world's machinery.

Jean Sullivan

Although the connections are not always obvious, personal change is inseparable from social and political change.

Harriet Lerner

Right livelihood is not just a philosophical ideal. It is a practical, achievable reality. Finding and maintaining right livelihood does require regular, consistent action, but the steps are clear and the results immediate.

Claude Whitmyer

The needle of our conscience is as good a compass as any.

Ruth Wolff

For evil to succeed, all it needs is for good men to do nothing.

Edmund Burke

No snowflake in an avalanche ever feels responsible.

Stanislaw Jerzy Lee

Do not expect Plato's ideal republic; be satisfied with even the smallest step forward, and consider this no small achievement.

Marcus Aurelius

If you assume that there's no hope, you guarantee that there will be no hope. If you assume that there is an instinct for freedom, that there are opportunities to change things, there's a chance you may contribute to making a better world. That's your choice.

Noam Chomsky

Idealism increases in direct proportion to one's distance from the problem.

John Galsworthy

Sentiment without action is the ruin of the soul.

Edward Abbey

The best reformers the world has ever seen are those who commence on themselves.

George Bernard Shaw

Instead of bucking your head against a stone wall . . . sit quietly with hands folded and wait for the wall to crumble. If you're willing to wait an eternity, it may happen in the twinkling of an eye.

For walls often give way quicker than the proud spirit which rules us. Don't sit and pray that it will happen! Just sit and watch it happen.

Henry Miller

Don't mourn, organize.

Joe Hill

Work for the triumph of the good, knowing you will lose.

Seneca

A group of political activists were attempting to show the master how their ideology would change the world. The master listened carefully. The following day he said, "An ideology is as good or bad as the people who make use of it. If a million wolves were to organize for justice would they cease to be a million wolves?"

Anthony de Mello

If Rosa Parks had moved to the back of the bus, you and I might never have heard of Dr. Martin Luther King.

Ramsey Clark

If Rosa Parks had taken a poll before she sat down in the bus in Montgomery, she'd still be standing.

Mary Frances Berry

Live your beliefs and you can turn the world around.

Henry David Thoreau

Paperwork, cleaning the house, . . . answering the phone, keeping patience and acting intelligently, which is to find some meaning in all that happens to us — these things, too, are the works of peace.

Dorothy Day

If only it were all so simple! If only there were evil people somewhere insidiously committing evil deeds, and it were necessary only to separate them from the rest of us and destroy them. But the line dividing good and evil cuts through the heart of every human being. And who is willing to destroy a piece of his own heart?

Aleksandr Solzhenitsyn

Not long ago, but before World War II was over, a young Negro girl was asked how she would punish Hitler. Answer: "Paint him black and bring him over here."

Walter Winchell

Is not one of our problems today that we have separated ourselves from the poor and the wounded and the suffering? We have too much time to discuss and theorize and have lost the yearning for God which comes when we are faced with the sufferings of people.

Jean Vanier

The causes we know everything about depend on causes we know very little about, which depend on causes we know absolutely nothing about.

Tom Stoppard

The real 1960s began on the afternoon of November 22, 1963. . . . It came to seem that Kennedy's murder opened some malign trapdoor in American culture, and the wild bats flapped out.

Lance Morrow

It is vain to say human beings ought to be satisfied with tranquility; they must have action, and they will make it if they cannot find it.

Charlotte Brontë

I am doomed to an eternity of compulsive work. No set goal achieved satisfies. Success only breeds a new goal. The golden apple devoured has seeds. It is endless.

Bette Davis

With the pride of the artist, you must blow against the walls of every power that exists the small trumpet of your defiance.

Norman Mailer

Diamonds are only chunks of coal / That stuck to their jobs, you see.

Minnie Richard Smith

Almost anything you do will seem insignificant, but it is very important that you do it.

Mohandas K. Gandhi

How we spend our days is, of course, how we spend our lives.

Annie Dillard

Don't worry about what the world wants from you; worry about what makes you come more alive. Because what the world really needs are people who are more alive.

Lawrence LeShan

We are like flies crawling across the ceiling of the Sistine Chapel: we cannot see what angels and gods lie underneath the threshold of our perceptions. We do not live in reality; we live in our paradigms, our habituated perceptions, our illusions; the illusions we share through culture we call reality, but the true historical reality of our condition is invisible to us.

William Irwin Thompson

We will go before God to be judged, and God will ask us, "Where are your wounds?" And we will say, "We have no wounds." And God will ask, "Was nothing worth fighting for?"

Allan Boesak

I don't believe in God, but I do believe in His saints.

Edith Wharton

In heaven, an angel is no one in particular.

George Bernard Shaw

My esteem in this country has gone up substantially. . . . Now when people wave at me they use all their fingers.

Jimmy Carter

As a young, little-known writer, Auden was once asked what effect fame might have upon him. "I believe," he said after a moment's reflection, "that I would always wear my carpet slippers." When fame did eventually come, Auden was always to be seen in carpet slippers, even when wearing evening dress.

The Little, Brown Book of Anecdotes

I cannot and will not cut my conscience to fit this year's fashions.

Lillian Hellman

If there are two courses of action, you should take the third.

Jewish proverb

We must combine the toughness of the serpent and the softness of the dove, a tough mind and a tender heart.

Martin Luther King Jr.

The deeds you do today may be the only sermon some people will hear today.

Saint Francis of Assisi

Eschew the monumental. Shun the epic. All the guys who can paint great big pictures can paint great small ones.

Ernest Hemingway

People seldom see the halting and painful steps by which the most insignificant success is achieved.

Anne Sullivan

The ark was built by amateurs, and the *Titanic* by the experts. Don't wait for the experts.

Murray Cohen

I cannot give you the formula for success, but I can give you the formula for failure, which is: Try to please everybody.

Herbert B. Swope

When a man is determined, what can stop him? Cripple him and you have a Sir Walter Scott. Put him in a prison cell and you have a John Bunyan. Bury him in the snows of Valley Forge and you have a George Washington. Have him born in abject poverty and you have a Lincoln. Put him in the grease pit of a locomotive roundhouse and you have a Walter P. Chrysler. Make him second fiddle in an obscure South African orchestra and you have a Toscanini. The hardships of life are sent not by an unkind destiny to crush, but to challenge.

Sam E. Roberts

How beggarly appear arguments before a defiant deed.

Walt Whitman

There are two great rules in life, the one general and other particular. The first is that everyone can in the end get what he wants if he only tries. This is the general rule. The particular rule is that every individual is more or less of an exception to the general rule.

Samuel Butler

I wasn't worried about a perfect game going into the ninth. It was like a dream. I was going on like I was in a daze. I never thought about it the whole time. If I'd thought about it I wouldn't have thrown a perfect game. I know I wouldn't.

Catfish Hunter

Our achievements speak for themselves. What we have to keep track of are our failures, discouragements, and doubts. We tend to forget the past difficulties, the many false starts, and the painful groping. We see our past achievements as the end result of a clean forward thrust, and our present difficulties as signs of decline and decay.

Eric Hoffer

What a strange machine man is! . . . You fill him with wine, fish, and radishes, and out come sighs, laughter, and dreams.

Nikos Kazantzakis

When I give food to the poor, they call me a saint. When I ask why the poor have no food, they call me a Communist.

Dom Hélder Câmara

Don't call me a saint. I don't want to be dismissed that easily.

Dorothy Day

What we cultivate and care about inwardly either freshens or poisons the bloodstream of humanity.

Robert Corin Morris

I don't believe in charity. I believe in solidarity. Charity is so vertical. It goes from the top to the bottom. Solidarity is horizontal. It respects the other person and learns from the other. I have a lot to learn from other people.

Eduardo Galeano

Get beyond love and grief. Exist for the good of man.

Ha Gakure

Q: Have you ever taken a serious political stand on anything?
A: Yes, for twenty-four hours I refused to eat grapes.

Woody Allen, *Sleeper*

We must be fond of this world, even in order to change it.

G.K. Chesterton

The world is a fine place and worth the fighting for.

Ernest Hemingway

I love America more than any other country in the world and, exactly for this reason, I insist on the right to criticize her perpetually.

James Baldwin

You begin saving the world by saving one man at a time; all else is grandiose romanticism or politics.

Charles Bukowski

No, no, we are not satisfied, and we will not be satisfied until justice rolls down like waters and righteousness like a mighty stream.

Martin Luther King Jr.

The ultimate aim of the quest . . . must be neither release nor ecstasy for oneself, but wisdom and power to serve others.

Joseph Campbell

The best thing against worry is to take care of others right away.

Carl Hilty

If one is going to change things, one has to make a fuss and catch the eye of the world.

Elizabeth Janeway

There are people who eat the earth and eat all the people on it, like in the Bible with the locusts. And other people who stand around and watch them eat it.

Lillian Hellman

People who love soft words and hate iniquity forget this, that reform consists in taking a bone away from a dog. Philosophy will not do this.

John Jay Chapman

Don't agonize. Organize.

Florynce R. Kennedy

To give up the task of reforming society is to give up one's responsibility as a free man.

Alan Paton

I suppose that even the most pleasurable of imaginable occupations, that of batting baseballs through the windows of the RCA Building, would pall a little as the days ran on.

James Thurber

I love the story about A.J. Muste, who, during the Vietnam War, stood in front of the White House night after night with a candle — sometimes . . . alone. A reporter interviewed him one evening as he stood there in the rain. "Mr. Muste," the reporter said, "do you really think you are going to change the policies of this country by standing out here alone at night with a candle?" A.J. responded, "Oh, I don't do this to change the country. I do this so the country won't change me."

Andrea Ayvazian

The place to improve the world is first in one's own heart and head and hands, and then work outward from there.

Robert M. Pirsig

Thinking about profound social change, conservatives always expect disaster, while revolutionaries confidently anticipate utopia. Both are wrong.

Carolyn Heilbrun

I'm a pessimist about probabilities; I'm an optimist about possibilities.

Lewis Mumford

When will our consciences grow so tender that we will act to prevent human misery rather than avenge it?

Eleanor Roosevelt

What I fear is being in the presence of evil and doing nothing. I fear that more than death.

Otilia de Koster

If there is no struggle, there is no progress. Those who profess to favor freedom, and yet deprecate agitation, are men who want crops without plowing up the ground. They want rain without thunder and lightning. They want the ocean without the awful roar of its many waters. This struggle may be a moral one, or it may be a physical one, or it may be both moral and physical — but it must be a struggle.

Frederick Douglass

᠗

To be revolutionary is to love your life enough to change it, to choose struggle instead of exile, to risk everything with only the glimmering hope of a world to win.

Andrew Kopkind

The question is not whether we will be extremist but what kind of extremist will we be.

Martin Luther King Jr.

You do not become a "dissident" just because you decide one day to take up this most unusual career. You are thrown into it by your personal sense of responsibility, combined with a complex set of external circumstances. You are cast out of the existing structures and placed in a position of conflict with them. It begins as an attempt to do your work well, and ends with being branded an enemy of society.

Václav Havel

It is dangerous to be right . . . when those in power are wrong.

Voltaire

Rebels and dissidents challenge the complacent belief in a just world, and . . . they are usually denigrated for their efforts. While they are alive, they may be called "cantankerous," "crazy," "hysterical," "uppity," or "duped." Dead, some of them become saints and heroes, the sterling characters of history. It's a matter of proportion. One angry rebel is crazy, three is a conspiracy, fifty is a movement.

Carol Tavris

The law is above the law, you know.

Dorothy Salisbury Davis

It is hard to believe that a man is telling the truth when you know that you would lie if you were in his place.

H.L. Mencken

This land is your land and this land is my land, sure, but the world is run by those that never listen to music anyway.

Bob Dylan

Freedom to cut down world's oldest trees / Freedom to make Indians get down on their knees / And pray to your God and obey your FBI / And freedom to protest if you're not too scared to die.

Allen Ginsberg

I'm not the heroic type. I was beaten up by Quakers.

Woody Allen

I think the greatest legacy of the 1960s was the general feeling that not only can you fight the powers that be, but you can win.

Abbie Hoffman

Don't let them tame you!

Isadora Duncan

I am, and always have been, and shall now always be a revolutionary writer, because our laws make law impossible; our liberties destroy all freedom; our property is organized robbery; our morality is an impudent hypocrisy; our wisdom is administered by inexperienced or malexperienced dupes, our power wielded by cowards and weaklings, and our honor false in all its points. I am an enemy of the existing order for good reasons.

George Bernard Shaw

Many persons have a wrong idea of what constitutes true happiness. It is not attained through self-gratification but through fidelity to a worthy purpose.

Helen Keller

The truth is tiny compared to the things you have to do.

Leonard Cohen

An unrectified case of injustice has a terrible way of lingering, restlessly, in the social atmosphere like an unfinished equation.

Mary McCarthy

The wheels of justice . . . they're square wheels.

Barbara Corcoran

None who have always been free can understand the terrible fascinating power of the hope of freedom to those who are not free.

Pearl S. Buck

Only very lowly and late have men come to realize that unless freedom is universal it is only extended privilege.

Christopher Hill

"Let the jury consider their verdict," the King said, for about the twentieth time that day. "No, no!" said the Queen. "Sentence first — verdict afterwards."

Lewis Carroll,
Alice's Adventures in Wonderland

Men simply copied the realities of their hearts when they built prisons.

Richard Wright

If you're condemned to death they have to give you one last meal of your choice. What is that all about? A group of people plans to kill you, so they want you to eat something you like? Do they think the food part will take your mind off the dying part?

George Carlin

The great thieves punish the little ones.

Thomas Fuller

To assert in any case that a man must be absolutely cut off from society because he is absolutely evil amounts to saying that society is absolutely good, and no one in his right mind will believe this.

Albert Camus

When the judge calls the criminal's name out, he stands up, and they are immediately linked by a strange biology that makes them both opposite and complementary. The one cannot exist without the other. Which is the sun and which is the shadow? It's well known some criminals have been great men.

Jean Genet

I am aware that no man is a villain in his own eyes.

James Baldwin

Your own wounds can be healed with weeping, / your own wounds can be healed with singing, / but the widow, the indian, the poor man, / the fisherman / stand bleeding right there in your doorway.

Pablo Neruda

When, at some point in our lives, we meet a real tragedy — which could happen to any one of us — we can react in two ways. Obviously, we can lose hope,

let ourselves slip into discouragement, into alcohol, drugs, and unending sadness. Or else we can wake ourselves up, discover in ourselves an energy that was hidden there, and act with more clarity, more force.

The Dalai Lama

Hope begins in the dark, the stubborn hope that if you just show up and try to do the right thing, the dawn will come. You wait and watch and work: you don't give up.

Anne Lamott

The nonviolent approach does not immediately change the heart of the oppressor. It first does something to the hearts and souls of those committed to it. It gives them new self-respect; it calls up resources of strength and courage that they did not know they had. Finally it reaches the opponent and so stirs his conscience that reconciliation becomes a reality.

Martin Luther King Jr.

People have the power to redeem the work of fools.

Patti Smith

One must give back the stare of the universe. Anybody can.

Hortense Calisher

The way to get things done is not to mind who gets the credit for doing them.

Benjamin Jowett

I slept and dreamt that life was joy. / I awoke and saw that life was service. / I acted and behold, service was joy.

Rabindranath Tagore

There is incredible value in being of service to others. I think if most of the people in therapy offices were dragged out to put their finger in a dike, take up their place in a working line, they would be relieved of terrible burdens.

Elizabeth Berg

Concern should drive us into action and not into a depression.

Karen Horney

His mother had often said, "When you choose an action, you choose the consequences of that action." She had emphasized the corollary of this axiom even more vehemently: when you desired a consequence, you had damned well better take the action that would create it.

Lois McMaster Bujold, *Memory*

Despair is a greater deceiver than hope.

Luc de Clapiers,
Marquis de Vauvenargues

You find lots of little things going on in every community in the country. If there is a world here in a hundred years, it will not be due to any big organization of any sort, no big political group, no big church, no big government. It is going to be saved by millions upon millions of little organizations. It might just be that what Jesus and Jeremiah and Mohammed and Buddha talked about will come true.

Pete Seeger

Reality is above all else a variable, and nobody is qualified to say that he or she knows exactly what it is. As a matter of fact, with a firm enough commitment, you can sometimes create a reality which did not exist before.

Margaret Halsey

All revolutionary changes are unthinkable until they happen — and then they are understood to be inevitable.

Theodore Roszak

I always had a decent sense of outrage.

Bella Abzug

There are two things to remember about a revolution: first, we're gonna get our asses kicked, and second, we're gonna win.

Source unknown

Only the truth is revolutionary.

Vladimir Lenin

Every revolutionary ends by becoming either an oppressor or a heretic.

Albert Camus

It is always the same: once you are liberated, you are forced to ask who you are.

Jean Baudrillard

I saw someone peeing in Jermyn Street the other day. I thought, is this the end of civilization as we know it? Or is it simply someone peeing in Jermyn Street?

Alan Bennett

Realize that for every ongoing war and religious outrage and environmental devastation and bogus Iraqi attack plan, there are a thousand counterbalancing acts of staggering generosity and humanity and art and beauty happening all over the world, right now, on a breathtaking scale, from flower box to cathedral. . . . Resist the temptation to drown in fatalism, to shake your head and sigh and just throw in the karmic towel. . . . Realize that this is the perfect moment to change the energy of the world, to step right up and crank your personal volume; right when it all seems dark and bitter and offensive and acrimonious and conflicted and bilious . . . there's your opening.

Mark Morford

Whatever you do, don't give up. Because all you can do once you've given up is bitch. I've known some great bitchers in my time. With some it's a passion; with others, an art.

Molly Ivins

[Hope is] a state of mind, not a state of the world. . . . Hope, in this deep and powerful sense, is not the same as joy that things are going well, or willingness to invest in enterprises that are obviously headed for early success, but rather an ability to work for something because it is good.

Václav Havel

Have patience! In time, even grass becomes milk.

Charan Singh

Do everything that you want to do, but always pick up the bill afterward.

Peggy Ramsey

It is easier to produce ten volumes of philosophical writings than to put one principle into practice.

Leo Tolstoy

Faith is not making religious-sounding noises in the daytime. It is asking your inmost self questions at night — and then getting up and going to work.

Mary Jean Irion

We must do what we conceive to be right and not bother our heads or burden our souls with whether we'll be successful. Because if we don't do the right thing, we'll do the wrong thing, and we'll be part of the disease and not part of the cure.

E.F. Schumacher

One must have teeth. Then love's like biting into an orange when the juice squirts in your teeth.

Bertolt Brecht

I never practice; I always play.

Wanda Landowska

Even if you're on the right track, you'll get run over if you just sit there.

Will Rogers

You will never find time for anything. If you want time, then you must make it.

Charles Buxton

It's not that I'm so smart, it's just that I stay with problems longer.

Albert Einstein

It's a little like wrestling a gorilla. You don't quit when you're tired; you quit when the gorilla is tired.

Robert Strauss

As you press on for justice, be sure to move with dignity and discipline, using only the weapons of love.

Martin Luther King Jr.

Nonviolence is not some exalted regimen that can be practiced only by a monk or a master; it also pertains to the way one interacts with a child, vacuums a carpet, or waits in line. . . . Whenever we separate ourselves from a given situation (for example, through inattentiveness, negative judgments, or impatience), we "kill" something valuable: . . . people, things, one's own composure, the moment itself. . . . These small-scale incidences of violence accumulate relentlessly, are multiplied on a social level, and become a source of the large-scale violence that can sweep down upon us so suddenly. . . . One need not wait until war is declared and bullets are flying to work for peace. . . . A more constant and equally urgent battle must be waged each day against the forces of one's own anger, carelessness, and self-absorption.

Kenneth Kraft

It is better to live a holy life than to talk about it. Lighthouses do not ring bells and fire cannons to call attention to their shining; they just shine.

D.L. Moody

Many are stubborn in pursuit of the path they have chosen, few in pursuit of the goal.

Friedrich Nietzsche

If you have an important point to make, don't try to be subtle or clever. Use a pile driver. Hit the point once. Then come back and hit it again. Then hit it a third time a tremendous whack.

Winston Churchill

Aim for the chopping block. If you aim for the wood, you will have nothing. Aim past the wood, aim through the wood; aim for the chopping block.

Annie Dillard

Fearlessness is the first requisite of spirituality. Cowards can never be moral.

Mohandas K. Gandhi

Resist much, obey little.

Walt Whitman

Fall seven times. Stand up eight.

Japanese proverb

He who limps is still walking.

Stanislaw Jerzy Lec

My conviction is that I have suffered for things that I am guilty of. I am suffering because I am a radical, and indeed I am a radical; I have suffered because I was an Italian, and indeed I am an Italian; I have suffered more for my family and for my beloved than for myself; but I am so convinced to be right that if you would execute me two times, and if I could be reborn two other times, I would live again to do what I have done already.

Bartolomeo Vanzetti

The mighty oak was once a little nut that stood its ground.

Source unknown

☙

The "kingdom of heaven" is a condition of the heart, not something that comes "upon the earth" or "after death."

Friedrich Nietzsche

Happiness is to take up the struggle in the midst of the raging storm and not to pluck the lute in the moonlight or recite poetry among the blossoms.

Ding Ling

Be natural in your meditation. Use up your own stock of piety and love before resorting to books. Remember that our God prefers the poverty of our heart to the most sublime thoughts borrowed from others.

Saint Peter Julian Eymard

Then the revelation came, silent, implacable, direct as a bullet. He did not look into the eyes of any fiery beast or see a burning bush.

Flannery O'Connor,
The Violent Bear It Away

No culture has yet solved the dilemma each has faced with the growth of a conscious mind: how to live a moral and compassionate existence when one is fully aware of the blood, the horror inherent in all life, when one finds darkness not only in one's own culture but within oneself. If there is a stage at which an individual life becomes truly adult, it must be when one grasps the irony in its unfolding and accepts responsibility for a life lived in the midst of such paradox. One must live in the middle of contradiction because if all contradiction were eliminated at once life would collapse. There are simply no answers to some of the great pressing questions. You continue to live them out, making your life a worthy expression of leaning into the light.

Barry Lopez

In the presence of fire, man never feels alone. The flames keep him company.

Oswald Spengler

Everywhere people ask, "What can I actually do?" The answer is as simple as it is disconcerting: we can each of us work to put our own inner house in order.

E.F. Schumacher

Anger or revolt that does not get into the muscles remains a figment of the imagination.

Simone de Beauvoir

The greatest challenge of the day is how to bring about a revolution of the heart, a revolution which has to start with each one of us. When we begin to take the lowest place, to wash the feet of others, to love our brothers with that burning love, that passion, which led to the Cross, then we can truly say, "Now I have begun."

Dorothy Day

The history of every country begins in the heart of a man or a woman.

Willa Cather

The major advances in civilization are processes which all but wreck the societies in which they occur.

Alfred North Whitehead

Long only for what you have.

André Gide

Fear . . . those prepared to die for the truth, for as a rule they will make others die with them. . . . Perhaps the mission of those who love mankind is to make people laugh at the truth, to make truth laugh, because the only truth lies in learning to free ourselves from insane passion for the truth.

Umberto Eco

When smashing monuments, save the pedestals — they always come in handy.

Stanislaw Jerzy Lee

Whatever it is, I'm against it.

Groucho Marx

And see, no longer blinded by our eyes.

Rupert Brooke

◌

That which issues from the heart alone will win the hearts of others to your own.

Johann Wolfgang von Goethe

You develop an instant global consciousness, a people orientation, an intense dis-satisfaction with the state of the world, and a compulsion to do something about it. From out there on the moon, international politics look so petty. You want to grab a politician by the scruff of the neck and drag him a quarter of a million miles out and say, "Look at that, you son of a bitch."

Edgar Mitchell

You can't derail a train by standing directly in front of it — or, not quite. But, a tiny piece of steel, properly placed . . .

Robert Creeley

We cannot avoid / Using power, / Cannot escape the compulsion / To afflict the world, / So let us . . . love powerfully.

Martin Buber

There is no economic problem and in a sense there never has been. But there is a moral problem and moral problems . . . have to be understood and transcended.

E.F. Schumacher

Only on paper has humanity yet achieved glory, beauty, truth, knowledge, virtue, and abiding love.

George Bernard Shaw

Passion and prejudice govern the world, only under the name of reason.

John Wesley

It's not when you realize that nothing can help you — religion, pride, anything — it's when you realize that you don't need any aid.

William Faulkner

The living of life, any life, involves great and private pain, much of which we share with no one.

Barry Lopez

One day a rabbi, in a frenzy of religious passion, rushed in before the ark, fell to his knees, and started beating his breast, crying, "I'm nobody! I'm nobody!" The cantor of the synagogue, impressed by this example of spiritual humility, joined the rabbi on his knees. "I'm nobody! I'm nobody!" The shamus (custodian), watching from the corner, couldn't restrain himself either. He joined the other two on his knees, calling out, "I'm nobody! I'm nobody!" At which point the rabbi, nudging the cantor with his elbow, pointed at the shamus and said, "Look who thinks he's a nobody."

Ram Dass and Paul Gorman

The caterpillar does all the work and the butterfly gets all the publicity.

George Carlin

We can be of little service to our fellows until we become disillusioned without being embittered.

F. Fraser Darling

One of the greatest evils of the day among those outside of prison is their sense of futility. Young people say, what is the sense of our small effort? They cannot see that we must lay one brick at a time, take one step at a time; we can be responsible only for the one action of the present moment. But we can beg for an increase of love in our hearts that will vitalize and transform all our individual actions, and know that God will take them and multiply them, as Jesus multiplies the loaves and fishes.

Dorothy Day

I would never betray a friend to serve a cause. Never reject a friend to help an institution. Great nations may fall in ruins before I would sell a friend to save them.

Edward Abbey

As long as we tolerate the division of mankind into power and profit organizations, and nations all continuously at one another's throats, we must each remind ourselves that though it is beautiful, each day is miserable. And act accordingly.

John Cage

The sun never knew how great it was till it struck the side of a building.

Louis Kahn

And then I think that unless one is oneself one cannot do anything much for others. With the best will in the world and even with a great deal of effort, one will always to a certain extent give them stones instead of bread — and both sides know it.

Isak Dinesen

Here's an answer to boredom and unhappiness: find a way to help someone.

Solomon Colodner

☙

It is not your obligation to complete your work, but you are not at liberty to quit.

The Talmud

I have been waiting twenty years for someone to say to me, "You have to fight fire with fire," so that I could reply, "That's funny — I always use water."

Howard Gossage

The monks of a neighboring monastery asked the master's help in a quarrel that had arisen among them. They had heard the master say he had a technique that was guaranteed to bring love and harmony to any group. On this occasion he revealed it. "Any time you are with anyone, or think of anyone, you must say to yourself: I am dying and this person too is dying, attempting the while to experience the truth of the words you are saying. If every one of you agrees to practice this, bitterness will die out, harmony will arise."

Anthony de Mello

It's a bit embarrassing to have been concerned with the human problem all one's life and find at the end that one has no more to offer by way of advice than "try to be a little kinder."

Aldous Huxley

I am done with great things and big things, great institutions and big success. I am for those tiny, invisible, molecular, moral forces that work from individual to individual, creeping through the crannies of the world like so many rootlets, or like the capillary oozing of water, which, if given time, will rend the hardest monuments of pride.

William James

Don't let me catch anyone talking about the universe in my department.

Ernest Rutherford

I have on my wall a great quote from Sir Laurence Olivier. He and Charlton Heston had done a play about twenty-five years ago, and they'd gotten slaughtered. Heston said, "Well, I guess you've just got to forget the bad reviews." And Olivier said, "No, you've got to forget the good ones."

William Goldman

We must have no illusions. We must not be naive. If we listen to the voice of God, we make our choice, get out of ourselves, and fight nonviolently for a better world. We must not expect to find it easy; we shall not walk on roses, people will not throng to hear us and applaud, and we shall not always be aware of divine protection. If we are to be pilgrims of justice and peace, we must expect the desert.

Dom Hélder Câmara

If we could only placate the world's rage with a drop of poetry or of love — but only the struggle, and the daring heart, are able to do that.

Pablo Neruda

Love does not help to understand / The logic of the bursting shell.

Edna St. Vincent Millay

Even stones have a love, a love that seeks the ground.

Meister Eckhart

I say to my breath once again, little breath come from in front of me, go away behind me, row me quietly now, as far as you can, for I am an abyss that I am trying to cross.

W.S. Merwin

He had stuffed his own emptiness with good works like a glutton.

Flannery O'Connor,
Everything That Rises Must Converge

In the last century, a tourist from America paid a visit to a renowned Polish rabbi, Hofetz Chaim. He was astonished to see that the rabbi's home was only a simple room filled with books, plus a table and a bench. "Rabbi," asked the tourist, "where is your furniture?" "Where is yours?" replied Hofetz Chaim. "Mine?" asked the puzzled American. "But I'm only passing through." "So am I," said the rabbi.

Tales of the Hasidim

If you are neutral in situations of injustice, you have chosen the side of the oppressor. If an elephant has his foot on the tail of a mouse and you say that you are neutral, the mouse will not appreciate your neutrality.

Desmond Tutu

I mark Henry James's sentence: Observe perpetually. Observe the oncome of age. Observe greed. Observe my own despondency. By that means it becomes serviceable.

Virginia Woolf

. . . a final comfort that is small, but not cold: the heart is the only broken instrument that works.

T.E. Kalem

The Bread In Your Cupboard

When someone steals another's clothes, we call him a thief. Should we not give the same name to one who could clothe the naked and does not? The bread in your cupboard belongs to the hungry; the coat hanging unused in your closet belongs to the one who needs it; the shoes rotting in your closet belong to the one who has no shoes; the money which you hoard up belongs to the poor.

Basil the Great

A man who sees another man on the street corner with only a stump for an arm will be so shocked the first time he'll give him sixpence. But the second time it'll be only a threepenny bit. And if he sees him a third time, he'll hand him over cold-bloodedly to the police.

Bertolt Brecht

The generosity of Tristan Bernard, who could never resist the entreaties of a beggar, was one of the causes of his own financial difficulties. One poor wretch . . . would always be found at Bernard's gate at certain fixed times. On one occasion, the old man's eyes widened with delight as he watched his benefactor take a sizable bill from his wallet instead of the usual coins. "We're leaving tomorrow for Normandy," explained Bernard, dropping the bill into the beggar's hat. "Here's two months' donation in advance. You have a right to your vacation, too."

The Little, Brown Book of Anecdotes

Charity is an ugly trick. It is a virtue grown by the rich on the graves of the poor. Unless it is accompanied by sincere revolt against the present social system, it is cheap moral swagger. In former times it was used as fire insurance by the rich, but now that the fear of Hell has gone . . . it is used either to gild mean lives with nobility or as a political instrument.

Rebecca West

Saintliness is also a temptation.

Jean Anouilh

It is good enough to talk of God whilst we are sitting here after a nice breakfast and looking forward to a nicer luncheon, but how am I to talk of God to the millions who have to go without two meals a day? To them God can only appear as bread.

Mohandas K. Gandhi

If you have never been hungry, you cannot know the either/or agony created by a single biscuit — either your brother gets it or you do. And if you do eat it, you know in your bones that you have stolen the food straight from his mouth. . . . This was the daily, debilitating side of poverty, . . . the perpetual scarcity that . . . makes the simplest act a moral dilemma.

Charles Johnson

For my part, I believe that the vainglorious and the violent will not inherit the earth. . . . In pursuance of that faith my friends and I take the hands of the dying in our hands. And some of us travel to the Pentagon, and others live in the Bowery and serve there, and others speak unpopularly and plainly of the fate of the unborn and of convicted criminals. It is all one.

Daniel Berrigan

Feeding the hungry is a greater work than raising the dead.

Saint John Chrysostom

The feeding of those that are hungry is a form of contemplation.

Simone Weil

When you're not used to comfort and good things to eat, you're intoxicated by them in no time. Truth's only too pleased to leave you. Very little's ever needed for Truth to let go of you. And after all, you're not really very keen to keep hold of it.

Louis-Ferdinand Céline

That lust for comfort, that stealthy thing that enters the house a guest, and then becomes a host, and then a master.

Khalil Gibran

Forgive us . . . for pasting stained glass on our eyes and our ears to shut out the cry of the hungry and the hurt of the world.

United Presbyterian Church's Litany for Holy Communion

There is tenderness only in the coarsest demand: that no one shall go hungry anymore.

Theodor Adorno

The decision to feed the world / is the real decision.

Adrienne Rich

He whose belly is full believes not him whose belly is empty.

Thomas Fuller

We are afraid of religion because it interprets rather than just observes. Religion does not confirm that there are hungry people in the world; it interprets the hungry to be our brethren whom we allow to starve.

Dorothee Sölle

The hunger of one is the shame of all.

Source unknown

When Christ said, "I was hungry and you fed me," he didn't mean only the hunger for bread and for food; he also meant the hunger to be loved. Jesus himself experienced this loneliness. He came amongst his own and his own received him not, and it hurt him then and it has kept on hurting him. The same hunger, the same loneliness, the same having no one to be accepted by and to be loved and wanted by. Every human being in that case resembles Christ in his loneliness; and that is the hardest part, that's real hunger.

Mother Teresa

Must the hunger become anger and the anger fury before anything will be done?

John Steinbeck

When a man tells you that he got rich through hard work, ask him: "Whose?"

Don Marquis

The rich are different from us.

F. Scott Fitzgerald

Yes, they have more money.

Ernest Hemingway, replying to F. Scott Fitzgerald

Indeed, I thought, slipping the silver into my purse, it is remarkable, remembering the bitterness of those days, what a change of temper a fixed income will bring about.

Virginia Woolf

Money helps, though not as much as you think when you don't have it.

Louise Erdrich

My husband's family was terribly refined. Within their circle you could know Beethoven, but God forbid if you *were* Beethoven.

Louise Nevelson

Making money ain't nothing exciting to me. You might be able to buy a little better booze than the wino on the corner, but you get sick just like the next cat, and when you die you're just as graveyard dead.

Louis Armstrong

Wouldn't you think some sociologist would have done a comparative study by now to prove, as I have always suspected, that there is a higher proportion of Undeserving Rich than Undeserving Poor?

Molly Ivins

Anyone who can live on welfare should be courted by Wall Street. He is a financial genius.

Joanna Clark

Americans live out their working lives, and most of their daily existence, not within a democratic system but instead within a hierarchical structure of subordination. To this extent, democracy is necessarily marginal . . . to their lives.

Robert A. Dahl

Clearly the most unfortunate people are those who must do the same thing over and over again, every minute, or perhaps twenty to the minute. They deserve the shortest hours and the highest pay.

John Kenneth Galbraith

Success is the American Dream we can keep dreaming because most people in most places . . . live wide awake in the terrible reality of poverty.

Ursula K. Le Guin

When shit becomes valuable, the poor will be born without assholes.

Brazilian proverb

I would almost say that my country is like a conquered province with foreign rulers, except that they are not foreigners and we are responsible for what they do.

Paul Goodman

I am still looking for the modern equivalent of those Quakers who ran successful businesses, made money because they offered honest products and treated their people decently, worked hard, spent honestly, saved honestly, gave honest value for money, put back more than they took out, and told no lies. This business creed, sadly, seems long forgotten.

Anita Roddick

I was sad because I had no shoes, until I met a man who had no feet. So I said, "Got any shoes you're not using?"

Steven Wright

The darkest hour in the history of any young man is when he sits down to study how to get money without honestly earning it.

Horace Greeley

In order that people may be happy in their work, these three things are needed: they must be fit for it; they must not do too much of it; and they must have a sense of success in it . . . a sure sense, or rather knowledge, that so much work has been done well, and fruitfully done, whatever the world may say or think about it.

John Ruskin

America was established not to create wealth but to realize a vision, to realize an ideal — to discover and maintain liberty among men.

Woodrow Wilson

I have two enemies in all the world, / Two twins, inseparably pooled: / The hunger of the hungry and the fullness of the full.

Marina Tsvetaeva

Rocks in the water don't know the misery of rocks in the sun.

Haitian proverb

The vices of the rich and great are called errors; and those of the poor and lowly only crimes.

Lord Byron

We must be careful that the people who make $5,000 a year are not pitted against those who make $25,000 a year by those who make $900,000.

Barbara A. Mikulski

If all the rich men in the world divided up their money amongst themselves, there wouldn't be enough to go round.

Christina Stead

Conservatives have historically seen people falling through the cracks in society and said, That's the way things work, survival of the fittest. Liberals see people falling through the cracks and say, We've got to do something about those people falling through the cracks, so we need a strong government that can provide programs and assist those people. Populists say there shouldn't be any cracks; let's fix them.

Jim Hightower

We say that time is money, meaning both are valuable. Both are a form of power. Usually, there is a reciprocal relationship between them; that is, abundance of money seems to go along with shortage of time, and abundance of time with shortage of money. Money is the wealth of the materialist, and works miracles in the realm of the physical. Time is the wealth of the pilgrim, and works miracles in all realms.

Ed Buryn

But lay up for yourself treasures in heaven, where neither moth nor rust doth corrupt, and where thieves do not break through nor steal.

Matthew 6:20

The tension between the call to the desert and to the marketplace arises not from the greater presence of God in one or the other, but from our varying psychological needs to apprehend him in different ways.

Sheila Cassidy

Rather than earn money, it was Thoreau's idea to reduce his wants so that he would not need to buy anything. As he went around town preaching this ingenious idea, the shopkeepers of Concord hoped he would drop dead.

Richard Armour

Money, it turned out, was exactly like sex. You thought of nothing else if you didn't have it, and thought of other things if you did.

James Baldwin

The greatest crimes are caused by surfeit, not by want. Men do not become tyrants so as not to suffer cold.

Aristotle

Every boy, in his heart, would rather steal second base than an automobile.

Tom Clark

There's a certain Buddhistic calm that comes from having . . . money in the bank.

Tom Robbins

She'd teach them [her children] these things are nothing, the clothes, toys, and furniture. These things fool people into thinking they must stay where the things are. Leave it all, she'd teach them, even . . . all your dreams of safe, calm places. Go with what is most terrifying. . . . Always choose love over safety, if you can tell the difference.

Josephine Humphreys,
Dreams of Sleep

We think that we must become acquisitive — though we call it by a better-sounding word. We call it evolution, growth, development, progress, and we say it is essential.

J. Krishnamurti

Our society is dedicated almost entirely to the celebration of the ego, with all its sad fantasies about success and power, and it celebrates those very forces of greed and ignorance that are destroying the planet.

Sogyal Rinpoche

Those who prize freedom only for the material benefits it offers have never kept it for long.

Alexis de Tocqueville

The labor of a human being is not a commodity or an article of commerce. You can't weigh the soul of a man with a bar of pig iron.

Samuel Gompers

Most successful people are unhappy. That's why they are successes — they have to reassure themselves about themselves by achieving something that the world will notice. . . . The happy people are failures because they are on such good terms with themselves that they don't give a damn.

Agatha Christie

Meetings are an addictive, highly self-indulgent activity that corporations and other large organizations habitually engage in only because they cannot actually masturbate.

Dave Barry

I asked a man in prison once how he happened to be there and he said he had stolen a pair of shoes. I told him that if he had stolen a railroad he would be a United States senator.

Mary "Mother" Jones

The law, in its majestic equality, forbids rich and poor alike to sleep under bridges, beg in the streets, or steal bread.

Anatole France

A broken heart is a very pleasant complaint for a man in London if he has a comfortable income.

George Bernard Shaw

Don't you know that if people could bottle the air they would? Don't you know there would be an American Air-bottling Association? And don't you know that they would allow thousands and millions to die for want of breath if they could not pay for air?

Robert Ingersoll

The truth is, we are all caught in the great economic system which is heartless.

Woodrow Wilson

Stripped of ethical rationalizations and philosophical pretensions, a crime is anything that a group in power chooses to prohibit.

Freda Adler

If you love the law and you love good sausage, don't watch either of them being made.

Betty Talmadge

The law is simply expediency wearing a long white dress.

Quentin Crisp

To be a poor man is hard, but to be a poor race in a land of dollars is the very bottom of hardships.

W.E.B. Du Bois

The equality of the capitalist and the laborer is the same as the equality of two fighters, when the hands of one are bound, while a gun is put into the hands of the other, and equal conditions are strictly observed for both in the fight.

Leo Tolstoy

That is what is so bizarre about the American legal system. Where else on earth would stealing from a phone booth be considered more serious than polluting the earth?

Laura Nader

Not every problem someone has with his girlfriend is necessarily due to the capitalist mode of production.

Herbert Marcuse

Every man thinks God is on his side. The rich and powerful know he is.

Jean Anouilh

God, we've been searching for you. What an incredible fortune there would be for you, God! Can you imagine the looks you'd get from your neighbors? But don't just sit there, God.

American Family Publishers, in a letter sent to the Bushnell (Florida) Assembly of God, announcing that "God" was a finalist for the $11 million top prize

The day is not far off when the economic problem will take the back seat where it belongs, and the arena of the heart and the head will be occupied, or reoccupied, by our real problems — the problems of life and of human relations.

John Maynard Keynes

There is poetry as soon as we realize that we possess nothing.

John Cage

True contentment depends not upon what we have; a tub was large enough for Diogenes, but the world was too small for Alexander.

Charles Caleb Colton

❧

Democracy forever teases us with the contrast between its ideals and its realities, between its heroic possibilities and its sorry achievements.

Agnes Repplier

All reformers, however strict their social conscience, live in houses just as big as they can pay for.

Logan Pearsall Smith

The degree of civilization in a society can be judged by entering its prisons.

Fyodor Dostoyevsky

You have to make more noise than anybody else, you have to make yourself more obtrusive than anybody else, you have to fill all the papers more than anybody else, in fact, you have to be there all the time and see that they do not

snow you under, if you are really going to get your reform realized.

Emmeline Pankhurst

Defend the poor and fatherless; do justice to the afflicted and needy.

Psalms 82:3

When you say fiscal responsibility, it seems to me that you really mean rich people keeping their money.

Alice Adams

We can have democracy in this country or we can have great wealth concentrated in the hands of a few, but we cannot have both.

Louis Brandeis

Democracy takes time. Dictatorship is quicker, but too many people get shot.

Jeffrey Archer

People who are much too sensitive to demand of cripples that they run races ask of the poor that they get up and act just like everyone else in society.

Michael Harrington

Thousands upon thousands are yearly brought into a state of real poverty by their great anxiety not to be thought poor.

William Cobbett

We wear more clothes than any people who have ever lived. We eat more different kinds of food than anyone since Louis XIV. What goes on in the corner drugstore the bazaars of Arabia couldn't match. What we find piled at the supermarkets is the harvest of the world in all seasons at the same time. And as we push through the aisles, grabbing this and that from every corner of the globe, with the Muzak sludge overhead, we should be the most contented people in the world. Are we?

Agnes de Mille

I like to go to Marshall Field's in Chicago just to see how many things there are in the world that I do not want.

Mother M. Madelava

When Mark Twain was an impoverished young reporter in Virginia City, he was walking along the street one day with a cigar box under his arm. He encountered a wealthy lady he knew, who said to him reproachfully, "You promised me that you would give up smoking."

"Madam," replied Twain, "this box does not contain cigars. I'm just moving."

The Little, Brown Book of Anecdotes

America is like one of those old-fashioned six-cylinder truck engines that can be missing two spark plugs and have a broken flywheel and a crankshaft that's five thousand millimeters off fitting properly, and two bad ball bearings, and still run. We're in that kind of situation. We can have substantial parts of the population committing suicide, and still run and look fairly good.

Thomas McGuane

My constituency is the desperate, the damned, the disinherited, the disrespected, and the despised.

Jesse Jackson

All this talk about equality. The only thing people really have in common is that they are all going to die.

Bob Dylan

How is it that you do not know how to interpret these times?

Luke 12:56

To feed men and not to love them is to treat them as if they were barnyard cattle. To love them and not to respect them is to treat them as if they were household pets.

Mencius

If a free society cannot help the many who are poor, it cannot save the few who are rich.

John F. Kennedy

America has the best-dressed poverty the world has ever known. . . . It is much easier in the United States to be decently dressed than it is to be decently housed, fed, or doctored.

Michael Harrington

When someone steals another's clothes, we call him a thief. Should we not give the same name to one who could clothe the naked and does not? The bread in your cupboard belongs to the hungry; the coat hanging unused in your closet belongs to the one who needs it; the shoes rotting in your closet belong to the one who has no shoes; the money which you hoard up belongs to the poor.

Basil the Great

Think of the worst experience you've ever had with a clerk in some government-service job — motor vehicles, hospital, whatever — and add the life-threatening condition of impending starvation or homelessness to the waiting line, multiply the anxiety by an exponent of ten, and you have some idea of what it's like in a welfare center.

Theresa Funiciello

We have grown literally afraid to be poor. We despise anyone who elects to be poor in order to simplify and save his inner life.

William James

I am on a platform at the train station, in the evening, waiting for an aunt from Bucharest. There are many people. I have a crescent roll, which I have not dared to eat because it seemed too enormous. I hold it in my hand, contemplating it, displaying it, congratulating myself for having it. When the train arrives at the station, our group begins to move, and I am left alone for a second. Out of nowhere, there emerges a little boy of about five or six who snatches away my roll! He watches me for a second, with a mischievous smile, then thrusts the roll into his mouth and disappears. I am so startled that I can neither speak nor move. That event revealed to me the terrible power of skill and daring.

Mircea Eliade

For those who have lived on the edge of poverty all their lives, the semblance of poverty affected by the affluent is both incomprehensible and insulting.

Lillian Breslow Rubin

When society does step in to help out a poor woman attempting to raise children on her own, all that it customarily has to offer is some government-surplus cheese, a monthly allowance so small it would barely keep a yuppie male in running shoes, and the contemptuous epithet "welfare cheat."

Barbara Ehrenreich

Rich folks always talks hard times.

Lillian Smith, *Strange Fruit*

To blame the poor for subsisting on welfare has no justice unless we are also willing to judge every rich member of society by how productive he or she is. Taken individual by individual, it is likely that there's more idleness and abuse of government favors among the economically privileged than among the ranks of welfare.

Norman Mailer

The four sons of my friend heard me say, and repeat: "This box of chocolates is for the four of you. One, two, three, four. Have you heard?" When I gave the box to the youngest, saying once again that it was for all, the little one opened it, and, pressing it to his chest, exclaimed, "It's mine, it's mine!" I felt as if I had just witnessed a meeting of the powerful of the earth.

Dom Hélder Câmara

Make all you can, save all you can, give all you can.

John Wesley

The relationship between our motives and our quality of mind is very subtle. Can we give truly without any expectation of getting something back, just for the joy of giving? Becoming very honest with ourselves is part of our training in morality.

Joseph Goldstein

Men feel that cruelty to the poor is a kind of cruelty to animals. They never feel that it is injustice to equals; nay, it is treachery to comrades.

G.K. Chesterton

As you are, so is the world.

Ramana Maharshi

If people are highly successful in their professions they lose their senses. Sight goes. They have no time to look at pictures. Sound goes. They have no time to listen to music. Speech goes. They have no time for conversation. They lose their sense of proportion — the relations between one thing and another. Humanity goes.

Virginia Woolf

Usually, terrible things done with the excuse that progress requires them are not really progress at all, but just terrible things.

Russell Baker

In a contest between new technology and old ways of life, it is the traditional rhythms that will hold. Traditional societies make up more than two-thirds of the world, the two-thirds that will not be going online to "save" time but will remain wedded to the knowledge that if the bus doesn't come that day, it will come someday. After all, there is nothing but time.

Gloria Naylor

The perception that we have "no time" is one of the distinctive marks of modern Western culture.

Margaret Visser

Reconsider your definitions. We are prone to judge success by the index of our salaries or the size of our automobiles rather than by the quality of our service and relationship to humanity.

Martin Luther King Jr.

What does a man need — really need? A few pounds of food each day, heat and shelter, six feet to lie down in, and some form of working activity that will yield a sense of accomplishment. That's all — in the material sense. And we know it. But we are brainwashed by our economic system until we end up in a tomb beneath a pyramid of time payments, mortgages, and preposterous gadgetry, playthings that divert our attention from the sheer idiocy of the charade.

Sterling Hayden

Many wealthy people are little more than janitors of their possessions.

Frank Lloyd Wright

I did not have 3,000 pairs of shoes. I had 1,060.

Imelda Marcos

Hell is made up of yearnings. The wicked don't roast on beds of nails; they sit on comfortable chairs and are tortured with yearnings.

Isaac Bashevis Singer

The earth was established to be in common for all, rich and poor. . . . Nature makes no distinctions among us at our birth, and none at our death. All alike she creates us, all alike she seals us in the tomb. Who can tell the dead apart? Open up the graves, and, if you can, tell which was a rich man.

Saint Ambrose

Would that there were an award for people who come to understand the concept of enough. Good enough. Successful enough. Thin enough. Rich enough. Socially responsible enough. When you have self-respect, you have enough, and when you have enough, you have self-respect.

Gail Sheehy

To be without some of the things you want is an indispensable part of happiness.

Bertrand Russell

Simplicity doesn't mean to live in misery and poverty. You have what you need, and you don't want to have what you don't need.

Charan Singh

Money frees you from doing things you dislike. Since I dislike doing nearly everything, money is handy.

Groucho Marx

The old Eskimo hunters she had known in her childhood thought the riches of life were intelligence, fearlessness, and love. A man with these gifts was rich.

Jean Craighead George,
Julie of the Wolves

I am immensely and continuously conscious of a world of nuclear bombs, of vast hunger, of curable injustice, of a meretricious press and cheap-jack television, of perilous and apparently endless international division, of unreasonable cruelty and suffering for which almost nobody cares, and of my own silly efforts to make money to provide me with irrelevant comforts or necessities like drink and to ensure some measure of security for my family. And I know that it is not the answer, because there is truthfully only one answer, which is absolute pacifism and absolute communism — not in the dreary, dogmatic party-political sense, but in the sense that my father would have called religious: the sense of mortal community. Not only do I know it; I knew it all along.

James Cameron

Who is rich? He that is content. Who is that? Nobody.

Benjamin Franklin

Never eat more than you can lift.

Miss Piggy

⌒

The dollar sign is the only sign in which the modern man appears to have any real faith.

Helen Rowland

Every time a man expects, as he says, his money to work for him, he is expecting other people to work for him.

Dorothy L. Sayers

If you put a chain around the neck of a slave, the other end fastens itself around your own.

Ralph Waldo Emerson

The only real struggle in the history of the world . . . is between the vested interest and social justice.

Arnold Toynbee

The poor have sometimes objected to being governed badly; the rich have always objected to being governed at all.

G.K. Chesterton

It's all very well to run around saying regulation is bad, get the government off our backs, etc. Of course our lives are regulated. When you come to a stop sign, you stop; if you want to go fishing, you get a license; if you want to shoot ducks, you can shoot only three ducks. The alternative is dead bodies at the intersection, no fish, and no ducks. OK?

Molly Ivins

Money is like fire, an element as little troubled by moralizing as earth, air, and water. Men can employ it as a tool, or they can dance around it as if it were the incarnation of a god. Money votes socialist or monarchist, finds a profit in pornography or translations from the Bible, commissions Rembrandt and underwrites the technology of Auschwitz. It acquires its meaning from the uses to which it is put.

Lewis H. Lapham

There is only one class in the community that thinks more about money than the rich, and that is the poor. The poor can think of nothing else.

Oscar Wilde

So you think that money is the root of all evil? Have you ever asked what is the root of money?

Ayn Rand

Capitalism is an art form, an Apollonian fabrication to rival nature. It is hypocritical for feminists and intellectuals to enjoy the pleasures and conveniences of capitalism while sneering at it. . . . Everyone born into capitalism has incurred a debt to it. Give Caesar his due.

Camille Paglia

Money is better than poverty, if only for financial reasons.

Woody Allen

Money does not corrupt people. What corrupts people is lack of affection. . . . Money is simply the bandage which wounded people put over their wounds.

Margaret Halsey

❧

You may break any written law in America with impunity. There is an unwritten law that you break at your peril. It is: do not attack the profit system.

Mary Heaton Vorse

Every civilizing step in history has been ridiculed as "sentimental," "impractical," or "womanish" . . . by those whose fun, profit, or convenience was at stake.

Joan Gilbert

A team effort is a lot of people doing what I say.

Michael Winner

When ideas go unexamined and unchallenged for a long enough time, they become mythological and very, very powerful. They create conformity. They intimidate.

E.L. Doctorow

It is difficult to get a man to understand something when his salary depends upon his not understanding it.

Upton Sinclair

The Duke of Cambridge protested that he wasn't arguing against change. He favored it, he said, when there was no alternative.

Source unknown

It's always been and always will be the same in the world: the horse does the work, and the coachman is tipped.

Source unknown

But it is not really difference the oppressor fears so much as similarity.

Cherríe Moraga

You know, it's not the world that was my oppressor, because what the world does to you . . . long enough and effectively enough, you begin to do to yourself.

James Baldwin

Power concedes nothing without demand. It never did, and it never will. Find out just what people will submit to, and you have found out the exact amount of injustice and wrong which will be imposed upon them; and this will continue till they have resisted with either words or blows, or with both. The limits of tyrants are prescribed by the endurance of those whom they oppress.

Frederick Douglass

Marge, it takes two to lie. One to lie and one to listen.

Homer Simpson

This is what the world honors: wealth, eminence, long life, a good name. This is what the world finds happiness in: a life of ease, rich food, fine clothes, beautiful sights, sweet sounds. . . . People who can't get these things fret a great deal and are afraid — this is a stupid way to treat the body. People who are rich wear themselves out rushing around on business. . . . People who are eminent spend night and day scheming and scrutinizing. . . . Man lives his life in company with worry, and if he lives a long time, . . . then he has spent that much time worrying. . . . This is a callous way to treat the body.

Chuang Tzu

Money destroys human roots wherever it is able to penetrate, by turning desire for gain into the sole motive. It easily manages to outweigh all other motives, because the effort it demands of the mind is so very much less. Nothing is so clear and so simple as a row of figures.

Simone Weil

The real measure of our wealth is how much we'd be worth if we lost all our money.

John Henry Jowett

We must, in short, make it economically possible for people to act upon their own best moral values.

Michael Harrington

⊘

Whenever people say, "We mustn't be sentimental," you can take it they are about to do something cruel. And if they add, "We must be realistic," they mean they are going to make money from it.

Brigid Brophy

Manners are the happy ways of doing things. . . . If they are superficial, so are the dewdrops which give such a depth to the morning meadows.

Ralph Waldo Emerson

A society based on cash and self-interest is not a society at all, but a state of war.

William Morris

Civilization has taught us to eat with a fork, but even now if nobody is around we use our fingers.

Will Rogers

One day she told me the story of her early life. Her first love affair took place when she was around eighteen. The young man was a year or two older and the procedure they adopted was to take off their clothes and, quite naked, climb two adjacent poplar trees. When they were as high as they could get, they would make them sway till their branches touched. They themselves never did.

Gerald Brenan

The perfect hostess will see to it that the works of male and female authors be properly separated on her bookshelves. Their proximity, unless they happen to be married, should not be tolerated.

Lady Gough's Etiquette

Civilization is the lamb's skin in which barbarism masquerades.

T.B. Aldrich

The great secret, Eliza, is not having bad manners or good manners or any other particular sort of manners, but having the same manner for all human souls: in short, behaving as if you were in Heaven, where there are no third-class carriages, and one soul is as good as another.

George Bernard Shaw,
Pygmalion

The question becomes: what is the appropriate behavior for a man or a woman in the midst of this world, where each person is clinging to his piece of debris? What is the proper salutation between people as they pass each other in this flood?

Leonard Cohen

The Bible tells us to love our neighbors and also to love our enemies — probably because generally they are the same people.

G.K. Chesterton

A society that presumes a norm of violence and celebrates aggression, whether in the subway, on the football field, or in the conduct of its business, cannot help making celebrities of the people who would destroy it.

Lewis Lapham

Always live in the ugliest house on the street. Then you don't have to look at it.

David Hockney

Behavior influences consciousness. Right behavior means right consciousness. Our attitude here and now influences the entire environment: our words, actions, ways of holding and moving ourselves, they all influence what happens around us and inside us. The actions of every instant, every day, must be right. . . . Every gesture is important. How we eat, how we put on our clothes, how we wash ourselves, how we go to the toilet, how we put things away, how we act with other people, family, wife, work. How we are — totally — in every single gesture.

Taisen Deshimaru

This is what you shall do: Love the earth and the sun and the animals, despise riches, give alms to everyone that asks, stand up for the stupid and crazy, devote your income and labor to others, hate tyrants, argue not concerning God, have patience and indulgence toward the people, take off your hat to nothing known or unknown or to any man or any number of men, . . . reexamine all you've been told at school or church or in any book, dismiss whatever insults your own soul, and . . . your very flesh shall be a great poem.

Walt Whitman

The first half of my life, I responded to arrogant people with anger and arrogance. Now I respond to their fragility with delicate care.

Theodore Isaac Rubin

Former Postmaster General J. Edward Day revealed in his book an ingenious way to stop long-winded telephone callers. Day suggests you hang up while you are talking. The other party will think you were accidentally cut off, because no one would hang up on his own voice.

Judith Martin, aka Miss Manners

☙

I Picked On The World

I realized either I was crazy or the world was crazy;
and I picked on the world. And of course I was right.

Jack Kerouac, *Vanity of Duluoz*

Politicians are the same all over; they promise to build a bridge even where there is no water.

Nikita Khrushchev

I confess I enjoy democracy immensely. It is incomparably idiotic, and hence incomparably amusing.

H.L. Mencken

Once, I thought to write a history of the immigrants in America. Then I discovered that the immigrants were American history.

Oscar Handlin

That men do not learn very much from the lessons of history is the most important of all the lessons that history has to teach.

Aldous Huxley

For a transitory enchanted moment, man must have held his breath in the presence of this continent, compelled into an aesthetic contemplation he neither understood nor desired, face to face for the last time in history with something commensurate to his capacity for wonder.

F. Scott Fitzgerald

Two centuries ago, a former European colony decided to catch up with Europe. It succeeded so well that the United States of America became a monster, in which the taints, the sickness, and the inhumanity of Europe have grown to appalling dimensions.

Frantz Fanon

A belief in a supernatural source of evil is not necessary; men alone are quite capable of every wickedness.

Joseph Conrad

A certain kind of rich man prefers the pleasures of moral or political dandyism. He feels obliged to hold views, espouse causes, restore order. The spectacle is nearly always comic.

Lewis H. Lapham

Most of us continue to work for wages in a highly unequal social system that denies us meaningful work and a decent return for our labor. That simple fact defines a set of common interests of immense democratic potential.

Charles Bergquist

One morning, Thomas Jefferson woke up in a modest Washington rooming house, dressed, and then left the house in order to attend his inauguration as third president. When he got back, duly sworn in, he found no space left for him at the dinner table. Quietly accepting the democratic principle of first come, first served, the president of the United States went up to his room without dinner.

Bartlett's Book of Anecdotes

In a consumer society, there are inevitably two kinds of slaves: the prisoners of addiction and the prisoners of envy.

Ivan Illich

There are good reasons why everybody should heed politicians' advice not to believe the media. One of the best is that the media report what politicians say.

Russell Baker

With words we govern men.

Benjamin Disraeli

Every violation of truth is not only a sort of suicide in the liar, but is a stab at the health of human society.

Ralph Waldo Emerson

Cinema, radio, television, and magazines are a school of inattention: people look without seeing, listen without hearing.

Robert Bresson

Stare. It is the way to educate your eye, and more. Stare, pry, listen, eavesdrop. Die knowing something. You are not here long.

Walker Evans

The function of freedom is to free somebody else.

Toni Morrison

The revolt of the poet is invariably conservative at its roots. . . . Not politically conservative, but imaginatively conservative, with a profound regard for what is given, as earth or air, sun or moon or stars, or the dreams of man.

Cid Corman

If, after all, men cannot always make history have a meaning, they can always act so that their own lives have one.

Albert Camus

I realized either I was crazy or the world was crazy; and I picked on the world. And of course I was right.

Jack Kerouac, *Vanity of Duluoz*

To die for an idea; it is unquestionably noble. But how much nobler it would be if men died for ideas that were true.

H.L. Mencken

There are a thousand hacking at the branches of evil to one who is striking at the root.

Henry David Thoreau

No society has been able to abolish human sadness; no political system can deliver us from the pain of living, from our fear of death, our thirst for the absolute. It is the human condition that directs the social condition, not vice versa.

Eugene Ionesco

During my eighty-seven years I have witnessed a whole succession of technological revolutions. But none of them has done away with the need for character in the individual or the ability to think.

Bernard M. Baruch

I feel so agitated all the time, like a hamster in search of a wheel.

Carrie Fisher

Panic is not an effective, long-term organizing strategy.

Starhawk

Try saying this silently to everyone and everything you see for thirty days . . . : "I wish you happiness now and whatever will bring happiness to you in the future." If we said it to the sky, we would have to stop polluting; if we said it when we see ponds and lakes and streams, we would have to stop using them as garbage dumps and sewers; if we said it to small children, we would have to stop abusing them, even in the name of training; if we said it to people, we would have to stop stoking the fires of enmity around us. Beauty and human warmth would take root in us like a clear, hot June day. We would change.

Joan Chittister

When eating a fruit, think of the person who planted the tree.

Vietnamese saying

One sister told me that, years before, my aunt [Sister Josephine] had summoned the young sisters from their morning prayer, led them to the house of a poor family whose mother lay ill. They cleaned, prepared breakfast, got the children off to school. "This is your prayer" was all she said to the sisters. "None of us ever forgot that," the sister said.

Daniel Berrigan

The notion of following your passion is worth indulging. Your passion is your source of power. . . . To live a really full life, you need to follow those paths . . . in defiance of all things conventional, perhaps. And of course it is at a price. You have to know that going in. But the price you pay, in my opinion, is not worth the time of day to think about. It's so important not to knee-pad around the world. You should never bow down to anything but those you love and respect. Ever. For anything.

Doug Peacock

Georges Clemenceau's contrariness was invaluable in shaking France out of its torpor during World War 1, but it was altogether less of an asset during the subsequent peace. This trait emerged even in trivial matters. Going into a grand garden party at Versailles, the bowler-hatted Clemenceau met the British foreign secretary, Lord Balfour, wearing a top hat. "They told me top hats would be worn," said the British diplomat. "They told me, too," said Clemenceau.

Bartlett's Book of Anecdotes

I wonder if you ever change human beings with arguments alone: either by peppering them with little sharp facts or by blowing them up with great guns of truth. You scare them, but do you change them? I wonder if you ever make any real difference in human beings without understanding them and loving them. For when you argue with a man (how much more with a woman) you are somehow trying to pull him down and make him less (and yourself more); but when you try to understand him, when you like him, how eager is he then to know the truth you have? . . . There is nothing in the world that people so much thrive upon, grow fine and rosy and robust upon . . . as being loved.

David Grayson

We are here to awaken from the illusion of our separateness.

Thich Nhat Hanh

☺

Americans are very friendly and very suspicious, that is what Americans are and that is what always upsets the foreigner who deals with them, they are so friendly how can they be so suspicious they are so suspicious how can they be so friendly but they just are.

Gertrude Stein

Sir, [the American colonists] are a race of convicts, and ought to be thankful for anything we allow them short of hanging.

Samuel Johnson

Every American carries in his bloodstream the heritage of the malcontent and the dreamer.

Dorothy Fuldheim

The average age of the world's greatest civilizations has been two hundred years. These nations have progressed through the following sequence: from bondage to spiritual faith; from spiritual faith to great courage; from great courage to liberty; from liberty to abundance; from abundance to selfishness; from selfishness to complacency; from complacency to apathy; from apathy to dependency; from dependency back into bondage.

Alexander Fraser Tytler

Half of the American people have never read a newspaper. Half have never voted for president. One hopes it is the same half.

Gore Vidal

We have, I fear, confused power with greatness.

Stewart L. Udall

Americans . . . believe in the future as if it were a religion; they believe that there is nothing they cannot accomplish, that solutions wait somewhere for all problems, like brides.

Frances Fitzgerald

A civilization which tends to concentrate wealth and power in the hands of a fortunate few, and to make of others mere human machines, must inevitably evolve anarchy and bring destruction.

Henry George

Tradition means giving votes to the most obscure of our classes — our ancestors. It is the democracy of the dead. Tradition refuses to submit to the small and arrogant oligarchy of those who merely happen to be walking around.

G.K. Chesterton

In the Soviet Union capitalism triumphed over communism. In this country capitalism triumphed over democracy.

Fran Lebowitz

Society never advances. It recedes as fast on one side as it gains on the other. It undergoes continual changes: it is barbarous, it is civilized, it is rich, it is scientific; but this change is not amelioration. For every thing that is given, something else is taken. Society acquires new arts and loses old instincts.

Ralph Waldo Emerson

The crucial disadvantage of aggression, competitiveness, and skepticism as national characteristics is that these qualities cannot be turned off at five o'clock.

Margaret Halsey

It is also supposed to be part of the American tradition that if we want to step out of line, we step out of line. Democracy isn't falling in line behind the president. Democracy is for people to think independently, be skeptical of government, look around and try to find out what's going on. And if they find out that government is deceiving them, to speak out as loudly as they can.

Howard Zinn

Every government, whatever its form, character, or color — be it absolute or constitutional, monarchy or republic, Fascist, Nazi, or Bolshevik — is by its very nature conservative, static, intolerant of change and opposed to it.

Emma Goldman

I think we are constantly faced with the same decision. The decision to be blindly obedient to authority versus the decision to try and change things by fighting the powers that be is always, throughout history, the only decision.

Abbie Hoffman

Ideally, one should have a great deal of courage and strength, but not boast or make a big show of it. Then, in times of need, one should rise to the occasion and fight bravely for what is right.

The Dalai Lama

Whatever America hopes to bring to pass in the world must first come to pass in the heart of America.

Dwight D. Eisenhower

We started from scratch, every American an immigrant who came because he wanted change. Why are we now afraid to change?

Eleanor Roosevelt

I'm tired of waiting. It's time for us to find our own voice, to do our own organizing, to push forward on reform, to push forward on issues of economic justice, and to make the United States of America, this good country, even better.

Paul Wellstone

My country tears of thee.

Lawrence Ferlinghetti

☺

We first crush people to the earth, and then claim the right of trampling on them forever, because they are prostrate.

Lydia Maria Child

In the next voyage of the *Mayflower*, after she carried the Pilgrims, she was employed in transporting a cargo of slaves from Africa.

Nathaniel Hawthorne

The Pilgrim Fathers landed on the shores of America and fell upon their knees. Then they fell upon the aborigines.

Source unknown

In the era of imperialism, businessmen became politicians and were acclaimed as statesmen, while statesmen were taken seriously only if they talked the language of successful businessmen.

Hannah Arendt

This republic was not established by cowards, and cowards will not preserve it.

Elmer Davis

We're far more concerned about the desecration of the flag than we are about the desecration of our land.

Wendell Berry

The great nations have always acted like gangsters, and the small nations like prostitutes.

Stanley Kubrick

We estimate the wisdom of nations by seeing what they did with their surplus capital.

Ralph Waldo Emerson

If I seem to take part in politics, it is only because politics encircle us today like the coil of a snake from which one cannot get out, no matter how much one tries. I wish therefore to wrestle with the snake.

Mohandas K. Gandhi

I look at the politics of this country as a game that is played on the people, this illusion of choice. It's interesting that the important things have been reduced in number: oil companies, communications, pharmaceuticals, insurance, banking, accounting, all these firms have been merged and reduced. The choices are very limited. But if you want a ba-

gel, we've got twenty-six flavors. There are four hundred kinds of mustard in this country. These are the illusions of choice. I don't really think choice is here to any substantive degree.

George Carlin

America: a country where everything is done to prove life isn't tragic.

Albert Camus

Haven't you ever noticed how highways always get beautiful near the state capital?

Shirley Ann Grau

The meeting of a customer and a clerk across the service counter in a store is as significant as two leaders of nations meeting over a conference table in search of peace. If peace and understanding is possible, it must occur in the moment that is present. It can occur only when relationship is real and unconditional. Relationship begins with thoughtless awareness, an openness that sees and hears with humility, and a consideration that has already forgiven all things that the mind might present as a barrier to unity.

Booker Jones

❧

The United States spends $50 billion annually on the development of defense and space technologies, but less than $2 billion on furthering our understanding of the environment. There is a perfectly straightforward reason why we have more sophisticated techniques for planting land mines in the desert than for planting corn on an erodible hillside.

Aaron Sachs

Myth: we have to save the earth. Frankly, the earth doesn't need to be saved. Nature doesn't give a hoot if human beings are here or not. The planet has survived cataclysmic and catastrophic changes for millions upon millions of years. Over that time, it is widely believed, 99 percent of all species have come and gone while the planet has remained. Saving the environment is really about saving our environment — making it safe for ourselves, our children, and the world as we know it. If more people saw the issue as one of saving themselves, we would probably see increased motivation and commitment to actually do so.

Robert M. Lilienfeld and William L. Rathje

The road to hell is paved.

Paul Ramsey

A nuclear power plant is infinitely safer than eating because three hundred people choke to death on food every year.

Dixy Lee Ray, former chair of the Atomic Energy Commission

An epoch will come when people will disclaim kinship with us as we disclaim kinship with the monkeys.

Khalil Gibran

The ground on which the ball bounces / Is another bouncing ball.

Delmore Schwartz

How would you describe the difference between modern war and modern industry — between, say, bombing and strip mining, or between chemical warfare and chemical manufacturing? The difference seems to be only that in war the victimization of humans is directly intentional and in industry it is accepted as a "trade-off."

Wendell Berry

She said there were two people you had to be true to — those people who came before you and those people who came after you.

Gayl Jones, *Eva's Man*

We are impressed with nature's power, but by projecting upon this power an image of the feminine, the mother, we reassure ourselves — for surely a mother will always be loving toward us, continue to feed us, clothe us, and carry away our wastes, and never kill us, no matter how much toxic waste we put in the soil or how many CFCs in the ozone. The sense of nature as inexhaustible mother encourages us to feel there are no limits to a finite planet, while the sense of nature as benign and ever-loving mother permits us to continue disregarding a crescendo of warnings.

Elizabeth Dodson Gray

Look twice before you leap.

Charlotte Brontë

The culture has moved to the point where I find myself in the far left without having gone there. I still feel like I'm putting up my father's old Indiana farmer's values. I think I'm a conservative. I don't think these guys that call themselves "conservatives" really are; these guys are high rollers and plungers and bet-the-farm-on-slender-things guys; they ain't conservatives. I think a conservative is somebody who cares about conserving the planet and the air and the water and the sky and the sun. It is something mean to say that mankind has fucked up the sunshine.

Stephen Gaskin

We must always be on the lookout for perverse dynamic processes which carry even good things to excess. It is precisely these excesses which become the most evil things in the world. The devil, after all, is a fallen angel.

Kenneth Boulding

Our noses too, and our eyes and ears, are political instruments, protesters. An aesthetic response is a political action. . . . We know instinctively, aesthetically, when a fish stinks, when the sense of beauty is offended. Standing for these moments — and these moments occur each day, within every airless office building, seated in each crippling chair, inundated by senseless noise and fattened on industrial food — standing for our responses, these aesthetic reverberations of truth in the soul, may be the primary civic act of the citizen, the origin of caution and of the precautionary principle itself, with its warnings to stop, look, and listen.

James Hillman

There is no reason to repeat bad history.

Eleanor Holmes Norton

What have we got here in America that we believe we cannot live without? We have the most varied and imaginative bathrooms in the world, we have kitchens with the most gimmicks, we have houses with every possible electrical gadget to save ourselves all kinds of trouble — all so that we can have leisure. Leisure, leisure, leisure! So that we don't go mad in the leisure, we have color TV. So that there will never, never, be a moment of silence, we have radio and Muzak. We can't stand silence, because silence includes thinking. And if we thought, we would have to face ourselves.

Agnes de Mille

By conforming to the norm, you perpetuate the norm.

Alex Vasquez

We started off trying to set up a small anarchist community, but people wouldn't obey the rules.

Alan Bennett

I wish they'd give me just one speck of proof that this world of theirs couldn't have been set up and handled better by a half dozen drugged idiots bound hand and foot at the bottom of a ten-mile well.

Kenneth Patchen

Maybe the technologists are right; maybe they can create conditions that will support 10 billion people on planet Earth, or even more. . . . It might be possible, for example, to farm the entire land surface and the oceans, too. . . . We could process sewage into bouillon cubes, eat algae, seaweed, plankton. All those things are theoretically possible. But . . . it seems like it would be a wretched world to live in — billions of humans packed into some sort of planetary food factory. Buckminster Fuller thought it could be done. But the question is, Should it be done? Who would want to live in such an ugly world?

Edward Abbey

⟋

Our inventions are wont to be pretty toys, which distract our attention from serious things. They are but improved means to an unimproved end.

Henry David Thoreau

Natives who beat drums to drive off evil spirits are objects of scorn to smart Americans who blow horns to break up traffic jams.

Mary Ellen Kelly

It is the virtue and the pathos of man that he aspires endlessly toward a better world; it is his weakness and his tragedy that he does nothing to bring such a world even one step nearer.

Ludwig Lewisohn

When great changes occur in history, when great principles are involved, as a rule the majority are wrong. The minority are usually right.

Eugene V. Debs

In America the word revolution is used to sell pantyhose.

Rita Mae Brown

What have we achieved in mowing down mountain ranges, harnessing the energy of mighty rivers, or moving whole populations about like chess pieces, if we ourselves remain the same restless, miserable, frustrated creatures we were before? To call such activity progress is utter delusion.

Henry Miller

To be a consumer is the most primitive level of being. It is to be a mouth, an eater, a devourer of things. . . . To discover the truth of who we are, we must discard the consumer mentality and reclaim our spiritual dignity.

David Frawley

It is one thing to decry the rat race. . . . That is the good and honorable work of moralists. It is quite another thing to quit the rat race, to drop out, to refuse to run any further — that is the work of the individualist. It is offensive because it is impolite; it makes the rebuke personal; the individualist calls not his or her behavior into question, but mine.

Paul Gruchow

The philosopher Diogenes was sitting on a curbstone, eating bread and lentils for his supper. He was seen by the philosopher Aristippus, who lived comfortably by flattering the king. Said Aristippus, "If you would learn to be subservient to the king, you would not have to live on lentils." Said Diogenes, "Learn to live on lentils, and you will not have to cultivate the king."

Louis I. Newman

The struggle to save the global environment is in one way much more difficult than the struggle to vanquish Hitler, for this time the war is with ourselves. We are the enemy, just as we have only ourselves as allies. In a war such as this, then, what is victory and how will we recognize it?

Al Gore

The atom bombs are piling up in the factories, the police are prowling through the cities, the lies are streaming from the loudspeakers, but the earth is still going round the sun.

George Orwell

A process which led from the amoeba to man appeared to philosophers to be obviously progress — though whether the amoeba would agree with this opinion is not known.

Bertrand Russell

The skylines lit up at dead of night, the air-conditioning systems cooling empty hotels in the desert, and artificial light in the middle of the day all have something both demented and admirable about them: the mindless luxury of a rich civilization, and yet of a civilization perhaps as scared to see the lights go out as was the hunter in his primitive night.

Jean Baudrillard

Perched on the loftiest throne in the world, we are still sitting on our own behind.

Michel Eyquem de Montaigne

Nonsense, it was all nonsense: this whole damned outfit, with its committees, its conferences, its eternal talk, talk, talk, was a great con trick; it was a mechanism to earn a few hundred men and women incredible sums of money.

Doris Lessing,
The Summer Before Dark

Long years must pass before the truths we have made for ourselves become our very flesh.

Paul Valéry

Memories are short; appetites for power and glory are insatiable. Old tyrants depart. New ones take their place. . . . It is all very baffling and trying.

Harry S. Truman

The charm, one might say the genius, of memory is that it is choosy, chancy, and temperamental; it rejects the edifying cathedral, and indelibly photographs the small boy outside, chewing a hunk of melon in the dust.

Elizabeth Bowen

Civilization is a stream with banks. The stream is sometimes filled with blood from people killing, stealing, shouting, and doing the things historians usually record — while, on the banks, unnoticed, people build homes, make love, raise children, sing songs, write poetry, and even whittle statues. The story of civilization is the story of what happened on the banks.

Will Durant

Our ignorance of history causes us to slander our own times.

Gustave Flaubert

The Middle Ages hangs over history's belt like a beer belly. It is too late now for aerobic dancing or cottage cheese lunches to reduce the Middle Ages. History will have to wear size forty-eight shorts forever.

Tom Robbins

We should remember that it is easy and foolish to sneer at the mistakes or barbarities of remote ages.

Hermann Hesse

One has but to observe a community of beavers at work in a stream to understand the loss in his sagacity, balance, cooperation, competence, and purpose which Man has suffered since he rose up on his hind legs. . . . He began to chatter and he developed Reason, Thought, and Imagination, qualities which would get the smartest group of rabbits or orioles in the world into inextricable trouble overnight.

James Thurber

Just as I was thinking that no century could possibly be dumber than the nineteenth, along comes the twentieth. I swear, the entire planet seemed to be staging some kind of stupidity contest.

Martin Amis

The second half of the twentieth century is a complete flop.

Isaac Bashevis Singer

The Buddha, the Godhead, resides quite as comfortably in the circuits of a digital computer or the gears of a cycle transmission as he does at the top of a mountain or in the petals of a flower.

Robert M. Pirsig

Do not despair of life. You have no doubt force enough to overcome your obstacles. Think of the fox, prowling through wood and field in a winter night for something to satisfy his hunger. . . . His race survives; I do not believe any of them ever committed suicide.

Henry David Thoreau

Many could forgo heavy meals, a full wardrobe, a fine house, et cetera; it is the ego they cannot forgo.

Mohandas K. Gandhi

To seek freedom is the only driving force I know. Freedom to fly off into that infinity out there. Freedom to dissolve; to lift off; to be like the flame of a candle, which, in spite of being up against the light of a billion stars, remains intact, because it never pretended to be more than what it is: a mere candle.

Carlos Castaneda

Some people just don't seem to realize, when they're moaning about not getting prayers answered, that no is the answer.

Nelia Gardner White

The man who is forever disturbed about the condition of humanity either has no problems of his own or has refused to face them.

Henry Miller

God don't make no mistakes. That's how He got to be God.

Archie Bunker, in the TV show
All in the Family

❧

Economics and politics are the governing powers of life today, and that's why everything is screwy.

Joseph Campbell

We who live beneath a sky still streaked with the smoke of crematoria have paid a high price to find out that evil is really evil.

François Mauriac

Humanity does not change much; in some ways it even improves. Our international football games are occasions for violence, but football began in England with a severed head for a ball.

Anthony Burgess

If someone tells you he's going to make a "realistic decision," you immediately understand that he's resolved to do something bad.

Mary McCarthy

The superior man understands what is right; the inferior understands what will sell.

Confucius

For what shall it profit a man, if he shall gain the whole world, and lose his own soul?

Mark 8:36

The present age is demented. It is possessed by a sense of dislocation, a loss of personal identity, an alternating sentimentality and rage which, in an individual patient, could be characterized as dementia.

Walker Percy

If we only wanted to be happy it would be easy; but we always want to be happier than other people, which is almost always difficult, since we think them happier than they are.

Charles de Montesquieu

We are not mad, we are human. We want to love, and someone must forgive us for the paths we take to love, for the paths are many and dark, and we are ardent and cruel in our journey.

Leonard Cohen

I would suggest that barbarism be considered as a permanent and universal human characteristic which becomes more or less pronounced according to the play of circumstances.

Simone Weil

We have two American flags always: one for the rich and one for the poor. When the rich fly it, it means that things are under control; when the poor fly it, it means danger, revolution, anarchy.

Henry Miller

In certain trying circumstances, urgent circumstances, desperate circumstances, profanity furnishes a relief denied even to prayer.

Mark Twain

She tended to be impatient with that sort of intellectual who, for all his brilliance, has never been able to arrive at the simple conclusion that to be reasonably happy you have to be reasonably good.

Carolyn Kizer,
A Slight Mechanical Failure

Practice charity, without holding in mind any conceptions about charity, for charity after all is just a word.

The Diamond Sutra

Think about it: It is easy to see God's beauty in a glorious sunset or in ocean waves crashing on a beach. But can you find the holiness in a struggle for life?

Harold Kushner

Beginning today, treat everyone you meet as if he or she were going to be dead by midnight. Extend to them all the care, kindness, and understanding you can muster, and do so with no thought of any reward. Your life will never be the same again.

Og Mandino

Our lives extend beyond our skins, in radical interdependence with the rest of the world.

Joanna Macy

⊘

Everything begins in mysticism and ends in politics.

Charles Péguy

Noncooperation with evil is as much a duty as cooperation with good.

Mohandas K. Gandhi

If we'd had the right technology back then, you would have seen Eva Braun on *The Donahue Show* and Adolf Hitler on *Meet the Press*.

Ed Turner

The average man votes below himself; he votes with half a mind or a hundredth part of one. A man ought to vote with the whole of himself, as he worships or gets married. A man ought to vote with his head and heart, his soul and stomach, his eye for faces and his ear for music; also (when sufficiently provoked) with his hands and feet. If he has ever seen a fine sunset, the crimson color of it should creep into his vote. . . . The question is not so much whether only a minority of the electorate votes. The point is that only a minority of the voter votes.

G.K. Chesterton

Choosing the lesser of two evils is still choosing evil.

Jerry Garcia

We assume that politicians are without honor. We read their statements, trying to crack the code. The scandal of their politics . . . [is] not so much that men in high places lie, only that they do so with such indifference, so endlessly, still expecting to be believed.

Adrienne Rich

When the ax comes into the forest, the trees, seeing the handle, say to each other, "He is one of us."

Hasidic proverb

His demeanor proclaimed a relaxed confidence that all men dreamed of and precious few obtained. His wit was obvious, his attention to others sincere, and his sense of humor legendary. I found myself disliking the son of a bitch at once.

Dan Simmons,
The Fall of Hyperion

As long as our civilization is essentially one of property, of fences, of exclusiveness, it will be mocked by delusions. Our riches will leave us sick; there will be bitterness in our laughter, and our wine will burn our mouth. Only that good profits which we can taste with all doors open, and which serves all men.

Ralph Waldo Emerson

Our Constitution was made only for a moral and religious people. It is wholly inadequate to the government of any other.

John Adams

Government is actually the worst failure of civilized man. There has never been a really good one, and even those that are most tolerable are arbitrary, cruel, grasping, and unintelligent.

H.L. Mencken

It may be true that the law cannot make a man love me, but it can keep him from lynching me, and I think that's pretty important.

Martin Luther King Jr.

I don't have general views about anything, except social injustice.

Marguerite Duras

Liberals feel unworthy of their possessions. Conservatives feel they deserve everything they've stolen.

Mort Sahl

One-fifth of the people are against everything all the time.

Robert F. Kennedy

I began the revolution with eighty-two men. If I had it to do again, I'd do it with ten or fifteen and absolute faith. It does not matter how small you are if you have faith and a plan of action.

Fidel Castro

The changes in our life must come from the impossibility to live otherwise than according to the demands of our conscience . . . not from our mental resolution to try a new form of life.

Leo Tolstoy

There is a story of a man who once stood before God, his heart breaking from the pain and injustice in the world. "Dear God," he cried out, "look at all the suffering, the anguish and distress in the world. Why don't you send help?" God responded, "I did send help. I sent you."

David J. Wolpe

Take your life in your own hands and what happens? A terrible thing: no one to blame.

Erica Jong

Most of us spend too much time on the last twenty-four hours and too little on the last six thousand years.

Will Durant

It is not enough to be busy: so are the ants. The question is, What are we busy about?

Henry David Thoreau

History is a child building a sand castle by the sea, and that child is the whole majesty of man's power in the world.

Heraclitus

Today every invention is received with a cry of triumph which soon turns into a cry of fear.

Bertolt Brecht

The unrecorded past is none other than our old friend, the tree in the primeval forest which fell without being heard.

Barbara Tuchman

The notion of progress in a single line without goal or limit seems perhaps the most parochial notion of a very parochial century.

Lewis Mumford

We already have the statistics for the future: the growth percentages of pollution, overpopulation, desertification. The future is already in place.

Günter Grass

You can't say that civilization don't advance . . . for in every war they kill you in a new way.

Will Rogers

Utopias are presented for our inspection as a critique of the human state. If they are to be treated as anything but trivial exercises of the imagination, I suggest there is a simple test we can apply. . . . We have to say to ourselves, "How would I myself live in this proposed society? How long would it be before I went stark staring mad?"

William Golding

For peace of mind, resign as general manager of the universe.

Larry Eisenberg

We pass the word around; we ponder how the case is put by different people; we read the poetry; we meditate over the literature; we play the music; we change our minds; we reach an understanding. Society evolves this way, not by shouting each other down, but by the unique capacity of unique, individual human beings to comprehend each other.

Lewis Thomas

The test of a civilization is in the way that it cares for its helpless members.

Pearl S. Buck

Ever since I could remember, I'd wished I'd been lucky enough to be alive at a great time — when something big was going on, like a crucifixion. And suddenly I realized I was.

Ben Shahn

Ideology, politics, and journalism, which luxuriate in failure, are impotent in the face of hope and joy.

P.J. O'Rourke

One generation passeth away, and another generation cometh: but the earth abideth forever.

Ecclesiastes 1:4

Saint Teresa of Avila described our life in this world as like a night at a second-class hotel.

Malcolm Muggeridge

Why do you hasten to remove anything which hurts your eye, while if something affects your soul you postpone the cure until next year?

Horace

It is easy to detect the bullshit in a jingle or an official euphemism for murder, but . . . I must keep my bullshit detector on when I say or write that I'm a good person who only wants peace and justice. Bullshit. I'm also a greedy person who wants a snazzy computer and a place in the country. I'm a demanding person who wants a clean environment, safe streets, and lower taxes. I'm an impossible person who wants instant nirvana, heaven on the cheap, sainthood in ten easy lessons. Perhaps you know people like me.

Mark O'Brien

No man chooses evil because it is evil; he only mistakes it for the happiness, the good that he seeks.

Mary Wollstonecraft Shelley

All things truly wicked start from an innocence.

Ernest Hemingway

Once, an old woman at my church said the secret is that God loves us exactly the way we are and that he loves us too much to let us stay like this — and I'm just trying to trust that.

Anne Lamott

In our time, political speech and writing are largely the defense of the indefensible.

George Orwell

He had the misleading air of open-hearted simplicity that people have come to demand of their politicians.

Rae Foley

The whole aim of practical politics is to keep the populace in a continual state of alarm (and hence clamorous to be led to safety) by menacing them with an endless series of hobgoblins, all of them imaginary.

H.L. Mencken

To be able to destroy with good conscience, to be able to behave badly and call your bad behavior "righteous indignation" — this is the height of psychological luxury, the most delicious of moral treats.

Aldous Huxley

Nearly all men can stand adversity, but if you want to test a man's character, give him power.

Abraham Lincoln

When someone behaves like a beast, he says, "After all, one is only human." But when he is treated like a beast, he says, "After all, one is human."

Karl Kraus

The devil can cite Scripture for his purpose.

William Shakespeare

Twaddle, rubbish, and gossip is what people want, not action. . . . The secret of life is to chatter freely about all one wishes to do and how one is always being prevented — and then do nothing.

Søren Kierkegaard

The besetting sin of most clever people is that it is much easier to say clever things than true ones.

Kenneth Boulding

If the truth doesn't save us, what does that say about us?

Lois McMaster Bujold

Before we can realize who we really are, we must become conscious of the fact that the person we think we are, here and now, is at best an impostor and a stranger.

Thomas Merton

The ingenuities we practice in order to appear admirable to ourselves would suffice to invent the telephone twice over on a rainy summer morning.

Brendan Gill

I sell mirrors in the city of the blind.

Kabir

He who cannot dance claims the floor is uneven.

Hindu saying

A mirror dreams only of another mirror.

Anna Akhmatova

In a virtuous community, men of sense and of principle will always be placed at the head of affairs. In a declining state of public morals, men will be so blinded to their true interests as to put the incapable and unworthy at the helm. It is therefore vain to complain of the follies or crimes of a government. We must lay our hands on our own hearts and say, "Here is the sin that makes the public sin."

Ralph Waldo Emerson

Politics is how you live your life, not whom you vote for.

Jerry Rubin

We speak of amnesia as if it were unusual.

Douglas Anderson

Let us not paralyze our capacity for good by brooding on man's capacity for evil.

David Sarnoff

I realize that if I wait until I am no longer afraid to act, write, speak, be, I'll be sending messages on a Ouija board, cryptic complaints from the other side.

Audre Lorde

My defenses were so great. . . . The cocky, chip-on-the-shoulder, macho, aggressive rock-and-roll hero who knew all the answers . . . was actually a terrified guy who didn't know how to cry. Simple.

John Lennon

So many objections may be made to everything, that nothing can overcome them but the necessity of doing something.

Samuel Johnson

So act that your principle of action might safely be made a law for the whole world.

Immanuel Kant

I attribute my success to this: I never gave or took an excuse.

Florence Nightingale

Hope is a bad thing. It means you are not what you want to be. It means that part of you is dead, if not all of you. It means that you entertain illusions. It's a sort of spiritual clap, I should say.

Henry Miller

Most of our platitudes notwithstanding, self-deception remains the most difficult deception. The tricks that work on others count for nothing in that very well-lit back alley where one keeps assignations with oneself.

Joan Didion

Monkeys are superior to men in this: when a monkey looks into a mirror, he sees a monkey.

Malcolm de Chazal

I lie to myself all the time. But I never believe me.

S.E. Hinton

Delusions of grandeur make me feel a lot better about myself.

Jane Wagner

Someday, somewhere, a guy is going to come to you and show you a nice, brand-new deck of cards on which the seal is never broken, and this guy is going to offer to bet you that the jack of spades will jump out of this deck and squirt cider in your ear. But, son, do not bet him, for as sure as you do you are going to get an ear full of cider.

Damon Runyon

Maturity consists in no longer being taken in by oneself.

Heimito von Doderer

⟨⟩

Advertisers are the interpreters of our dreams. . . . Like the movies, they infect the routine futility of our days with purposeful adventure. Their weapons are our weaknesses: fear, ambition, illness, pride, selfishness, desire, ignorance. And these weapons must be kept bright as a sword.

E.B. White

It is pretty obvious that the debasement of the human mind caused by a constant flow of fraudulent advertising is no trivial thing. There is more than one way to conquer a country.

Raymond Chandler

Real events don't have endings, / Only the stories about them do.

James Galvin

The media transforms the great silence of things into its opposite.

Michel de Certeau

Elvira always lied first to herself before she lied to anybody else, since this gave her a conviction of moral honesty.

Phyllis Bottome, *Under the Skin*

Deception and "con games" are a way of life in all species and throughout nature. Organisms that do not improve their ability to deceive — and to detect deception — are less apt to survive.

Harriet Lerner

I will never again go to people under false pretenses even if it is to give them the Holy Bible. I will never again sell anything, even if I have to starve.

Henry Miller

A linguistics professor was lecturing to his class one day. "In English," he said, "a double negative forms a positive. In some languages, though, such as Russian, a double negative is still a negative. However, there is no language wherein a double positive can form a negative." A voice from the back of the room piped up, "Yeah, right."

Source unknown

I wanted only to try to live in accord with the promptings which came from my true self. Why was that so very difficult?

Hermann Hesse, *Demian*

A lie will easily get you out of a scrape, and yet, strangely and beautifully, rap-

ture possesses you when you have taken the scrape and left out the lie.

C.E. Montague

Falsehood is invariably the child of fear in one form or another.

Aleister Crowley

Political language . . . is designed to make lies sound truthful and murder respectable and to give an appearance of solidity to pure wind.

George Orwell

Each day a few more lies eat into the seed with which we are born, little institutional lies from the print of newspapers, the shock waves of television, and the sentimental cheats of the movie screen.

Norman Mailer

Freedom of the press is guaranteed only to those who own one.

A.J. Liebling

The sorrows of humanity are no one's sorrows. . . . A thousand people drowned in floods in China is news; a solitary child drowned in a pond is tragedy.

Josephine Tey

We should never forget that everything Adolf Hitler did in Germany was "legal" and everything the Hungarian freedom fighters did in Hungary was "illegal."

Martin Luther King Jr.

How do you describe the sorting out on arriving at Auschwitz, the separation of children who see a father or mother going away, never to be seen again? How do you express the dumb grief of a little girl and the endless lines of women, children, and rabbis being driven across the Polish or Ukrainian landscapes to their deaths? No, I can't do it. And . . . I don't understand how Europe's most cultured nation could have done that. For these men who killed with submachine guns in the Ukraine were university graduates. Afterwards, they went home and read a poem by Heine. So what happened?

Elie Wiesel

Truth will not be ignored. It will rise up and consume us.

Katharine Wylde

Then I will speak upon the ashes.

Sojourner Truth, when told of a threat to burn down the hall where she was about to speak

Before Buddha or Jesus spoke, the nightingale sang, and long after the words of Jesus and Buddha are gone into oblivion, the nightingale still will sing. Because it is neither preaching nor teaching nor commanding nor urging. It is just singing.

D.H. Lawrence

Truth and Falsehood were bathing. Falsehood came out of the water first and dressed herself in Truth's clothes. Truth, unwilling to put on the garments of Falsehood, went naked.

Source unknown

There are three truths: my truth, your truth, and the truth.

Chinese proverb

You will never be happy if you continue to search for what happiness consists of. You will never live if you are looking for the meaning of life.

Albert Camus

[The philosopher] Wittgenstein writes about a man who, not being certain of an item he reads in the newspaper, buys one hundred copies of the paper to reassure himself of its truth.

Richard Kehl

The fact is I don't trust a man who uses the word evil eighteen times in ten minutes. If you're half evil, nothing soothes you more than to think the person you are opposed to is totally evil.

Norman Mailer

I just don't know why they're shooting at us. All we want to do is bring them democracy and white bread. Transplant the American Dream. Freedom. Achievement. Hyperacidity. Affluence. Flatulence. Technology. Tension. The inalienable right to an early coronary sitting at your desk while plotting to stab your boss in the back.

Hawkeye, in the TV show M*A*S*H

All civilization ever does is hide the blood and cover up hate with pretty words.

Ursula K. Le Guin

How many times have you tried to shield yourself by reading the newspaper, watching television, or just spacing out? That is the $64,000 question: how much have you connected with yourself at all in your whole life?

Chögyam Trungpa Rinpoche

The most delusional fantasies can be made to masquerade as sanity if you've got the political power to reinforce them.

Penny Skillman

Of course it's the same old story. Truth usually is the same old story.

Margaret Thatcher

Never apologize for showing feeling, my friend. Remember that when you do so you apologize for truth.

Benjamin Disraeli

Make yourself an honest man, and then you may be sure there is one less rascal in the world.

Thomas Carlyle

All the information I have about myself is from forged documents.

Vladimir Nabokov

You only lie to two people in your life: your girlfriend and the police. Everybody else you tell the truth to.

Jack Nicholson

Whatever games are played with us, we must play no games with ourselves, but deal in our privacy with the last honesty and truth.

Ralph Waldo Emerson

There are very few human beings who receive the truth, complete and staggering, by instant illumination. Most of them acquire it fragment by fragment, on a small scale, by successive developments, cellularly, like a laborious mosaic.

Anaïs Nin

Believe those who are seeking the truth; doubt those who find it.

André Gide

All affirmations are true in some sense, false in some sense, meaningless in some sense, true and false in some sense, true and meaningless in some sense, and true and false and meaningless in some sense.

Sri Syadasti

What difference is there, do you think, between those in Plato's cave who can only marvel at the shadows and images of various objects, provided they are content and don't know what they miss, and the philosopher who has emerged from the cave and sees the real things?

Desiderius Erasmus

Einstein's space is no closer to reality than Van Gogh's sky. . . . The scientist's discoveries impose his own order on chaos, as the composer or painter imposes his; an order that always refers to limited aspects of reality, and is biased by the observer's frame of reference, which differs from period to period, as a Rembrandt nude differs from a nude by Monet.

Arthur Koestler

[The formula] "two times two is five" is sometimes also a most charming thing.

Fyodor Dostoyevsky

We believe as much as we can. We would believe everything if we only could.

William James

And what if it were true after all? Tell me, and what if it were true?

Levi Yitzhak

⟲

Every human being's essential nature is perfect and faultless, but after years of immersion in the world we easily forget our roots and take on a counterfeit nature.

Lao Tzu

We do not err because truth is difficult to see. It is visible at a glance. We err because this is more comfortable.

Aleksandr Solzhenitsyn

The truth about our childhood is stored up in our body, and although we can repress it, we can never alter it. Our intellect can be deceived, our feelings manipulated, our perceptions confused, and our body tricked with medication. But someday the body will present its bill, for it is as incorruptible as a child who, still whole in spirit, will accept no compromises or excuses, and it will not stop tormenting us until we stop evading the truth.

Alice Miller

Penetrate deeply into the secret existence of anyone about you, even of the man or woman whom you count happiest, and you will come upon things

they spend all their efforts to hide. Fair as the exterior may be, if you go in, you will find bare places, heaps of rubbish that can never be taken away, cold hearths, desolate altars, and windows veiled with cobwebs.

Myrtle Reed

Disillusion is an extraordinarily interesting state of being, having immediate and far-reaching effects. It is a sacred state, a state that has power. . . . The experience of disillusion stops thought. And with the screen of associations quieted, only then, the mind is receptive . . . and can experience a moment of more precise knowledge.

Carla Needleman

Much sheer effort goes into avoiding the truth: left to itself, it sweeps in like the tide.

Fay Weldon

Why tell lies when one is going to die?

Edward Dahlberg

If you have integrity, nothing else matters. If you don't have integrity, nothing else matters.

Alan Simpson

Truth should not be forced; it should simply manifest itself, like a woman who has in her privacy reflected and coolly decided to bestow herself upon a certain man.

John Updike

I have never but once succeeded in making him tell a lie, and that was by a subterfuge. "Moore," I said, "do you always speak the truth?" "No," he replied. I believe this to be the only lie he ever told.

**Bertrand Russell on
George Edward Moore**

After a second's astonishment, Kate let the lie stand. Like most lies it was much easier than the truth, and to contradict it might turn out to be a very wearying affair.

**Ursula Reilly Curtiss,
*The Wasp***

Truth is a great flirt.

Franz Liszt

Today I bent the truth to be kind, and I have no regret, for I am far surer of what is kind than I am of what is true.

Robert Brault

On their return journey from the South Pole, Scott's party was beset by fearful blizzards. Oates suffered badly from frost-bitten feet, which were turning gangrenous. He begged to be left behind so as not to slow up the others. His companions would not hear of it, and they struggled on for another day. The following morning the blizzard was still raging. Oates said, "I am just going outside and may be some time." He then walked out of the tent and vanished forever into the storm.

The Little, Brown Book of Anecdotes

Don't be yourself. Be someone a little nicer.

Mignon McLaughlin

What is always speaking silently is the body.

Norman O. Brown

If stories come to you, care for them. And learn to give them away where they are needed. Sometimes a person needs a story more than food to stay alive. That is why we put these stories in each other's memory. This is how people care for themselves.

Barry Lopez

I was raised by . . . people who regard telling one story when two would do as a sign someone is not really trying.

Linda Ellerbee

Who then tells a finer tale than any of us? Silence does.

Isak Dinesen

What was once called the objective world is a sort of Rorschach ink blot, into which each culture, each system of science and religion, each type of personality, reads a meaning only remotely derived from the shape and color of the blot itself.

Lewis Mumford

You can't judge Hollywood by superficial impressions. After you get past the artificial tinsel you get down to the real tinsel.

Samuel Goldwyn

Television knows no night. It is perpetual day. TV embodies our fear of the dark, of night, of the other side of things.

Jean Baudrillard

I secretly understood: the primitive appeal of the hearth. Television is — its irresistible charm — a fire.

John Updike

It is a medium of entertainment which permits millions of people to listen to the same joke at the same time, and yet remain lonesome.

T.S. Eliot

Educational television should be absolutely forbidden. It can only lead to unreasonable expectations and eventual disappointment when your child discovers that the letters of the alphabet do not leap up out of books and dance around the room with royal blue chickens.

Fran Lebowitz

I hate television. I hate it as much as peanuts. But I can't stop eating peanuts.

Orson Welles

Television is actually closer to reality than anything in books. The madness of TV is the madness of human life.

Camille Paglia

Television, despite its enormous presence, turns out to have added pitifully few lines to the communal memory.

Justin Kaplan

I find television very educational. Every time someone switches it on, I go into another room and read a good book.

Groucho Marx

She claimed I had something she called Star Trek Amnesia. She said I would

purposely forget having seen an episode until the last ten minutes of the show, then I'd say, "Oh yeah, I remember this," but by then it was too late, I'd just go ahead and finish it.

Cass Nevada

The heroic hours of life do not announce their presence by drum and trumpet, challenging us to be true to ourselves. . . . Some little, unassuming, unobtrusive choice presents itself before us slyly and craftily, glib and insinuating, in the modest garb of innocence. To yield to its blandishments is so easy.

Benjamin Cardozo

There are only two industries which refer to their customers as "users" — drugs and computers.

Edward R. Tufte

But they are useless. They can only give you answers.

Pablo Picasso, on computers

Love and compassion predominate in the world. And this is why unpleasant events make "news"; compassionate activities are so much a part of daily life that they are taken for granted and, therefore, largely ignored.

The Dalai Lama

The sky is not less blue because the blind man does not see.

Danish proverb

I use devotional objects to foster patience, just as the beads of a rosary are devotional tools to foster mindfulness. My tools to cultivate patience are fossils that friends have given me. I have a small trilobite, an ancient marine mammal, and another that may be an early form of the nautilus, and recently I received a tiny fish that's 600 million years old. I look at those and handle them, and that's helpful to me.

David Steindl-Rast

We are all prisoners, but some of us are in cells with windows and some without.

Khalil Gibran

⌒

You can no more win a war than you can win an earthquake.

Jeannette Rankin

Human beings are perhaps never more frightening than when they are convinced beyond doubt that they are right.

Laurens van der Post

If I got to make just one law, it would be that the men who make the decisions to drop bombs would first, every time, have to spend one whole day taking care of a baby. We were not made to do this killing thing, I swear. Back up. It's a big mistake.

Barbara Kingsolver

I suffer more from the humiliations inflicted by my country than from those inflicted on her.

Simone Weil

To the blessed work of making weapons we assign our finest intellect and the largest share of our treasure, and in the magnificence of an aircraft carrier or a cruise missile we find our moral and aesthetic equivalent of the Sistine ceiling and Chartres Cathedral.

Lewis H. Lapham

They wrote in the old days that it is sweet and fitting to die for one's country. But in modern war, there is nothing sweet nor fitting in your dying. You will die like a dog for no good reason.

Ernest Hemingway

Inaction may be the highest form of action.

Jerry Brown

America is addicted to wars of distraction.

Barbara Ehrenreich

All wars are civil wars, because all men are brothers.

François de Salignac
de la Mothe Fénelon

It is isolation that is critical to war. You can't be abusive when you realize your connectedness.

David Kadlec

Never think that wars are irrational catastrophes: they happen when wrong ways of thinking and living bring about intolerable situations.... The root causes of conflict are usually to be found in some wrong way of life in which all parties have acquiesced, and for which everybody must, to some extent, bear the blame.

Dorothy L. Sayers

War would end if the dead could return.

Stanley Baldwin

It is my intention to make my entire life a rejection of, a protest against the crimes and injustices of war and political tyranny which threaten to destroy the whole race of man and the world with him. . . . I make monastic silence a protest against the lies of politicians, propagandists, and agitators, and when I speak it is to deny that my faith and my Church can ever seriously be aligned with these forces of injustice and destruction. But it is true, nevertheless, that the faith in which I believe is also invoked by many who believe in war, believe in racial injustices, and believe in self-righteous and lying forms of tyranny. My life must, then, be a protest against these also, and perhaps against these most of all.

Thomas Merton

If any question why we died, / Tell them, because our fathers lied.

Rudyard Kipling

◌

Profits are springing, like weeds, from the fields of the dead.

Rosa Luxemburg

Show me who makes a profit from war, and I'll show you how to stop the war.

Henry Ford

After each war, there is a little less democracy to save.

Brooks Atkinson

What difference does it make to the dead, the orphans, and the homeless, whether the mad destruction is wrought under the name of totalitarianism or the holy name of liberty or democracy?

Mohandas K. Gandhi

Men love war because it allows them to look serious. Because they imagine it is the one thing that stops women from laughing at them.

John Fowles

They were going to look at war, the red animal — war, the blood-swollen god.

Stephen Crane,
The Red Badge of Courage

I shall die, but that is all I shall do for Death.

Edna St. Vincent Millay

In a war of ideas, it is people who get killed.

Stanislaw Jerzy Lec

Society highly values its normal man. It educates children to lose themselves and to become absurd, and thus be normal. Normal men have killed perhaps one hundred million of their fellow normal men in the last fifty years.

R.D. Laing

I can use up twenty-five thousand men a month.

Napoleon Bonaparte

Men are willing to be dead if they can only be dead in a pile.

Max Eastman

We used to wonder where war lived, what it was that made us so vile. And now we realize that we know where it lives, that it is inside ourselves.

Albert Camus

Peace is the ego's greatest enemy because, according to the ego's interpretation of reality, war is the guarantee of its survival. The ego becomes strong in strife.

A Course in Miracles

Very few people chose war. They chose selfishness and the result was war. Each of us, individually and nationally, must choose: total love or total war.

Dave Dellinger

Nonviolence means avoiding not only external physical violence but also internal violence of spirit. You not only refuse to shoot a man, but you refuse to hate him.

Martin Luther King Jr.

I wondered why somebody didn't do something for peace. Then I realized that I am somebody.

Source unknown

True patriotism hates injustice in its own land more than anywhere else.

Clarence Darrow

To survive it is often necessary to fight, and to fight you have to dirty yourself.

George Orwell

Sacredness of human life! The world has never believed it! It has been with life that we have settled our quarrels; won wives, gold, and land; defended ideas; imposed religions. We have held that a death toll was a necessary part of every human achievement, whether sport, war, or industry. A moment's rage over the horror of it, and we have sunk into indifference.

Ida Tarbell

The nonviolent revolution begins in your mind. You must first redefine yourself. When people redefine themselves, slavery is dead. Then the power structure makes a motion, but doesn't get a second.

James Bevel

Political crises are moral crises.

Octavio Paz

Violence does not and cannot exist by itself; it is invariably intertwined with the lie.

Aleksandr Solzhenitsyn

The only people on earth who do not see Christ and his teachings as nonviolent are Christians.

Mohandas K. Gandhi

...this sadness / of never understanding ourselves / and of threatening ourselves with death ...

Pablo Neruda

☾

All the wrong people remember Vietnam. I think all the people who remember it should forget it, and all the people who forgot it should remember it.

Michael Herr

Nothing is worse than war? Dishonor is worse than war. Slavery is worse than war.

Winston Churchill

War is bestowed like electroshock on the depressive nation: thousands of volts jolting the system, an artificial galvanizing, one effect of which is loss of memory. War comes . . . as absolute failure of imagination, scientific and political. That a war can be represented as helping a people to "feel good" about themselves, their country, is a measure of that failure.

Adrienne Rich

A violent act pierces the atmosphere, leaving a hole through which the cold, damp draft of its memory blows forever.

Jane Stanton Hitchcock

It is simply not true that war never settles anything.

Felix Frankfurter

There's a consensus out that it's OK to kill when your government decides who to kill. If you kill inside the country, you get in trouble. If you kill outside the country, right time, right season, latest enemy, you get a medal.

Joan Baez

We are the unwilling, led by the unqualified, doing the unnecessary for the ungrateful.

Graffiti, U.S. air base, Vietnam, 1970

Nobody deserves reparation more than the Vietnamese. We savaged them though

they had never hurt us, and we have made no reparation to them, nothing. We are the richest people in the world and they are among the poorest and we cannot find it in our hearts, our honor, to give them help — because the government of Vietnam is communist. And perhaps because they won.

Martha Gellhorn

In America all too few blows are struck into flesh. We kill the spirit here, we are experts at that. We use psychic bullets and kill each other cell by cell.

Norman Mailer

Rambo isn't violent. I see Rambo as a philanthropist.

Sylvester Stallone

The chief nonhuman species that practice war, with organized armies engaging in deadly combat, are certain varieties of ant. Those social insects some 60 million years ago had invented all the major institutions of "civilization," including "kingship" (actually, queenship), military conquest, the division of labor, the segregation of functions and castes, to say nothing of the domestication of other species, and even the beginnings of agriculture. Civilized man's chief contribution to this anthill complex was to add the powerful stimulant of irrational fantasy.

Lewis Mumford

To say that war is madness is like saying that sex is madness: true enough, from the standpoint of a stateless eunuch, but merely a provocative epigram for those who must make their arrangements in the world as given.

John Updike

Wars make for better reading than peace does.

A.J.P. Taylor

Does my behavior in respect of love effect nothing? That is because there is not enough love in me. Am I powerless against untruthfulness and the lies which have their being all around me? The reason is that I myself am not truthful enough.... Is my love of peace misunderstood and scorned? That means that I am not yet sufficiently peace-loving.

Albert Schweitzer

✆

We seem to have a compulsion these days to bury time capsules in order to give those people living in the next century or so some idea of what we are like. I have prepared one of my own. In it, I have placed some rather large samples of dynamite, gunpowder, and nitroglycerin. My time capsule is set to go off in the year 3000. It will show them what we are really like.

Alfred Hitchcock

If a woman gets nervous, she'll eat or go shopping. A man will attack a country — it's a whole other way of thinking.

Elayne Boosler

A real patriot is the fellow who gets a parking ticket and rejoices that the system works.

Bill Vaughan

"Among the Reasons God May Temporarily Be Unavailable to Bless America": . . . (5) because God has had it up to here with the assumption that prayers for national exemption from pain and tragedy deserve an answer; (6) because God is too busy processing Americans' prayers for their high-school football teams; . . . (9) because God takes for granted that the bombs falling on Kabul are America's real prayers; (10) because such a tasteless and lurid efflorescence of red, white, and blue (including flags wrapped around church steeples) gives God a massive headache.

Peter Laarman

The United States is like the guy at the party who gives cocaine to everybody and still nobody likes him.

Jim Samuels

Men grow tired of sleep, love, singing, and dancing sooner than of war.

Homer

People who consider themselves so different from their named enemies should plant a crop and work a field together. During the labor, they would talk about children and find the common ground of parenting. At the harvest, they would hold cooperation in their hands as they offer up with pride a melon or squash.... Has the society of human beings become too complex to realize such simplicity?

Booker Jones

Independence? That's a middle-class blasphemy. We are all dependent on one another, every soul of us on earth.

George Bernard Shaw

Do not wait for leaders; do it alone, person to person.

> Mother Teresa

Time to plant tears, says the almanac.

> Elizabeth Bishop

The presence of the dead person is imaginary, but his absence is very real: henceforth it is his way of appearing.

> Simone Weil

There are years when nothing happens and years in which centuries happen.

> Carlos Fuentes

The practice of terror serves the true believer not only to cow and crush his opponents but also to invigorate and intensify his own faith.

> Eric Hoffer

The first and greatest commandment is, Don't let them scare you.

> Elmer Davis

Those who would give up essential liberty to purchase a little temporary safety deserve neither liberty nor safety.

> Benjamin Franklin

Chief Roman Nose of the Cheyenne, and his people, believed he was immortal, and he, and they, were right every day of his life except one.

> Richard Paul Haight

The great courage is to stare as squarely at the light as at death.

> Albert Camus

Without your wound where would your power be? . . . The very angels themselves cannot persuade the wretched and blundering children on earth as can one human being broken on the wheels of living. In love's service, only the wounded soldiers can serve.

> Thornton Wilder

Whenever I despair, I remember that the way of truth and love has always won. There may be tyrants and murderers, but in the end they always fall. Think of it, always.

> Mohandas K. Gandhi

After the game, the king and pawn go into the same box.

> Italian proverb

Now you know the worst / we humans have to know / about ourselves, and I am sorry.

> Wendell Berry

Even for our enemies in misery, there should be tears in our eyes.

> Charan Singh

You do not see the river of mourning because it lacks one tear of your own.

> Antonio Porchia

☺

The function of the state is twofold and contradictory: it keeps peace and unleashes war. This ambiguity is in us as human beings. Individuals, groups, classes, nations, and governments, all of them, all of us, are doomed to divergence, dispute, dissension; we are also doomed to dialogue and negotiation.

Octavio Paz

There is always a well-known solution to every human problem — neat, plausible, and wrong.

H.L. Mencken

Seek simplicity, and distrust it.

Alfred North Whitehead

If there is a sin against life, it consists perhaps not so much in despairing of life as in hoping for another life and in eluding the implacable grandeur of this life.

Albert Camus

Expecting life to treat you well because you are a good person is like expecting an angry bull not to charge because you are a vegetarian.

Shari R. Barr

No, I'm really a very good man, but I'm a very bad wizard.

L. Frank Baum,
The Wizard of Oz

It was absolutely marvelous working for [physicist Wolfgang] Pauli. You could ask him anything. There was no worry that he would think a particular question was stupid, since he thought all questions were stupid.

Victor Weisskopf

There ain't no answer. There ain't going to be any answer. There never has been an answer. That's the answer.

Gertrude Stein

The universe was a vast machine yesterday; it is a hologram today. Who knows what intellectual rattle we'll be shaking tomorrow.

R.D. Laing

Existence is a strange bargain. Life owes us little; we owe it everything. The only true happiness comes from squandering ourselves for a purpose.

William Cowper

If the only prayer you say in your entire life is "Thank you," that would suffice.

Meister Eckhart

Traveler, there is no path, / Paths are made by walking.

Antonio Machado

The world is before you and you need not take it or leave it as it was when you came in.

James Baldwin

Knowing you are alive is feeling the planet buck under you, rear, kick, and try to throw you; you hang on to the ring. It is riding the planet like a log downstream, whooping. Or, conversely, you step aside from the dreaming fast loud routine and feel time as a stillness about you, and hear the silent air asking in so thin a voice: Have you noticed yet that you will die? Do you remember, remember, remember? Then you feel your life as a weekend, a weekend you cannot extend, a weekend in the country.

Annie Dillard

We must blow on the coals of the heart.

Archibald MacLeish

He found an enormous old umbrella in the trunk. . . . The bright satin material had been eaten away by moths. "Look what's left of our circus clown's umbrella," said the Colonel with one of his old phrases. Above his head, a mysterious system of little metal rods opened. "The only thing it's good for now is to count the stars."

Gabriel García Márquez,
No One Writes to the Colonel

There is nothing stable in the world; uproar's your only music.

John Keats

All the gods are dead except the god of war.

Eldridge Cleaver

After the earthquake and the fire comes the still, small voice.

Dorothy Thompson

For as long as space endures, and for as long as living beings remain, until then may I, too, abide to dispel the misery of the world.

The Dalai Lama

The man who thinks only of his own salvation is as good as a coal drawn out of the fire.

James Jones

Great ideas, it has been said, come into the world as gently as doves. Perhaps then, if we listen attentively, we can hear, amid the uproar of empires and nations, a faint flutter of wings, the gentle stir-ring of life and hope. Some will say that this hope lies in a nation; others, in a person. I believe, rather, that it is awak-ened and nourished by millions of soli-tary individuals whose deeds and works every day negate frontiers and the crud-est implications of history.

Albert Camus

The Indians have never accepted human life as ordinary, as something that can be managed in a controlled or painless manner. They realize that life tests the deepest qualities within the human per-sonality, qualities that emerge in heroic combat not merely with others but also with oneself and with the powers of the universe.

Thomas Berry

There can be no deep disappointment where there is not deep love.

Martin Luther King Jr.

I pray for the strength to accept that lives most often end in tragedy, that quests don't always work, that under-standing is a long and lonely hunt, that I can't reason my way to love, eat gold, or live forever. And that none of this mat-ters. I pray to understand that I am here to find my way back to God, whatever that takes, and all the rest, save love and duty, is an illusion.

John Taylor Gatto

Patience is a hard discipline. It is not just waiting until something happens over which we have no control: the arrival of the bus, the end of the rain, the return of a friend, the resolution of a conflict. Patience is not waiting passively until someone else does something. Patience asks us to live the moment to the fullest, to be completely present to the moment, to taste the here and now, to be where we are. When we are impatient, we try to get away from where we are. We behave as if the real thing will happen tomorrow, later, and somewhere else. Let's be patient and trust that the treasure we look for is hidden in the ground on which we stand.

Henri J.M. Nouwen

Patience — and the mulberry leaf becomes a silk gown.

Chinese proverb

Erv had a gift for optimism. He believed what he wanted to; he could be strong-willed in that way. Ruth said that if Erv tossed a ball in the air three times, tried to hit it three times with a bat, and three times missed, he would, undisturbed, conclude: Wow, what a pitcher.

Steve Fishman

For all your ills I give you laughter.

Rabelais

᠍

Every Blade Of Grass

Every blade of grass has its angel that bends over it and whispers, "Grow, grow."

The Talmud

They can crush all the roses they want to, but they will not be able to postpone the spring.

Octavio Paz

Every blade of grass has its angel that bends over it and whispers, "Grow, grow."

The Talmud

If the landscape reveals one certainty, it is that the extravagant gesture is the very stuff of creation. After the one extravagant gesture of creation in the first place, the universe has continued to deal exclusively in extravagances, flinging intricacies and colossi down aeons of emptiness. . . . The whole show has been on fire from the word go.

Annie Dillard

Nothing is more humbling than to look with a strong magnifying glass at an insect so tiny that the naked eye sees only the barest speck and to discover that nevertheless it is sculpted and articulated and striped with the same care and imagination as a zebra. Apparently it does not occur to nature whether or not a creature is within our range of vision, and the suspicion arises that even the zebra was not designed for our benefit.

Rudolf Arnheim

Now I see the secret of making the best persons. It is to grow in the open air and to eat and sleep with the earth.

Walt Whitman

Take long walks in stormy weather or through deep snow in the fields and woods, if you would keep your spirits up. Deal with brute nature. Be cold and hungry and weary.

Henry David Thoreau

We are nature. We are nature seeing nature. We are nature with a concept of nature. Nature weeping. Nature speaking of nature to nature.

Susan Griffin

I believe in God, only I spell it Nature.

Frank Lloyd Wright

If you study Japanese art, you see a man who is undoubtedly wise, philosophic, and intelligent who spends his time how? In studying the distance between the earth and the moon? No. In studying the policy of Bismarck? No. He studies a single blade of grass. But this blade of grass leads him to draw every plant and then the seasons, the wide aspect of the countryside, then animals, then the human figure. So he passes his life, and life is too short to do the whole.

Vincent van Gogh

The worm in the radish doesn't think there is anything sweeter.

Sholom Aleichem

The world has not to be put in order, the world is order incarnate. It is for us to put ourselves in unison with this order.

Henry Miller

We made the smell of banana in chemistry once, and I nearly cried because it actually smelled like bananas and was so simple and so fake.

Eve Babitz

Like it or not, we are slaves of the hour and its colors and forms, subjects of the sky and the earth. Even that part of us that burrows deepest into itself, disdaining its surroundings, does not burrow along the same paths when it rains as when the sky is clear.

Fernando Pessoa

Hope and fear cannot alter the seasons.

Chögyam Trungpa Rinpoche

Wind moving through grass so that the grass quivers. This moves me with an emotion I don't even understand.

Katherine Mansfield

The losing of Paradise is enacted over and over again by the children of Adam and Eve. We clothe our souls with messages and doctrines and lose the touch of the great life in the naked breast of nature.

Rabindranath Tagore

Except during the nine months before he draws his first breath, no man manages his affairs as well as a tree does.

George Bernard Shaw

Some people want to see God with their eyes as they see a cow, and love him as they love their cow — they love their cow for the milk and cheese and profit it brings them.

Meister Eckhart

It is one of the secrets of nature in its mood of mockery that fine weather lays a heavier weight on the mind and hearts of the depressed and the inwardly tormented than does a really bad day with dark rains sniveling continuously and sympathetically from a dirty sky.

Muriel Spark

The mystical is not how the world is, but that it is.

Ludwig Wittgenstein

To the dull mind all nature is leaden. To the illuminated mind the whole world burns and sparkles with light.

Ralph Waldo Emerson

There are dangers in sentimentalizing nature. Most sentimental ideas imply, at bottom, a deep if unacknowledged disrespect. It is no accident that we Americans, probably the world's champion sentimentalizers about nature, are at one and the same time probably the world's most voracious and disrespectful destroyers of wild and rural countryside.

Jane Jacobs

To put it rather bluntly, I am not the type who wants to go back to the land; I am the type who wants to go back to the hotel.

Fran Lebowitz

Nothing in the nature around us is evil. This needs to be repeated since one of the human ways of talking oneself into inhuman acts is to cite the supposed cruelty of nature.

John Berger

He felt with the force of a revelation that to throw up the clods of earth manfully is as beneficent as to revolutionize the world. It was not the matter of the work, but the mind that went into it that counted — and the man who was not content to do small things well would leave great things undone.

Ellen Glasgow,
The Voice of the People

I go about looking at horses and cattle. They eat grass, make love, work when they have to, bear their young. I am sick with envy of them.

Sherwood Anderson

It's hard for me to get used to these changing times. I can remember when the air was clean and sex was dirty.

George Burns

Nature never said to me: Do not be poor. Still less did she say: Be rich. Her cry to me was always: Be independent.

Sébastien-Roch Nicolas de Chamfort

The sun and the moon and the stars would have disappeared long ago . . . had they happened to be within the reach of predatory human hands.

Havelock Ellis

We cannot cheat on DNA. We cannot get round photosynthesis. We cannot say, I am not going to give a damn about phytoplankton. All these tiny mechanisms provide the preconditions for our planetary life. To say we do not care is to say in the most literal sense that we choose death.

Barbara Ward

It is impossible to care for each other more or differently than we care for the earth. . . . The earth is what we all have in common. It is what we are made of and what we live from, and we cannot damage it without damaging those with whom we share it. But I believe it goes farther than that. There is an uncanny resemblance between our behavior toward each other and our behavior toward the earth. . . . By some connection we do not recognize, the willingness to exploit one becomes the willingness to exploit the other.

Wendell Berry

If the Sun & Moon should Doubt / They'd immediately Go out.

William Blake

The world has signed a pact with the devil; it had to. . . . The terms are clear: if you want to live, you have to die; you cannot have mountains and creeks without space, and space is a beauty married to a blind man. The blind man is Freedom, or Time, and he does not go anywhere without his great dog Death. The world came into being with the signing of the contract.

Annie Dillard

Everything we meet is equally important and unimportant.

Thomas A. Clark

There is nothing useless in nature; not even uselessness itself.

Michel Eyquem de Montaigne

Most things come and go, however good to watch; a few things stay and matter to the end. Rain, for instance.

Reynolds Price

☙

We manipulate nature as if we were stuffing an Alsatian goose. We create new forms of energy; we make new elements; we kill crops; we wash brains. I can hear them in the dark sharpening their lasers.

Erwin Chargaff

I asked him once, "Would you like us to have a dishwashing machine so you wouldn't have to dry dishes?" He said, "Certainly not. It makes a hell of a noise. I like to dry the dishes as you wash them. We always have a good time talking."

Sophia Mumford, on her late husband, Lewis

The mind of the most logical thinker goes so easily from one point to another that it is not hard to mistake motion for progress.

Margaret Collier Graham

I think that human exertion will have no appreciable effect upon humanity. Man is now only more active — not more happy, nor more wise — than he was six thousand years ago.

Edgar Allan Poe

An environmental setting developed over millions of years must be considered to have some merit. Anything so complicated as a planet, inhabited by more than a million and a half species of plants and animals, all of them living together in a more or less balanced equilibrium in which they continually use and reuse the same molecules of the soil and air, cannot be improved by aimless and uninformed tinkering.

E.F. Schumacher

Such gardens are not made / By singing, "Oh, how beautiful!" and sitting in the shade.

Rudyard Kipling

Break with the outside world, live like a bear.

Gustave Flaubert

I believe in the forest, and in the meadow, and in the night in which the corn grows.

Henry David Thoreau

I am against nature. I don't dig nature at all. I think nature is very unnatural. I think the truly natural things are dreams, which nature can't touch with decay.

Bob Dylan

In nature there are neither rewards nor punishments — there are consequences.

R.D. Ingersoll

Why do you go and build a monument to a man who sends electricity through a wire? Does not nature do that millions of times over? Is not everything already existing in nature? What is the value of your getting it? It is already there.

Swami Vivekananda

We have for too long accepted a traditional way of looking at nature, at nature's creatures, which has blinded us to their incredible essence, and which has made us incomparably lonely. It is our loneliness as much as our greed which can destroy us.

Joan McIntyre

There is no shame when one is foolish with a tree No bird ever called me crazy No rock scorns me as a whore The earth means exactly what it says.

Chrystos

Be humble for you are made of dung. Be noble for you are made of stars.

Serbian proverb

The air pushes around you, fills with birds, yellow wings, and eyes.

Stephen Dobyns

When I get sick of what men do, I have only to walk a few steps in another direction to see what spiders do. Or what the weather does. This sustains me very well indeed.

E.B. White

The rain surrounded the whole cabin with . . . a whole world of meaning, of secrecy, of silence, of rumor. Think of it: all that speech pouring down, selling nothing, judging nobody, drenching the thick mulch of dead leaves, soaking the trees, filling the gullies and crannies of the wood with water, washing out the places where men have stripped the hillside. What a thing it is to sit absolutely alone in the forest at night, cherished by this wonderful, unintelligent, perfectly innocent speech, the most comforting speech in the world. . . . Nobody started it, nobody is going to stop it. It will talk as long as it wants, the rain. As long as it talks I am going to listen.

Thomas Merton

There are many fine things about nature, but it does no talking.

Chuang Chou

It gives one a feeling of confidence to see nature still busy with experiments, still dynamic, and not through nor satisfied because a Devonian fish managed to end as a two-legged character with a straw hat. There are other things brewing and growing in the oceanic vat. It pays to know this. It pays to know that there is just as much future as there is past. The only thing that doesn't pay is to be sure of man's own part in it. There are things down there still coming ashore.

Loren Eiseley

Great art picks up where nature ends.

Marc Chagall

[Frank Lloyd Wright] and I walked up to the high ground [to a potential building site for a new home] where there was an old orchard above a pasture which faces north and has an endless view over the hills. He took one look and then peed and said, "Good spot"; and we walked down the hill back to the house.

Arthur Miller

☉

If you're going to care about the fall of the sparrow, you can't pick and choose who's going to be the sparrow. It's everybody.

Madeleine L'Engle

If God didn't want man to hunt, he wouldn't have given us plaid shirts.

Johnny Carson

I tend to be suspicious of people whose love of animals is exaggerated; they are often frustrated in their relationships with humans.

Camilla Koffler

To me nature is . . . spiders and bugs, and . . . big fish eating little fish, and . . . plants eating plants, and animals eating animals. It's like an enormous restaurant, that's the way I see it.

Woody Allen

Mankind's true moral test, its fundamental test (which lies deeply buried from view), consists of its attitude toward those who are at its mercy: animals. And in this respect mankind has suffered a fundamental debacle, a debacle so fundamental that all others stem from it.

Milan Kundera

A Robin Red breast in a Cage / Puts all Heaven in a Rage.

William Blake

The country before us was now thronged with buffalo. . . . They were crowded so densely together that in the distance their rounded backs presented a surface of uniform blackness.

Frances Parkman, on the American West in 1847

Last night we had a bouillabaisse which I couldn't touch because of the terror of its preparation. The secret is to throw live sea creatures into a boiling pot. And we saw a lobster who, while turning red in his death, reached out a claw to snatch and gobble a dying crab. Thus, in this hot stew of the near-dead and burning, one expiring fish swallows another expiring fish while the cook sprinkles saffron onto the squirming.

Ned Rorem

A peasant becomes fond of his pig and is glad to salt away its pork. What is significant, and is so difficult for the urban stranger to understand, is that the two statements are connected by an and, and not by a but.

John Berger

The animal shall not be measured by man. In a world older and more complete than ours, they move finished and complete, gifted with extensions of the senses we have lost or never attained, living by voices we shall never hear. They are not brethren, they are not underlings; they are other nations, caught with ourselves in the net of life, fellow prisoners of the splendor and travail of the earth.

Henry Beston

A duck's legs, though short, cannot be lengthened without pain to the duck; a crane's legs, though long, cannot be shortened without misery to the crane.

Chuang Tzu

Ants are as much like human beings as to be an embarrassment. They farm fungi, raise aphids as livestock, launch armies into war, use chemical sprays to alarm and confuse enemies, capture slaves, . . . engage in child labor, . . . exchange information ceaselessly. They do everything but watch television.

Lewis Thomas

Abu Yazid made his periodic journey to purchase supplies at the bazaar in the city of Hamadan — a distance of several hundred miles. When he returned home, he discovered a colony of ants in the cardamom seeds. He carefully packed the seeds up again and walked back across the desert to the merchant from whom he had bought them. His intent was not to exchange the seeds but to return the ants to their home.

Sufi legend retold by James P. Carse

Love is the extremely difficult realization that something other than oneself is real.

Iris Murdoch

I have sometimes thought of the final cause of dogs having such short lives and I am quite satisfied it is in compassion to the human race; for if we suffer so much in losing a dog after an acquaintance of ten or twelve years, what would it be if they were to live double that time?

Sir Walter Scott

In order to really enjoy a dog, one doesn't merely try to train him to be semihuman. The point of it is to open oneself to the possibility of becoming partly a dog.

Edward Hoagland

To be sure, the dog is loyal. But why, on that account, should we take him as an example? He is loyal to men, not to other dogs.

Karl Kraus

Cats are smarter than dogs. You can't get eight cats to pull a sled through snow.

Jeff Valdez

Be a good animal, true to your animal instincts.

D.H. Lawrence

When an animal has nothing to do, it goes to sleep. When a man has nothing to do, he may ask questions.

Bernard J.F. Lonergan

When the visitor arrived he found the holy man in prayer. He sat so still that not even a hair on his head moved. When the holy man had finished his prayer, the visitor asked where he had learned such stillness. He replied, "From my cat. She was watching a mouse hole with even greater concentration than you have seen in me." The holy man's cat was seeking something with all her heart and soul. If we are making little headway on our spiritual quest, perhaps we should ask ourselves if we are seeking our goal with the same passion that a cat seeks a mouse.

Edward Hays

☺

My mother thought it would make us feel better to know animals had no souls, and thus their deaths were not to be taken so seriously. But it didn't help, and when I think of some of the animals I have known, I wonder. The only really "soulful" eyes in the world belong to the dog or cat who sits on your lap or at your feet, commiserating when you cry.

Liz Smith

Animals give us their constant, unjaded faces, and we burden them with our bodies and civilized ordeals.

Gretel Ehrlich

It was quite incomprehensible to me . . . why in my evening prayers I should pray for human beings only. So when my mother had prayed with me and had kissed me goodnight, I used to add silently a prayer that I had composed myself for all living creatures. It ran thus: "O Heavenly Father, protect and bless all things that have breath; guard them from all evil, and let them sleep in peace."

Albert Schweitzer

I once heard it said — and the saying has haunted me ever since — that if animals believed in the Devil, he would look remarkably like a human being.

Lord Bishop of Manchester

The lower animals are our brethren. I include among them the lion and the tiger. We do not know how to live with these carnivorous beasts and poisonous reptiles because of our ignorance. When man learns better, he will learn to befriend even these. Today he does not even know how to befriend a man of a different religion or from a different country.

Mohandas K. Gandhi

In nothing does man, with his grand notions of heaven and charity, show forth his innate, wild animalism more clearly than in his treatment of his brother beasts. From the shepherd with his lambs to the red-handed hunter, it is the same: no recognition of rights — only murder in one form or another.

John Muir

It can truly be said: Men are the devils of the earth, and the animals are the tormented souls.

Arthur Schopenhauer

I ask people why they have deer heads on their walls, and they say, "Because it's such a beautiful animal." There you go. Well, I think my mother's attractive, but I have photographs of her.

Ellen DeGeneres

We call them dumb animals, and so they are, for they cannot tell us how they feel, but they do not suffer less because they have no words.

Anna Sewell

Many things that human words have upset are set at rest again by the silence of animals. Animals move through the world like a caravan of silence. A whole world, that of nature and that of animals, is filled with silence. Nature and animals seem like protuberances of silence. The silence of animals and the silence of nature would not be so great and noble if it were merely a failure of language to materialize. Silence has been entrusted to the animals and to nature as something created for its own sake.

Max Picard

The charm which Henry [Thoreau] uses for bird and frog and mink is patience. They will not come to him, or show him aught, until he becomes a log among logs, sitting still for hours in the same place; then they come around him and to him, and show themselves at home.

Ralph Waldo Emerson

The sense of smell in the animal is what intuition is to the human spirit. It tells you of the invisible, of what cannot be detected by any other means. It tells you the things that are not there, yet are coming. You see into the blind, opaque past and round the corner of time.

Laurens van der Post

Some animals, like some men, leave a trail of glory behind them. They give their spirit to the place where they have lived, and remain forever a part of the rocks and streams and the wind and sky.

Marguerite Henry

The basis of all animal rights should be the Golden Rule: we should treat them as we would wish them to treat us, were any other species in our dominant position.

Christine Stevens

A prisoner lived in solitary confinement for ten years. He saw and spoke to no one, and his meals were served through an opening in the wall. One day, an ant came into his cell. The man contemplated it in fascination as it crawled around the room. He held it in the palm of his hand the better to observe it, gave it a grain or two. . . . It suddenly struck him that it had taken him ten long years of solitary confinement to open his eyes to the loveliness of an ant.

Anthony de Mello

And They Were Both Naked, The Man And His Wife

And they were both naked, the man and his wife, and they were not ashamed.

Genesis 2:25

We have so many words for states of mind, and so few words for the states of the body.

Jeanne Moreau

Our body is precious. It is a vehicle for awakening. Treat it with care.

The Buddha

We have attempted to separate the spiritual and the erotic, thereby reducing the spiritual to a world of flattened affect, a world of the ascetic who aspires to feel nothing.

Audre Lorde

The sick do not ask if the hand that smooths their pillow is pure, nor the dying care if the lips that touch their brow have known the kiss of sin.

Oscar Wilde

Fear has a smell, as love does.

Margaret Atwood

Passionate love is not peculiar to the human species, for it penetrates through all existing things — celestial, elemental, vegetable, and mineral.

Avicenna

The great majority of us are required to live a life of constant, systematic duplicity. Your health is bound to be affected if, day after day, you say the opposite of what you feel, if you grovel before what you dislike and rejoice at what brings you nothing but misfortune. Our nervous system isn't just a fiction, it's a part of our physical body, and our soul exists in space inside us, like the teeth in our mouth. It can't be forever violated with impunity.

Boris Pasternak

If anything is sacred, the human body is sacred.

Walt Whitman

When he urinated, it sounded like night prayer.

F. Scott Fitzgerald

It is so much more difficult to live with one's body than with one's soul. One's body is so much more exacting: what it won't have, it won't have, and nothing can make bitter into sweet.

D.H. Lawrence

I honor shit for saying: We go on.

Maxine Kumin

The body has its own way of knowing, a knowing that has little to do with logic, and much to do with truth; little to do with control, and much to do with acceptance; little to do with division and analysis, and much to do with union.

Marilyn Sewell

I had to face the facts; I was pear-shaped. I was a bit depressed because I hate pears. Specially their shape.

Charlotte Bingham

Everything on earth [is] beautiful, everything, except what we ourselves think and do when we forget the higher purposes of life and our own human dignity.

Anton Chekhov

It is my opinion that humans are largely what they make of themselves; in other words, "human nature" is not so much an empirical reality as a process of self-construction. This means that if people become what they think they are, what they think they are is exceedingly important.

Linda Marie Fedigan

We saw men haying far off in the meadow, their heads waving like the grass which they cut. In the distance, the wind seemed to bend all alike.

Henry David Thoreau

How idiotic civilization is! Why be given a body if you have to keep it shut up in a case like a rare, rare fiddle?

Katherine Mansfield

The human body is not a thing or substance, given, but a continuous creation. The human body is an energy system . . . which is never a complete structure; never static; is in perpetual inner self-construction and self-destruction; we destroy in order to make it new.

Norman O. Brown

To strengthen the mind you must harden the muscles.

Michel Eyquem de Montaigne

There are so many things that can provide us with peace. Next time you take a shower or a bath, I suggest you hold your big toes in mindfulness. . . . When we hold our toes in mindfulness . . . we will find that our bodies have been very kind to us. We know that any cell in our toes can turn cancerous, but our toes have been behaving very well, avoiding that kind of problem. Yet we have not been nice to them at all. These kinds of practices can bring us happiness.

Thich Nhat Hanh

Happiness is always a byproduct. It is probably a matter of temperament, and for anything I know it may be glandular. But it is not something that can be demanded from life, and if you are not happy, you had better stop worrying about it and see what treasures you can pluck from your own brand of unhappiness.

Robertson Davies

☉

I will praise thee, for I am fearfully and wonderfully made.

Psalms 139:14

The strongest, surest way to the soul is through the flesh.

Mabel Dodge

God bless the roots! Body and soul are one.

Theodore Roethke

Many things about our bodies would not seem to us so filthy and obscene if we did not have the idea of nobility in our heads.

G.C. Lichtenberg

Teeth. What goddamn things they were. We had to eat. And eat and eat again. We are all disgusting, doomed to our dirty little tasks. Eating and farting and scratching and smiling and celebrating holidays.

Charles Bukowski, *Pulp*

Never, never eat anything out of a carton, even if you are at home alone with the shades drawn. Doing so is wicked and constitutes Miss Manners' one exception to the generally genial rule about violations of etiquette not counting if you don't get caught.

Judith Martin, aka Miss Manners

Our own physical body possesses a wisdom which we who inhabit the body lack. We give it orders which make no sense.

Henry Miller

Greed, like the love of comfort, is a kind of fear.

Cyril Connolly

The body is the soul. We ignore its aches, its pains, its eruptions, because we fear the truth. The body is God's messenger.

Erica Jong

Every man is the builder of a temple, called his body, to the god he worships, after a style purely his own, nor can he get off by hammering marble instead. We are all sculptors and painters, and our material is our own flesh and blood and bones.

Henry David Thoreau

Why do people / lavish decoration / on this set of bones / destined to disappear / without a trace?

Ikkyu

I just can't stand to look plain, 'cause that don't fit my personality. I may be a very artificial-looking person, but the good news is, I'm very real on the inside.

Dolly Parton

Beauty is one of the rare things that do not lead to doubt of God.

Jean Anouilh

It has been said that a pretty face is a passport. But it's not; it's a visa, and it runs out fast.

Julie Burchill

All God's children are not beautiful. Most of God's children are, in fact, barely presentable.

Fran Lebowitz

Nothing ruins a face so fast as double-dealing. Your face telling one story to the world. Your heart yanking your face to pieces, trying to let the truth be known.

Jessamyn West

Was she so loved because her eyes were so beautiful, or were her eyes so beautiful because she was so loved?

Anzia Yezierska

Beauty is unbearable, drives us to despair, offering us for a minute the glimpse of an eternity that we should like to stretch out over the whole of time.

Albert Camus

I can tell you only that beauty cannot be expressed or explained in a theory or an idea, that it moves by its own law, that it is God's way of comforting His broken children.

Mark Helprin

Beauty is indeed a good gift of God; but that the good may not think it is a great good, God dispenses it even to the wicked.

Saint Augustine

A man finds room in the few square inches of the face for the traits of all his ancestors; for the expression of all his history, and his wants.

Ralph Waldo Emerson

A face that has the marks of having lived intensely, that expresses some phase of life, some dominant quality or intellectual power, constitutes for me an interesting face. For this reason, the face of an older person, perhaps not beautiful in the strictest sense, is usually more appealing than the face of a younger person who has scarcely been touched by life.

Doris Ulmann

To seek after beauty as an end is a wild goose chase, a will-o'-the-wisp, because it is to misunderstand the very nature of beauty, which is the normal condition of a thing being as it should be.

Ade Bethune

I'm tired of all this nonsense about beauty being only skin-deep. That's deep enough. What do you want — an adorable pancreas?

Jean Kerr

Cure yourself of the affliction of caring how you appear to others. Concern yourself only with how you appear before God, concern yourself only with the idea God may have of you.

Miguel de Unamuno

Beauty is an ecstasy; it is as simple as hunger. There is really nothing to be said about it. It is like the perfume of a rose: you can smell it and that is all.

W. Somerset Maugham

A woman watches her body uneasily, as though it were an unreliable ally in the battle for love.

Leonard Cohen

It is because we don't know who we are, because we are unaware that the kingdom of heaven is within us, that we behave in the generally silly, the often insane, the sometimes criminal ways that are so characteristically human.

Aldous Huxley

Oh that this too too solid flesh would melt, thaw, and resolve itself into a dew.

William Shakespeare

Beauty is life when life unveils her holy face.

Khalil Gibran

A beautiful woman who is pleasing to men is good only for frightening fish when she falls into the water.

Zen proverb

And they were both naked, the man and his wife, and they were not ashamed.

Genesis 2:25

It would be nice to live in a society where the genitals were really considered beautiful. It seems to me any other way of seeing is obscene. After all, there they are. Why not like them?

Carol Emshwiller

The power pervades the universe. It whirls the galaxies on their paths, it blossoms as the rose, it shines in beauty when man meets woman.

Rick Strauss

The soul, like the body, lives by what it feeds on.

Josiah Gilbert Holland

Along came Paul, impotent old fussbudget. He could eat like a horse, but for some reason he either couldn't or wouldn't function sexually, or took no pleasure in it if he did. So sex became a sin.

Jack Woodford

In the sweaty, passionate, filthy embrace, in all of its delicious and time-dissolving power, in the midst of that embrace there is no difference, no separation between the spiritual and the profane. But it's reached through the profane rather than through the spiritual, at least in my canon. That is the portal, that is the door into the whole affair. In that moment there is no separation, there is no spirit and flesh, there's no conflict, there never was.

Leonard Cohen

Where does one person end and another person begin?

Iris Murdoch

Love and life cannot help but marry and stay married with an exhausting violence of fidelity.

Kate O'Brien

We live in an atmosphere of shame. We are ashamed of everything that is real about us; ashamed of ourselves, of our relatives, of our incomes, of our accents, of our opinions, of our experience, just as we are ashamed of our naked skins.

George Bernard Shaw

There's always the hyena of morality at the garden gate, and the real wolf at the end of the street.

D.H. Lawrence

You can't do anything with anybody's body to make it dirty to me. Six people, eight people, one person — you can only do one thing to make it dirty: kill it. Hiroshima was dirty.

Lenny Bruce

Nature is an endless combination and repetition of a very few laws. She hums the old well-known air through innumerable variations.

Ralph Waldo Emerson

Nudists are fond of saying that when you come right down to it, everyone is alike, and, again, that when you come right down to it, everyone is different.

Diane Arbus

Your body is the ground metaphor of your life, the expression of your existence. It is your Bible, your encyclopedia, your life story. Everything that happens to you is stored and reflected in your body. Your body knows; your body tells. The relationship of your self to your body is indivisible, inescapable, unavoidable. In the marriage of flesh and spirit, divorce is impossible, but that doesn't mean that the marriage is necessarily happy or successful.

Gabrielle Roth

I am a little world.

John Donne

Measure your health by your sympathy with morning and spring. If there is no response in you to the awakening of nature — if the prospect of an early morning walk does not banish sleep, if the warble of the first bluebird does not thrill you — know that the morning and spring of your life are past. Thus may you feel your pulse.

Henry David Thoreau

There are those who so dislike the nude that they find something indecent in the naked truth.

F.H. Bradley

Body and spirit are twins: God only knows which is which.

Algernon Charles Swinburne

☺

Others, like me, are just learning how, just beginning to sample the powerful religion of ordinary life, of freshly mopped floors and stacked dishes and clothes blowing on the line.

Adair Lara

Cooking is like love. It should be entered into with abandon or not at all.

Harriet Van Horne

What I love about cooking is that after a hard day, there is something comforting about the fact that if you melt butter and add flour and then hot stock, it will get thick!

Nora Ephron

There is a famous document of Christian mysticism called *Practicing the Presence*, in which a monk would experience his union with the Christ in doing very simple things — baking bread, washing dishes, cleaning the floor, and so on. In New Age circles this sometimes gets misinterpreted. The assumption is that the act itself is the practicing of the presence, as in "My practice is baking bread." This can be a good thing to do in a skillful way, but what makes something a practice is not just the ordinary doing of it. It is the sense that in this moment we are giving ourselves, in love, to the universe through this action. . . . If I am washing this dish, I wash it with the sense that I am caressing the consciousness of a multitude of beings, that I am touching my beloved.

David Spangler

Simplicity of living means meeting life face to face. It means confronting life clearly, without unnecessary distractions, without trying to soften the awesomeness of our existence or mask the deeper magnificence of life with pretentious, distracting, and unnecessary accumulations.

Duane Elgin

There is more simplicity in the man who eats caviar on impulse than in the man who eats Grape-Nuts on principle.

G.K. Chesterton

The act of putting into your mouth what the earth has grown is perhaps your most direct interaction with the earth.

Frances Moore Lappé

Edible: Good to eat and wholesome to digest, as a worm to a toad, a toad to a snake, a snake to a pig, a pig to a man, and a man to a worm.

Ambrose Bierce

Americans can eat garbage, provided you sprinkle it liberally with ketchup, mustard, chili sauce, Tabasco sauce, cayenne pepper, or any other condiment which destroys the original flavor of the dish.

Henry Miller

If sometimes our poor people have had to die of starvation, it is not that God didn't care for them, but because you and I didn't give, were not an instrument in the hands of God, to give them that bread, to give them that clothing; because we did not recognize him, when once more Christ came in distressing disguise, in the hungry man, in the lonely man, in the homeless child, and seeking for shelter.

Mother Teresa

I eat to live, to serve, and also, it happens, to enjoy, but I do not eat for the sake of enjoyment.

Mohandas K. Gandhi

Let the number of guests not exceed twelve . . . so chosen that their occupations are varied, their tastes similar, . . . the dining room brilliantly lighted, the cloth pure white, the temperature between 60 and 68, the men witty and not pedantic, the women amiable and not too coquettish; the dishes exquisite but few, the wines vintage; . . . the coffee hot; . . . the drawing room large enough to give those who must have it a game of cards while leaving plenty of room for after-dinner talk; . . . the tea not too strong, the toast artistically buttered; . . . the signal to leave not before eleven; and everyone in bed at midnight.

Anthelme Brillat-Savarin

What is patriotism but the love of the good things we ate in our childhood?

Lin Yutang

All recipes are built on the belief that somewhere at the beginning of the chain there is a cook who did not use them. This is the great nostalgia of our cuisine, ever invoking an absent mother-cook who once laid her hands on the body of the world for us and worked it into food. The promise of every cookbook is that it offers a way back onto her lap.

John Thorne

There is no love sincerer than the love of food.

George Bernard Shaw

I don't mind that I'm fat. You still get the same money.

Marlon Brando

⟡

I can reason down or deny everything, except this perpetual Belly; feed he must and will, and I cannot make him respectable.

Ralph Waldo Emerson

The belly is the reason why man does not so easily take himself for a god.

Friedrich Nietzsche

There are many ways of eating, for some eating is living, for some eating is dying, for some thinking about ways of eating gives to them the feeling that they have it in them to be alive and to be going on living, to some to think about eating makes them know that death is always waiting that dying is in them.

Gertrude Stein

Society is composed of two great classes — those who have more dinners than appetite, and those who have more appetite than dinners.

Sébastien-Roch Nicolas de Chamfort

A hungry man is not a free man.

Adlai Stevenson

Upscale people are fixated with food simply because they are now able to eat so much of it without getting fat, and the reason they don't get fat is that they maintain a profligate level of calorie expenditure. The very same people whose evenings begin with melted goat cheese . . . get up at dawn to run, break for a midmorning aerobics class, and watch the evening news while racing on a stationary bicycle.

Barbara Ehrenreich

One can be conscious of the body with head consciousness, and this is true of so many people who engage in physical culture. . . . The body is seen then as the instrument of the ego.

Alexander Lowen

Nobody, but nobody, is as fat as she thinks she is.

Cynthia Heimel

A few of his disciples had decided to do a "grape cure" and eat nothing but grapes and grape juice for a while. Paramahansa Yogananda smiled when he heard about this and remarked, "Devotion is the greatest purifier." His disciple Donald Walters asked, "Is it your wish then, Sir, that we break this fast?" "Well, I don't want you to break your wills," said Yogananda, "now that you have set them in this way. But your time would be better spent if you worked on developing devotion. A pure heart is the way to God, not a pure stomach."

William Ashoka Ross

There is a type of person in whose mind God is always getting mixed up with vitamins.

Manly P. Hall

Clearly, some time ago makers and consumers of American junk food passed jointly through some kind of sensibility barrier in the endless quest for new taste sensations. Now they are a little like those desperate junkies who have tried every known drug and are finally reduced to mainlining bathroom-bowl cleanser in an effort to get still higher.

Bill Bryson

Bread that must be sliced with an ax is bread that is too nourishing.

Fran Lebowitz

My mother made me eat broccoli. I hate broccoli. I am the president of the United States. I will not eat any more broccoli.

George H.W. Bush

My grandmother would sometimes choke on her food, and have to go out on the side porch in Shillington, where one or another member of the family would follow and hammer on her back while she clung, gagging, to the porch rail. . . . I also would choke now and then. My album of sore moments includes a memory of crouching above my tray in the Lowell House dining hall at Harvard, miserably retching at something in my throat that would not go up or down, while half-swallowed milk dribbled from my mouth and the other students at the table silently took up their trays and moved away. On the edge of asphyxia, I sympathized with them and wished that I, too, could shun me.

John Updike

We never repent having eaten too little.

Thomas Jefferson

The trouble with eating Italian food is that five or six days later you're hungry again.

George Miller

That's something I've noticed about food: whenever there's a crisis, if you can get people to eating normally, things get better.

Madeleine L'Engle

Then the cook enters and approaches our table. He bows low before me. He is grateful to me, he explains, because since his years as a cook in a Buddhist monastery, he has had little opportunity to cook vegetarian food for anyone who appreciates it. The wild mushrooms, he tells me, were picked in a nearby forest. The greens are from gardens known for the quality of their vegetables. He bows slowly, and thanks me once again. I stumble over my own words of gratitude as he quietly disappears into the kitchen. I never see him again. I didn't sleep that night. The cook's reverence and humility sliced through years of protective hardness and caught me without warning. His food was saturated with love, and its nurturance was almost too much to bear.

Anne Scott

This was the dawn of plastic eating in America. . . . We doted on Velveeta. Spam. Canned ravioli. Instant puddings. Instant anything. The farther a thing was from the texture, flavor, and terrifying unpredictability of real food, the better.

Shirley Abbott

Fake food — I mean those patented substances chemically flavored and mechanically bulked out to kill the appetite and deceive the gut — is unnatural, almost immoral, a bane to good eating and good cooking.

Julia Child

For the first time in the history of the world, every human being is now subjected to contact with dangerous chemicals, from the moment of conception until death.

Rachel Carson

I'm not a vegetarian because I love animals. I'm a vegetarian because I hate plants.

A. Whitney Brown

I want nothing to do with natural foods. At my age I need all the preservatives I can get.

George Burns

We may find in the long run that tinned food is a deadlier weapon than the machine gun.

George Orwell

We do not understand the earth in terms either of what it offers us or of what it requires of us, and I think it is the rule that people inevitably destroy what they do not understand. . . . Our model citizen is a sophisticate who before puberty understands how to produce a baby, but at the age of thirty will not know how to produce a potato.

Wendell Berry

One of the joys our technological civilization has lost is the excitement with which seasonal flowers and fruits were welcomed; the first daffodil, strawberry, or cherry are now things of the past, along with their precious moment of arrival. Even the tangerine — now a satsuma or clementine — appears de-pipped months before Christmas.

Derek Jarman

Once, perhaps, the God-intoxicated few could abscond to the wild frontiers, the forests, the desert places to keep alive the perennial wisdom that they harbored. But no longer. They must now become a political force or their tradition perishes. Soon enough, there will be no solitude left for the saints to roam but its air will shudder with a noise of great engines that drowns out all prayers.

Theodore Roszak

Humans — despite their artistic pretensions, their sophistication, and their many accomplishments — owe their existence to a six-inch layer of topsoil and the fact that it rains.

Source unknown

It seems to me that our three basic needs for food and security and love are so mixed and mingled and entwined that we cannot straightly think of one without the others.

M.F.K. Fisher

There's little risk in becoming overly proud of one's garden, because gardening by its very nature is humbling. It has a way of keeping you on your knees.

JoAnn R. Barwick

To own a bit of ground, to scratch it with a hoe, to plant seeds and watch their renewal of life — this is the commonest delight of the race, the most satisfactory thing a man can do.

Charles Dudley Warner

Gardening is not a rational act. What matters is the immersion of the hands in the earth, that ancient ceremony of which the Pope kissing the tarmac is merely a pallid vestigial remnant. In the spring, at the end of the day, you should smell like dirt.

Margaret Atwood

Whoever could make two ears of corn, or two blades of grass to grow upon a spot of ground where only one grew before, would deserve better of mankind, and do more essential service to his country, than the whole race of politicians put together.

Jonathan Swift

Have you become a farmer? Is it not pleasanter than to be shut up within four walls and delving eternally with the pen?

Thomas Jefferson

When one tugs at a single thing in nature, he finds it attached to the rest of the world.

John Muir

Lyda was an exuberant, even a dramatic gardener. . . . She was always holding up a lettuce or a bunch of radishes with an air of resolute courage, as though she had shot them herself.

Renata Adler, *Speedboat*

Sex is good, but not as good as fresh sweet corn.

Garrison Keillor

The miraculous is not extraordinary but the common mode of existence. It is our daily bread. Whoever really has considered the lilies of the field or the birds of the air and pondered the improbability of their existence in this warm world within the cold and empty stellar distances will hardly balk at the turning of water into wine — which was, after all, a very small miracle. We forget the greater and still continuing miracle by which water (with soil and sunlight) is turned into grapes.

Wendell Berry

The grandeur of nature is only the beginning. Beyond the grandeur is God.

Abraham Joshua Heschel

Go into the kitchen to shake the chef's hand. If he is thin, have second thoughts about eating there; if he is thin and sad, flee.

Ferand Point

The first thing I did when I made the decision to kill myself was to stop dieting. Let them dig a wider hole.

Gail Parent

To lengthen thy life, lessen thy meals.

Benjamin Franklin

We arrive eager, we stuff ourselves and go away depressed and disappointed and probably feeling a bit queasy into the bargain. . . . A greedy start and a stupefied finish. Waiters, who are constantly observing this cycle, must be the most disillusioned of men.

Iris Murdoch

Life itself is the proper binge.

Julia Child

As we talked of freedom and justice one day for all, we sat down to steaks. I am eating misery, I thought, as I took the first bite. And spit it out.

Alice Walker

We often mistake a desire of the body for a yearning of the soul.

Harry Austryn Wolfson

Such is life. It is no cleaner than a kitchen; it reeks of a kitchen; and if you mean to cook your dinner, you must expect to soil your hands. The real art is getting them clean again.

Honoré de Balzac

The best foods are the products of infinite and wearying trouble. The trouble need not be taken by the consumer, but someone, ever since the Fall, has had to take it.

Rose Macaulay

If we mammals don't get something to eat every day or two, our temperature drops, all our signs fall off, and we begin to starve. Living at biological red alert, it's not surprising how obsessed we are with food.

Diane Ackerman

Cheese that is required by law to append the word food to its title does not go well with red wine or fruit.

Fran Lebowitz

What a piece of bread looks like / depends on whether you are hungry or not.

Rumi

This is the heart of whole-body eating. Be there when you eat. . . . Taste it. Savor it. . . . Rejoice in it. See how it makes your body feel. Take in all the sensations. But don't just eat the food. Eat the ambiance. Eat the colors. Eat the aromas. Eat the conversation. Eat the company sitting next to you. Eat the entire experience. . . . We don't just hunger for food alone.

Marc David

Those boys could hear a meat bone being dropped into soup half a mile away. If a man brushed a crumb from his beard, there was their knock on his door.

Joanne Greenberg,
Rites of Passage

Even crumbs are bread.

Danish proverb

Contemplating that suffering which is unbearable to us, and is unbearable to others, too, can produce bodhi [awake] mind, which arises from the compassion that wishes to free all living beings from suffering.

The Dalai Lama

☺

The toughest part of being on a diet is shutting up about it.

Gerald Nachman

As she is a woman, and as she is an American, she was dieting.

Katharine Whitehorn

Food is the most primitive form of comfort.

Sheilah Graham

All food starting with p is comfort food, I thought: pasta, potato chips, pretzels, peanut butter, pastrami, pizza, pastry.

Sara Paretsky, *Killing Orders*

There is such a thing as food and such a thing as poison. But the damage done by those who pass off poison as food is far less than that done by those who generation after generation convince people that food is poison.

Paul Goodman

If a fly gets into the throat of one who is fasting, it is not necessary to pull it out.

Ayatollah Khomeini

If one doesn't have a character like Abraham Lincoln or Joan of Arc, a diet simply disintegrates into eating exactly what you want to eat, but with a bad conscience.

Maria Augusta Trapp

Eating is never so simple as hunger.

Erica Jong

Addiction, obesity, and starvation (anorexia nervosa) are political problems, not psychiatric: each condenses and expresses a contest between the individual and some other person or persons . . . over the control of the individual's body.

Thomas Szasz

You can never get enough of what you don't really want.

Eric Hoffer

Women should try to increase their size rather than decrease it, because I believe the bigger we are, the more space we'll take up, and the more we'll have to be reckoned with. I think every woman should be fat like me.

Roseanne Barr

Jack Sprat could eat no fat, / His wife could eat no lean. / A real sweet pair of neurotics.

Jack Sharkey

A monk asked Chao-chou, "I have just entered the monastery: please give me some guidance." Chao-chou said, "Have you eaten your rice gruel?" The monk said, "Yes, I've eaten." Chao-chou said, "Then go wash your bowl."

Zen story

Man does not live by bread alone, but he also does not live long without it.

Frederick Buechner

No man was ever more than about nine meals away from crime or suicide.

Eric Sevareid

A man with money to pay for a meal can talk about hunger without demeaning himself. . . . But for a man with no money hunger is a disgrace.

Vicki Baum

In the last twenty-four hours about forty thousand children, most of them under five, have died in the world. More than 80 percent of those deaths are from preventable diseases like tetanus, measles, whooping cough, acute respiratory infection, and diarrhea. Such deaths are often associated with malnutrition.

New Internationalist

Food for all is a necessity. Food should not be a merchandise, to be bought and sold as jewels are bought and sold by those who have the money to buy. Food is a human necessity, like water and air, and it should be available.

Pearl S. Buck

In the Fiji islands, it appears, cannibalism is now familiar. They eat their own wives and children. We only devour widows' houses, and great merchants outwit and absorb the substance of small ones, and every man feeds on his neighbor's labor if he can. It is a milder form of cannibalism.

Ralph Waldo Emerson

Crime is a logical extension of the sort of behavior that is often perfectly respectable in legitimate business.

Robert Rice

There is a crime here that goes beyond denunciation. There is a sorrow here that weeping cannot symbolize. There is a failure here that topples all our successes. The fertile earth, the straight tree rows, the sturdy trunks, and the ripe fruit. And children dying of pellagra must die because a profit cannot be taken from an orange. And coroners must fill in the certificate — died of malnutrition — because the food must rot, must be forced to rot. . . . In the eyes of the people there is the failure, and in the eyes of the hungry there is a growing wrath. In the souls of the people the grapes of wrath are filling and growing heavy, growing heavy for the vintage.

John Steinbeck,
The Grapes of Wrath

☙

Tolstoy's illness dried him up, burnt something out of him. Inwardly he seemed to become lighter, more transparent, more resigned. His eyes are still keen, his glance piercing. He listens attentively, as though recalling something which he has forgotten, or as though waiting for something new and unknown.

Maxim Gorky

Some people think that doctors and nurses can put scrambled eggs back into the shell.

Dorothy Canfield Fisher

The great secret, known to internists . . . is that most things get better by themselves; most things, in fact, are better in the morning.

Lewis Thomas

There is this noteworthy difference between savage and civilized: that while a sick, civilized man may be six months convalescing, generally speaking, a sick savage is almost half well again in a day.

Herman Melville

The term clinical depression finds its way into too many conversations these days. One has a sense that a catastrophe has occurred in the psychic landscape.

Leonard Cohen

There is a healthy way to be ill.

George Sheehan

Illness is the night-side of life, a more onerous citizenship. Everyone who is born holds dual citizenship, in the kingdom of the well and in the kingdom of the sick.

Susan Sontag

Why is there evil in the world? That is the supreme question of all religions and philosophies, and . . . the question "Why is there sickness?" is just another form of it. . . . Sickness and health are not simply physical states that the methods of science will eventually analyze completely and make understandable. They are rooted in the deepest and most mysterious strata of Being.

Andrew Weil

Life's sharpest rapture is surcease of pain.

Emma Lazarus

Who would imagine that someone could recover from a terminal case of cancer by receiving massive doses of radiation, or drugs first developed for chemical warfare, much less by watching funny movies? I have begun to suspect that . . . anything and everything can kill and heal, whether it is digitalis in heart medicine, a lover's touch, or God's grace.

Kat Duff

We have had for three weeks past a warm visit from the sun (my almighty physician), and I find myself almost reestablished.

Thomas Jefferson

Red meat and gin.

Julia Child, when asked, at eighty-four, to what she credited her longevity

The Church says: The body is a sin. Science says: The body is a machine. Advertising says: The body is a business. The body says: I am a fiesta.

Eduardo Galeano

The body repeats the landscape. They are the source of each other and create each other.

Meridel Le Sueur

When I go into my garden with a spade, and dig a bed, I feel such an exhilaration and health that I discover that I have been defrauding myself all this time in letting others do for me what I should have done with my own hands.

Ralph Waldo Emerson

Nothing in all nature is so lovely and so vigorous, so perfectly at home in its environment, as a fish in the sea. Its surroundings give to it a beauty, quality, and power which are not its own. We take it out, and at once a poor, limp, dull thing, fit for nothing, is gasping away its life. So the soul, sunk in God, living the life of prayer, is supported, filled, transformed in beauty, by a vitality and a power which are not its own.

Evelyn Underhill

The healthy, the strong individual, is the one who asks for help when he needs it — whether he's got an abscess on his knee or in his soul.

Rona Barrett

As a confirmed melancholic, I can testify that the best and maybe the only antidote for melancholia is action. However, like most melancholics, I suffer also from sloth.

Edward Abbey

The greatest force in the human body is the natural drive of the body to heal itself — but that force is not independent of the belief system, which can translate expectations into psychological change. Nothing is more wondrous about the 15 billion neurons in the human brain than their ability to convert thoughts, hopes, ideas, and attitudes into chemical substances. Everything begins, therefore, with belief.

Norman Cousins

All my life I've been a hypochondriac. Even as a little boy, I'd eat my M&Ms one at a time with a glass of water.

Richard Lewis

I am walking down the street in Manhattan, Fifth Avenue in the lower sixties, women with shopping bags on all sides. I realize with some horror that for the last fifteen blocks I have been counting how many women have better and how many women have worse figures than I do. Did I say fifteen blocks? I meant fifteen years.

Pam Houston

Of all the infirmities we have, the most savage is to despise our being.

Michel Eyquem de Montaigne

Nothing comes from nothing, / The darkness from the darkness. Pain comes from the darkness / And we call it wisdom. It is pain.

Randall Jarrell

Today in America — and every day in America — 76 million Valium will be swallowed. In addition, some 30 million people will glue themselves to soap operas on television. It would seem that our culture is not well adapted to deal with pain.

Matthew Fox

I believe my pain.

Theodore Roethke

The least pain in our little finger gives us more concern and uneasiness than the destruction of millions of our fellow beings.

William Hazlitt

When it is dark enough, you can see the stars.

Ralph Waldo Emerson

It is only great pain, that slow protracted pain which takes its time and in which we are, as it were, burned with green wood, that compels us philosophers to descend into our ultimate depths and to put from us all trust, all that is good-hearted, palliated, gentle, average, wherein perhaps our humanity previously reposed. I doubt whether such pain "improves" — but I do know it deepens us.

Friedrich Nietzsche

Illness is the doctor to whom we pay most heed; to kindness, to knowledge, we make promises only; pain we obey.

Marcel Proust

Health of body and mind is a great blessing, if we can bear it.

John Henry Newman

When a man dies, he does not die just of the disease he has: he dies of his whole life.

Charles Péguy

Dearest Lord, may I see you today and every day in the person of your sick, and whilst nursing them, minister unto you. Though you hide yourself behind the unattractive disguise of the irritable, the exacting, the unreasonable, may I still recognize you and say: "Jesus, my patient, how sweet it is to serve you."

Mother Teresa

To punish drug takers is like a drunk striking the bleary face he sees in the mirror. Drugs will not be brought under control until society itself changes, enabling men to use them as primitive man did: welcoming the visions they provided not as fantasies, but as intimations of a different, and important, level of reality.

Brian Inglis

When you stop drinking, you have to deal with this marvelous personality that started you drinking in the first place.

Jimmy Breslin

No drug, not even alcohol, causes the fundamental ills of society. If we're looking for the causes of our troubles, we shouldn't test people for drugs; we should test them for stupidity, ignorance, greed, and love of power.

P.J. O'Rourke

He who is of calm and happy nature will hardly feel the pressure of age, but to him who is of opposite disposition, youth and age are equally a burden.

Plato

If you enter into healing, be prepared to lose everything. Healing is a ravaging force to which nothing seems sacred or inviolate. As my original pain releases itself in healing, it rips to shreds the structures and foundations I built in weakness and ignorance. Ironically and unjustly, only I can pay the price of having lived a lie. I am experiencing the bizarre miracle of reincarnating, more lucidly than at birth, in the same lifetime.

Ely Fuller

A sense of reverence is necessary for psychological health. If a person has no sense of reverence, no feeling that there is anyone or anything that inspires awe, it generally indicates an ego inflation that cuts the conscious personality off completely from the nourishing springs of the unconscious.

Robert Johnson

How refreshing, the whinny of a pack-horse unloaded of everything!

Zen saying

If the desire to be honest is greater than the desire to be "good" or "bad," then the terrific power of one's vices will become clear. And behind the vice the old forgotten fear will come up (the fear of being excluded from life) and behind the fear the pain (the pain of not being loved) and behind this pain of loneliness the deepest and most profound and most hidden of all human desires: the desire to love and to give oneself in love and to be part of the living stream we call brotherhood. And the moment love is discovered behind hatred, all hatred disappears.

Fritz Kunkel

Compassion for myself is the most powerful healer of them all.

Theodore Isaac Rubin

Every form of addiction is bad, no matter whether the narcotic be alcohol or morphine or idealism.

Carl Jung

I was forever Billy Hamill's son, but I no longer wanted to be the next edition of Billy Hamill. He had his life and I had mine. If there were patterns, endless repetitions, cycles of family history, if my father was the result of his father and his father's father, on down through the generations into the Irish fogs, I could no longer accept any notion of predestination. Someone among the males of this family had to break the pattern. It might as well be me. I didn't have that drink. Twenty years have gone by, and I've never had one since.

Pete Hamill

You know, we come up with all kinds of things, but still the wound does not heal, still the reality is suffering. We come up with all kinds of new drugs, all kinds of new approaches. Yes, there are all kinds of human decencies to embrace, and we should really try to be nice to one another, but nothing dissolves this sense of irritation and unsatisfactoriness that we all feel. Nobody gets over that.

Leonard Cohen

It is not heroin or cocaine that makes one an addict; it is the need to escape from a harsh reality. There are more television addicts, more baseball and football addicts, more movie addicts, and certainly more alcohol addicts in this country than there are narcotics addicts.

Shirley Chisholm

Old habits are strong and jealous.

Dorothea Brande

A drug is neither moral nor immoral — it's a chemical compound. The compound itself is not a menace to society until a human being treats it as if consumption bestowed a temporary license to act like an asshole.

Frank Zappa

A Coke at snack time, a drink before dinner, a cup of coffee after dinner, a cigarette with coffee — very relaxing. Four shots of drugs. Domesticated ones.

Adam Smith

Here is a mental treatment guaranteed to cure every ill that flesh is heir to: sit for half an hour every night and mentally forgive everyone against whom you have any ill will or antipathy.

Charles Fillmore

[The Greek physician] Galen was called to attend the wife of a Roman aristocrat. Her doctor had been treating her for an organic complaint, but she had not improved. Galen, while taking her pulse, mentioned the name of an actor with whom her name was linked in the gossip of the town. Her pulse immediately bounded. Then Galen leaned down and whispered something in her ear that made her laugh. That laugh began her cure.

The Little, Brown Book of Anecdotes

Never go to a doctor whose office plants have died.

Erma Bombeck

☉

The tragedy of old age is not that one is old, but that one is young.

Oscar Wilde

A man of fifty is responsible for his face.

Edwin M. Stanton

I'm at that age now where just putting my cigar in its holder is a thrill.

George Burns

Time engraves our faces with all the tears we have not shed.

Natalie Clifford Barney

Eighty years old! No eyes left, no ears, no teeth, no legs, no wind! And when all is said and done, how astonishingly well one does without them!

Paul Cladel

They went to the bathroom and got their teeth. They went down to the sitting room . . . and ate large pieces of . . . cake.

V.S. Naipaul,
The Nightwatchman's Occurrence Book

The hardest years in life are those between ten and seventy.

Helen Hayes

The view after seventy is breathtaking. What is lacking is someone, anyone, of the older generation to whom you can turn when you want to satisfy your curiosity about some detail of the landscape of the past. There is no longer any older generation. You have become it, while your mind was mostly on other matters.

William Maxwell

[Opening words of a lecture.] If there are any of you at the back who do not hear me, please don't raise your hands because I am also nearsighted.

W.H. Auden

Old age is an insult. It's like being smacked.

Lawrence Durrell

Old age was growing inside me. It kept catching my eye from the depths of the mirror. I was paralyzed sometimes as I saw it making its way toward me so steadily when nothing inside me was ready for it.

Simone de Beauvoir

Life goes on, having nowhere else to go.

Diane Ackerman

When I was young, I admired clever people. Now that I am old, I admire kind people.

Abraham Joshua Heschel

Certainly the effort to remain unchanged, young, when the body gives so impressive a signal of change as the menopause, is gallant; but it is a stupid, self-sacrificial gallantry, better befitting a boy of twenty than a woman of forty-five or fifty. Let the athletes die young and laurel-crowned. Let the soldiers earn the Purple Hearts. Let women die old, white-crowned, with human hearts.

Ursula K. Le Guin

The whiter my hair becomes, the more ready people are to believe what I say.

Bertrand Russell

Sins become more subtle as you grow older: you commit sins of despair rather than of lust.

Piers Paul Read

Old people are fond of giving good advice; it consoles them for no longer being capable of setting a bad example.

François de la Rochefoucauld

A clay pot sitting in the sun will always be a clay pot. It has to go through the white heat of the furnace to become porcelain.

Mildred Witte Struven

Now that I am sixty, I see why the idea of elder wisdom has passed from currency.

John Updike

Old women snore violently. They are like bodies into which bizarre animals have crept at night; the animals are vicious, bawdy, noisy. How they snore! There is no shame to their snoring. Old women turn into old men.

Joyce Carol Oates

Everything we feel is made of time. All the beauties of life are shaped by it.

Peter Shaffer

We often hear of the beauties of old age, but the only old age that is beautiful is the one the man has been long preparing for by living a beautiful life. Every one of us is right now preparing for old age. There may be a substitute somewhere in the world for Good Nature, but I do not know where it can be found. The secret of salvation is this: keep sweet, be useful, and keep busy.

Elbert Hubbard

Even if our efforts of attention seem for years to be producing no result, one day a light that is in exact proportion to them will flood the soul.

Simone Weil

A man lives with himself for seventy years, and doesn't know who he is.

Israel Salanter Lipkin

He who would be a great soul in the future, must be a great soul now.

Ralph Waldo Emerson

We all want to be happy, and we're all going to die. . . . You might say these are the only two unchallengeably true facts that apply to every human being on this planet.

William Boyd

Here is a test to find whether your mission on earth is finished: if you're alive, it isn't.

Richard Bach

All our final resolutions are made in a state of mind which is not going to last.

Marcel Proust

From the rise, he looks out over his place. This is it. This is all there is in the world — it contains everything there is to know or possess, yet everywhere people are knocking their brains out trying to find something different, something better. His kids all scattered, looking for it. Everyone always wants a way out of something like this, but what he has here is the main thing there is — just the way things grow and die, the way the sun comes up and goes down every day. These are the facts of life. They are so simple, they are almost impossible to grasp.

Bobbie Ann Mason,
from the short story "Spence and Lila"

Eternity is not something that begins after you are dead. It is going on all the time. We are in it now.

Charlotte Perkins Gilman

When hungry, eat your rice; when tired, close your eyes. Fools may laugh at me, but wise men know what I mean.

Lin-Chi

Time will teach us more than all our thoughts.

Benjamin Disraeli

The older woman's love is not love of herself, nor of herself mirrored in a lover's eyes, nor is it corrupted by need. It is a feeling of tenderness so still and deep and warm that it gilds every grass blade and blesses every fly. It includes the ones who have a claim on it, and a great deal else besides. I wouldn't have missed it for the world.

Germaine Greer

Doggedly Blundering Toward Heaven

For the wonderful thing about saints is that they were human. They lost their tempers, got hungry, scolded God, were egotistical or testy or impatient in their turns, made mistakes and regretted them. Still, they went on doggedly blundering toward heaven.

Phyllis McGinley

At the moment you are most in awe of all there is about life that you don't understand, you are closer to understanding it all than at any other time.

Jane Wagner

A mystic is a person who is puzzled before the obvious but who understands the nonexistent.

Elbert Hubbard

The thing that astonished him was that cats should have two holes cut in their coat exactly at the place where their eyes are.

G.C. Lichtenberg

One may explain water, but the mouth will not become wet. One may expound fully on the nature of fire, but the mouth will not become hot.

Takuan Sōhō

Chance furnishes me what I need. I am like a man who stumbles along; my foot strikes something. I bend over and it is exactly what I want.

James Joyce

Chance is perhaps the pseudonym of God when he does not wish to sign his work.

Anatole France

I would rather live in a world where my life is surrounded by mystery than live in a world so small that my mind could comprehend it.

Harry Emerson Fosdick

"Is there any point to which you would wish to draw my attention?"

"To the curious incident of the dog in the nighttime."

"The dog did nothing in the nighttime."

"That was the curious incident," remarked Sherlock Holmes.

Sir Arthur Conan Doyle,
The Memoirs of Sherlock Holmes

The Buddha always told his disciples not to waste their time and energy in metaphysical speculation. Whenever he was asked a metaphysical question, he remained silent. Instead, he directed his disciples toward practical efforts. . . . He once said, "Suppose a man is struck by a poisoned arrow and the doctor wishes to take the arrow out immediately. Suppose the man does not want the arrow removed until he knows who shot it, his age, his parents, and why he shot it. What would happen? If he were to wait until all these questions have been answered, the man might die first." Life is so short. It must not be spent in endless metaphysical speculation that does not bring us any closer to the truth.

Thich Nhat Hanh

There is a fifth dimension beyond those known to man. It is a dimension vast as space and timeless as infinity. It is the middle ground between light and shadow, between the pit of his fears and the summit of his knowledge. This is the dimension of imagination. It is an area called the Twilight Zone.

Rod Serling

If there is one door in the castle you have been told not to go through, you must.

Otherwise you'll just be rearranging furniture in rooms you've already been in.

Anne Lamott

๏

The first mystery is simply that there is a mystery, a mystery that can never be explained or understood, only encountered from time to time. Nothing is obvious. Everything conceals something else.

Lawrence Kushner

The universe is the language of God.

Lorenz Oken

I'm astounded by people who want to "know" the universe when it's hard enough to find your way around Chinatown.

Woody Allen

I don't think, in our kind of society, we'll be able to develop a full-blown mystical religion or concept of God because we seek instant gratification, fast food, endless talk, and noise. The silence in mysticism is alien. People want to do a few courses in mysticism, rather like the way you do French before going on holiday, and emerge a mystic. Mysticism isn't like that.

Karen Armstrong

Joan of Arc: I hear voices telling me what to do. They come from God.
Robert: They come from your imagination.
Joan: Of course. That is how the messages of God come to us.

George Bernard Shaw,
Saint Joan

O you who love clear edges / more than anything, watch the edges that blur.

Adrienne Rich

When nothing is for sure, we remain alert, perennially on our toes. It is more exciting not to know which bush the rabbit is hiding behind than to behave as though we knew everything.

Carlos Castaneda

What if you slept? And what if, in your sleep, you dreamed? And what if, in your dream, you went to heaven and there plucked a strange and beautiful flower? And what if, when you awoke, you had the flower in your hand? Ah, what then?

Samuel Taylor Coleridge

Everything that happens is at once natural and inconceivable.

E.M. Cioran

If one looks at a thing with the intention of trying to discover what it means, one ends up no longer seeing the thing itself, but thinking of the question that has been raised. One cannot speak about mystery; one must be seized by it.

René Magritte

There are times when you want to stop working at faith and just be washed in a blowing wind that tells you everything.

Don DeLillo

Nothing that is worth doing can be achieved in our lifetime; therefore we must be saved by hope. Nothing which is true or beautiful or good makes complete sense in any immediate context of history; therefore we must be saved by faith. Nothing we do, however virtuous, can be accomplished alone; therefore we must be saved by love.

Reinhold Niebuhr

Look. This is your world! You can't not look. There is no other world. This is your world; it is your feast. You inherited this; you inherited these eyeballs; you inherited this world of color. Look at the greatness of the whole thing. Look! Don't hesitate — look! Open your eyes. Don't blink, and look, look — look further.

Chögyam Trungpa Rinpoche

Sakyamuni once cried out in pity for a yogi by the river who had wasted twenty years of his human existence in learning how to walk on water, when the ferryman might have taken him across for a small coin.

Richard Kehl

We do not know what anything is. The summarization of our existence is Mystery, absolute, unqualified confrontation with what we cannot know. And no matter how sophisticated we become by experience, this will always be true of us.

Da Free John

Deep down, all of us are probably aware that some kind of mystical evolution . . . is our true task. Yet we suppress the notion with considerable force because to admit it is to admit that most of our political gyrations, religious dogmas, social ambitions, and financial ploys are not merely counterproductive but trivial.

Tom Robbins

Listen to your life. See it for the fathomless mystery that it is. In the boredom and pain of it no less than in the excitement and gladness; touch, taste, smell your way to the holy and hidden heart of it, because in the last analysis all moments are key moments, and life itself is grace.

Frederick Buechner

Mysticism and exaggeration go together. A mystic must not fear ridicule if he is to push all the way to the limits of humility or the limits of delight.

Milan Kundera

I am glad that my master lived / in a one-story / house / when I began . . . to traverse / the early stages of / love. / For when he would speak / of the wonders and the beauty of creation / . . . I could not control my happiness and would commence / an ecstatic dance / that most always resulted in a / . . . dive, head first, / out of his / window. . . . And you only broke your big nose / seventeen times.

Hafiz

Mystics and schizophrenics find themselves in the same ocean, but the mystics swim whereas the schizophrenics drown.

R.D. Laing

☽

We are not born all at once, but by bits. The body first, and the spirit later. . . . Our mothers are racked with the pains of our physical birth; we ourselves suffer the longer pains of our spiritual growth.

Mary Antin

Alas, O Lord, to what a state dost Thou bring those who love Thee!

Saint Teresa of Avila

We are not human beings trying to be spiritual. We are spiritual beings trying to be human.

Jacquelyn Small

Spirituality is the sacred center out of which all life comes, including Mondays and Tuesdays and rainy Saturday afternoons in all their mundane and glorious detail. . . . The spiritual journey is the soul's life commingling with ordinary life.

Christina Baldwin

Slipping / on my shoes, / boiling water, / toasting bread, / buttering the sky: / that should be enough contact / with God in one day / to make anyone crazy.

Hafiz

They lied to you, sold you ideas of good and evil, gave you distrust of your body, . . . invented words of disgust for your molecular love, mesmerized you with inattention, bored you with civilization.

Hakim Bey

We do not have too much intellect and too little soul, but too little precision in matters of the soul.

Robert Musil

Who can order the Holy? It is like a rain forest, dripping, lush, fecund, wild. We enter its abundance at our peril, for here we are called to the wholeness for which we long, but which requires all we are and can hope to be.

Marilyn Sewell

If an angel were ever to tell us anything of his philosophy, I believe many propositions would sound like 2 x 2 = 13.

G.C. Lichtenberg

In the greatest confusion there is still an open channel to the soul. It may be difficult to find because by midlife it is overgrown, and some of the wildest thickets that surround it grow out of what we describe as our education. But the channel is always there, and it is our business to keep it open, to have access to the deepest part of ourselves.

Saul Bellow

The human soul is virtually indestructible, and its ability to rise from the ashes remains as long as the body draws breath.

Alice Miller

A person is neither a thing nor a process but an opening through which the Absolute can manifest.

Martin Heidegger

If the soul could have known God without the world, the world would never have been created.

Meister Eckhart

Christ and Moses standing in the back of Saint Pat's, looking around. Confused, Christ is, at the grandeur of the interior, the baroque interior, the rococo baroque interior. Because his route took him through Spanish Harlem, and he is wondering what the hell fifty Puerto Ricans were doing living in one room when that stained-glass window is worth ten G's a square foot.

Lenny Bruce

The fall of man stands as a lie before Beethoven, / A truth before Hitler.

Gregory Corso

When we speak of treading the path of the dharma . . . it does not mean that we become religious, calm, and good. Trying to be calm, trying to be good, is also an aspect of striving, of neuroticism.

Chögyam Trungpa Rinpoche

We must seek God in error and forgetfulness and foolishness.

Meister Eckhart

Every decision you make is a mistake.

Edward Dahlberg

We are built to make mistakes, coded for error.

Lewis Thomas

The soul that projects itself entirely into activity, and seeks itself outside itself in the work of its own will, is like a madman who sleeps on the sidewalk in front of his house instead of living inside where it is quiet and warm.

Thomas Merton

Without mystical experience . . . religion is a corpse.

William McNamara

We all carry within us our places of exile, our crimes, and our ravages. But our task is not to unleash them on the world; it is to fight them in ourselves and in others.

Albert Camus

In our darkness, there is not a place for beauty. Every place is for beauty.

Rene Char

If there be anywhere on earth a lover of God who is always kept safe from falling, I know nothing of it, for it was not shown me. But this was shown: that in falling and rising again we are always kept in the same precious love.

Julian of Norwich

Nothing burns in hell but the self.

Theologia Germanica

☽

I believe in original sin. I find people profoundly bad and irresistibly funny.

Joe Orton

The truth is that everything is One, and this of course is not a numerical one.

Philip Kapleau

No matter how convinced a Buddhist is that the world is an illusion, she invariably leaves a room by walking through a doorway rather than through a wall.

Bruce Gregory

Spirituality is not a course in literature.

Stewart Brinton

In the Garden, God had given Adam a test. It was the test of faith — faith that God's will can be fulfilled without knowledge, without any additions. But Adam wanted to know, and so, fell from his creator. We face the same test every day. We fail when we step back from each situation. Instead of trusting that the will of God can speak through us, we want to know God, to define Him as a truth found in a specific place, or in one path of action, as though all of God's will could be conveyed through a single channel.

Eliezer Shore

Let a man get up and say, "Behold, this is the truth," and instantly I perceive a sandy cat filching a piece of fish in the background. "Look, you have forgotten the cat," I say.

Virginia Woolf, *The Waves*

Good God, how much reverence can you have for a Supreme Being who finds it necessary to include such phenomena as phlegm and tooth decay in His divine system of creation?

Joseph Heller, *Catch-22*

Everything in this world has a hidden meaning. . . . Men, animals, trees, stars, they are all hieroglyphics. . . . When you see them, you do not understand them. You think they are really men, animals, trees, stars. It is only years later . . . that you understand.

Nikos Kazantzakis,
Zorba the Greek

Life is this simple: we are living in a world that is absolutely transparent and God is shining through it all the time. This is not just a fable or a nice story. It is true. If we abandon ourselves to God and forget ourselves, we see it sometimes, and we see it maybe frequently. God is manifest everywhere, in everything — in people and in things and in nature and in events. It becomes very

obvious that God is everywhere and in everything and we cannot be without God. It's impossible. It's simply impossible.

Thomas Merton

It would be good to remember that culture or knowledge is something much lighter than one would imagine. Lighter, and more ambivalent.

Witold Gombrowicz

There is a crack in everything God has made.

Ralph Waldo Emerson

Never make a god of your religion.

Sir Arthur Helps

The question of bread for myself is a material question, but the question of bread for my neighbor is a spiritual question.

Nikolai Berdyaev

Given that all religions preach brotherhood, love of your fellow man, and tolerance for all people without exception, why is it that all the world's different religions have never been able to achieve unity?

Frank Zappa

It has never been more difficult to hear the unflattering voice of the truth — and never more difficult, once having heard it, to follow it — because there is nothing in the world around us that supports our choice.

Sogyal Rinpoche

Jesus promised those who would follow his leadings only three things: that they should be absurdly happy, entirely fearless, and always in trouble.

Maltbie Babcock

Normally, he was the happiest of men. He asked so little of life that its frugal bounty amazed and delighted him. . . . He believed in miracles and frequently observed them, and nothing astonished him. His imagination was as wild as a small boy's and his faith ultimate. In ordinary life he was, quite frankly, hardly safe out.

Margery Allingham,
The Tiger in the Smoke

I cannot believe in a God who wants to be praised all the time.

Friedrich Nietzsche

Some believers who were sitting around a fountain taunted Saint John of God about his faith and poured scorn on his belief in miracles. John, who was a very burly fellow, answered, "Is it not a miracle enough that God prevents me from throwing you into the water?"

Source unknown

Sophia wished that Florence would not talk about the Almighty as if his real name was Godfrey, and God was just Florence's nickname for him.

Nancy Mitford, *Pigeon Pie*

It always comes back to the same necessity: go deep enough and there is a bedrock of truth, however hard.

May Sarton

The sun, I tell you, is alive, and more alive than I am, or a tree is. It may have blazing gas, as I have hair and a tree has leaves. But I tell you, it is the Holy Ghost in full raiment, shaking and walking, and alive as a tiger is, only more so, in the sky.

D.H. Lawrence

Our quaint metaphysical opinions, in an hour of anguish, are like playthings by the bedside of a child deathly sick.

Samuel Taylor Coleridge

What is truth? I don't know, and I'm sorry I raised the point.

Edward Abbey

Once I had abandoned the search for everyone else's truth, I quickly discovered that the job of defining my own truth was far more complex than I had anticipated.

Ingrid Bengis

Have you ever really looked anybody in the face?

J. Krishnamurti

I have only three enemies. My favorite enemy, the one most easily influenced for the better, is the British nation. My second enemy, the Indian people, is far more difficult. But my most formidable opponent is a man named Mohandas K. Gandhi. With him, I seem to have very little influence.

Mohandas K. Gandhi

Yet it is in our idleness, in our dreams, that the submerged truth sometimes comes to the top.

Virginia Woolf

〇

Every morning the *New York Times* is out on the front step, and I wake up and get my tea and decide whether to meditate first or read the *New York Times* first. If the *New York Times* is first, by the time I'm to page four, I am already engaged in the pain and the suffering, the greed and the fear. If I meditate first and come into a kind of spacious awareness, I have a perspective that gives me some leverage so that I don't just keep drowning in it. It doesn't mean nonaction; it means that the action comes from a quieter space inside.

Ram Dass

The detached observer is as much entangled as the active participant.

Theodore Adorno

There's an alternative. There's always a third way, and it's not a combination of the other two ways. It's a different way.

David Carradine

Give me the madman's sudden insight and the child's spiritual dignity.

Theodore Roethke

Work is hard. Distractions are plentiful. And time is short.

Adam Hochschild

It does no good to think moralistically about how much time we waste. Wasted time is usually good soul time.

Thomas Moore

Perhaps a feature of the crucified face lurks in every mirror; perhaps the face died, was erased so that God may be all of us. Who knows but that tonight we may see it in the labyrinth of dreams, and tomorrow not know that we saw it.

Jorge Luis Borges

My feeling is that there is nothing in life but refraining from hurting others and comforting those who are sad.

Olive Schreiner

We have now sunk to a depth at which the restatement of the obvious is the first duty of intelligent men.

George Orwell

A rabbi was asked to adjudicate a case. The first man presented his argument, and the rabbi, after hearing the evidence, said to him, "You are right!" Then the second man presented his argument, and the rabbi, after hearing his evidence, said, "You are right!" At this point, the rabbi's wife turned to her husband and asked, "How can both of these men be right?" The rabbi thought for a moment and then said, "Darling, you are right!"

Source unknown

The armies of Rome disappeared more than a millennium ago, but the force of the life of a single human whom Roman soldiers put to death continues to shape the development of our species. Who had the power?

Gary Zukav

The well of Providence is deep. It's the buckets we bring to it that are small.

Mary Webb

Faith and doubt both are needed, not as antagonists but working side by side, to take us around the unknown curve.

Lillian Smith

Colors are the deeds and sufferings of light.

Johann Wolfgang von Goethe

Our roots are in the dark; the earth is our country. Why did we look up for blessing — instead of around, and down? What hope we have lies there. Not in the sky full of orbiting spy-eyes and weaponry, but in the earth we have looked down upon. Not from above, but from below. Not in the light that blinds, but in the dark that nourishes, where human beings grow human souls.

Ursula K. Le Guin

There is often in people to whom "the worst" has happened an almost transcendent freedom, for they have faced "the worst" and survived it.

Carol Pearson

O world, I cannot hold thee close enough.

Edna St. Vincent Millay

I cannot believe that the inscrutable universe turns on an axis of suffering; surely the strange beauty of the world must somewhere rest on pure joy!

Louise Bogan

Rabbi Yoshua ben Levi asked Elijah, "When will the Messiah come?"

Elijah replied, "Go and ask him yourself."

"Where is he?"

"Sitting at the gates of the city."

"How shall I know him?"

"He is sitting among the poor covered with wounds. The others unbind all their wounds and bind them up again. But he unbinds one at a time and then binds it up again, saying to himself, 'Perhaps I shall be needed. If so, I must always be ready so as not to delay for a moment.'"

The Talmud

⌒

The most fundamental of divisions is that between the intellect, which can only do its work by saying continually, "Thou fool," and the religious genius which makes all equal.

William Butler Yeats

What the world expects of Christians is that Christians should speak out, loud and clear; that they should voice their condemnation in such a way that never a doubt, never the slightest doubt, could arise in the heart of the simplest person; that they should get away from abstraction and confront the blood-stained face history has taken on today.

Albert Camus

If we find fullness of joy in the thought that God is, we should find the same fullness in the knowledge that we ourselves are not, for it is the same thought.

Simone Weil

Of course, if one can escape grief and pain and ensure joy and peace by denying God, the attempt can be made. But even atheists have misery, grief, and pain.

Atheism is not more profitable than theism. The atheist simply transfers the burden from the head to the shoulders, denying that there is a head. The burden has to be borne, but only with greater hardship.

Sai Baba

We find the most terrible form of atheism, not in the militant and passionate struggle against the idea of God himself, but in the practical atheism of everyday living, in indifference and torpor. We often encounter these forms of atheism among those who are formally Christians.

Nikolai Berdyaev

Isolation has led me to reflection, reflection to doubt, doubt to a more sincere and intelligent love of God.

Marie Lenéru

At midnight I abruptly awakened. At first my mind was foggy. . . . Then all at once I was struck as though by lightning, and the next instant heaven and earth crumbled and disappeared. Instantaneously, like surging waves, a tremendous delight welled up in me, a veritable hurricane of delight, as I laughed loudly and wildly, "There's no reasoning here, no reasoning at all! Ha! Ha! Ha!" The empty sky split in two, then opened its enormous mouth and began to laugh uproariously: "Ha! Ha! Ha!"

Koun Yamada

It often happens that I wake at night and begin to think about a serious problem and decide I must tell the pope about it.

Then I wake up completely and remember that I am the pope.

Pope John XXIII

What good is it to me if Mary gave birth to the Son of God fourteen hundred years ago, and I do not also give birth to the Son of God in my time and in my culture? We are all meant to be mothers of God. God is always needing to be born.

Meister Eckhart

He who shall introduce into public affairs the principles of primitive Christianity will revolutionize the world.

Benjamin Franklin

The highest condition of the religious sentiment is when . . . the worshiper not only sees God everywhere, but sees nothing which is not full of God.

Harriet Martineau

Years ago, my mother gave me a bullet. I put it in my breast pocket. Two years after that I was walking down the street when a berserk evangelist heaved a Gideons Bible out a hotel-room window, hitting me in the chest. The Bible would have gone through my heart if it wasn't for the bullet.

Woody Allen

If Jesus Christ were to come today, people would not even crucify him. They would ask him to dinner, and hear what he had to say, and make fun of it.

Thomas Carlyle

Jesus is not a blue-eyed right-winger. . . . Jesus is the one who entered the world among the dispossessed and the outcasts to announce an entirely new way of thinking and living. The way of Jesus and the prophets . . . moves us beyond the familiar options of abandoning the poor, controlling the poor, or even "helping" the poor from places of isolation and comfort. Instead, it leads us to a new relationship with one another, a deep reconnection, a restoration of the shattered covenant.

Jim Wallis

Though it is possible to utter words only with the intention to fulfill the will of God, it is very difficult not to think about the impression which they will produce on men and not to form them accordingly. But deeds you can do quite unknown to men, only for God. And such deeds are the greatest joy that a man can experience.

Leo Tolstoy

⊘

Two prisoners whose cells adjoin communicate with each other by knocking on the wall. The wall is the thing which separates them but it is also their means of communication. It is the same with us and God. Every separation is a link.

Simone Weil

He became an infidel, hesitating between two mosques.

Turkish proverb

The world is not a prison-house but a kind of spiritual kindergarten where millions of bewildered infants are trying to spell God with the wrong blocks.

Edwin Arlington Robinson

Looking for God is like seeking a path in a field of snow; if there is no path and you are looking for one, walk across it and there is your path.

Thomas Merton

Whatever you say about God you should be able to say standing over a pit full of burning babies.

Elie Wiesel

A devotee once complained to the great nineteenth-century saint Sri Ramakrishna about not having had any deep experiences of God. Sri Ramakrishna took him by the hand and led him to the ashram's bathing pond. They both walked into the water until they were about waist deep, and Sri Ramakrishna then pushed the man's head underwater with great force and held him there for nearly a minute. The man struggled and struggled, and finally the saint released his grip and the man emerged urgently from the water, gasping for breath. Sri Ramakrishna said to him, "When you want God as much as you wanted that next breath, you will see God."

Bo Lozoff

I have some obsession with how God exists. Is he an essential god or an existential god; is he all-powerful or is he, too, an embattled existential creature who may succeed or fail in his vision?

Norman Mailer

There is really no difference between matter, mind, and spirit. There are only different phases of experiencing the One. This very world is seen by the five senses as matter, by the very wicked as hell, by the good as heaven, and by the perfect as God.

Swami Vivekananda

Only our concept of Time makes it possible for us to speak of the Day of Judgment by that name; in reality it is a summary court in perpetual session.

Franz Kafka

When God sneezed, I didn't know what to say.

Henny Youngman

The true saint lives in the midst of other people. He rises in the morning; he eats and sleeps when needed. He buys and sells in the marketplace just like everyone else. He marries, has children, and meets with his friends. Yet never for an instant does he forget God.

Abu Sa'id

The essential self is innocent, and when it tastes its own innocence knows that it lives forever.

John Updike

There are some faults so nearly allied to excellence that we can scarce weed out the vice without eradicating the virtue.

Oliver Goldsmith

We cannot make a religion for others, and we ought not to let others make a religion for us. Our own religion is what life has taught us.

Dean Inge

God does not die on the day when we cease to believe in a personal deity, but we die on the day when our lives cease to be illumined by the steady radiance, renewed daily, of a wonder, the source of which is beyond all reason.

Dag Hammarskjöld

You must concentrate upon and consecrate yourself wholly to each day, as though a fire were raging in your hair.

Taisen Deshimaru

The search is what anyone would undertake if he were not sunk in the everydayness of his own life. . . . To become aware of the possibility of the search is to be on to something. Not to be on to something is to be in despair.

Walker Percy

Guard the mysteries! Constantly reveal them!

Lew Welch

Penetrating so many secrets, we cease to believe in the unknowable. But there it sits, nevertheless, calmly licking its chops.

H.L. Mencken

I think we are responsible for the universe, but that doesn't mean we decide anything.

René Magritte

If triangles made a god, they would give him three sides.

Charles de Montesquieu

Truth can be found everywhere, even on the lips of drunkards, in the noisiest of taverns.

Elie Wiesel

Any God I ever felt in church I brought in with me.

Alice Walker,
The Color Purple

Men with faith can face martyrdom while men without it feel stricken when they are not invited to dinner.

Walter Lippmann

Until God has taken possession of him, no human being can have faith, but only simple belief; and it hardly matters whether or not he has such a belief, because he will arrive at faith equally well through incredulity.

Simone Weil

None of us has lived up to the teachings of Christ.

Eleanor Roosevelt

Talk to me about the truth of religion and I'll listen gladly. Talk to me about the duty of religion and I'll listen submissively. But don't come talking to me about the consolations of religion or I shall suspect that you don't understand.

C.S. Lewis, after the death
of his wife

How else but through a broken heart /
May Lord Christ enter in?

Oscar Wilde

Nobody can deny but religion is a comfort to the distressed, a cordial to the sick, and sometimes a restraint on the wicked; therefore whoever would argue or laugh it out of the world without giving some equivalent for it ought to be treated as a common enemy.

Lady Mary Worley Montagu

If the question could be put to a popular vote, I do not believe a single state would vote for the coming of Jesus to reign here as he reigns in heaven. I do not believe a single county, a single ward in this city, or a single precinct in this country would vote for his coming. . . . The Republican party would vote for the biggest blackguard on earth rather than for him. The Democrats would vote solidly against him. Even the Prohibitionists wouldn't want him here. I see some of you shaking your heads. Well, shake 'em. I'm talking facts.

Dwight L. Moody

What is religion? That which is never spoken.

Henry David Thoreau

Religion has made us meditate constantly on the crucifixion and never on the resurrection.

D.H. Lawrence

Dogma can in no way limit a limitless God.

Flannery O'Connor

It is good to be born in a church, but it is bad to die there. It is good to be born a child, but bad to remain a child. Churches, ceremonies, symbols are good for children; but when the child is grown up, he must burst, either the church or himself. . . . The end of all religion is the realization of God.

Swami Vivekananda

God is not a continent, like Antarctica, lying off somewhere, inert, without relation to human life till some Scott or Amundsen or Byrd finds him. God is not a mountain peak to which travelers must go and which they climb step by step. God is like the air we breathe or the earth beneath our feet. To discover God is simply to awaken to reality. It is like a plant discovering the sun and the rain that drew it from the earth or like children discovering the parents who gave them birth and love and nurture.

Luther A. Weigle

I studiously avoided all so-called holy men. I did so because I had to make do with my own truth, not accept from others what I could not attain on my own. I would have felt it as a theft had I attempted to learn from the holy men and to accept their truth for myself. Neither in Europe can I make any borrowings from the East, but must shape my life out of myself — out of what my inner being tells me, or what nature brings to me.

Carl Jung

Perhaps the most lasting pleasure in life is the pleasure of not going to church.

Dean Inge

Whilst you live, a little religion seems enough; but believe me, it requires a great deal when you come to die.

Geraldine Jewsbury

My father . . . considered a walk among the mountains as the equivalent of churchgoing.

Aldous Huxley

A religious awakening which does not awaken the sleeper to love has aroused him in vain.

Jessamyn West

There is no religion without love, and people may talk as much as they like about their religion, but if it does not teach them to be good and kind to man and beast, it is all a sham.

Anna Sewell

In Louisville, at the corner of Fourth and Walnut, in the center of the shopping district, I was suddenly overwhelmed with the realization that I loved all those people, that they were mine and I theirs, that we could not be alien to one another even though we were total strangers. It was like waking from a dream of separateness, of spurious self-isolation in a special world, the world of renunciation and supposed holiness. . . . This sense of liberation from an illusory difference was such a relief and such a joy to me that I almost laughed out loud. . . . I have the immense joy of being a member of a race in which God became incarnate. . . . There is no way of telling people that they are all walking around shining like the sun.

Thomas Merton

That life . . . that she had complained against, had murmured at, had raged at and defied — nonetheless she had loved it so, joyed in it so, both in good days and evil, that not one day had there been when it would not have seemed hard to give it back to God, nor one grief that she could have forgone without regret.

Sigrid Undset, *The Cross*

Heaven and Hell are in the present moment, and we are either in Heaven or Hell as we live out our lives each day.

Charles Scot Giles

Each activity of daily life in which we stretch ourselves on behalf of others is a prayer of action — the times when we scrimp and save in order to get the children something special; the times when we share our car with others on rainy mornings, leaving early to get them to work on time; the times when we keep up correspondence with friends or answer one last telephone call when we are dead tired at night. These times and many more like them are lived prayer.

Richard J. Foster

Faith and philosophy are air, but events are brass.

Herman Melville

Earth's crammed with Heaven, and every common bush afire with God.

Elizabeth Barrett Browning

That the world is, is the mystical.

Ludwig Wittgenstein

But then, at the moment of my greatest despair, from my unconscious there came a sequence of words, like a strange disembodied oracle from a voice that was not mine: "The only real security in life lies in relishing life's insecurity." Even if it meant being crazy and out of step with all that seemed holy, I had decided to be me.

M. Scott Peck

Whenever I travel I like to keep the seat next to me empty. I found a great way to do it. When someone walks down the aisle and says to you, "Is someone sitting there?" just say, "No one — except the Lord."

Carol Leifer

How is it, Lord, that we are cowards in everything save in opposing thee?

Saint Teresa of Avila

There is in man a fear of joy as keen as the fear of suffering, because true joy precludes the pleasant feeling of self-importance just as suffering precludes all the comforts of self-pity. No man can know the one without the other.

Helen Luke

In the fight between you and the world, back the world.

Frank Zappa

The problem is that ego can convert anything to its own use, even spirituality. Ego is constantly attempting to acquire and apply the teachings of spirituality for its own benefit.

Chögyam Trungpa Rinpoche

Don't be humble. You're not that great.

Golda Meir

That Christianity is identical with democracy is the hardest of gospels; there is nothing that so strikes men with fear as the saying that they are all the sons of God.

G.K. Chesterton

Until it was decided by dictate that you're not allowed to see things other people don't see, hear things other people don't hear, or smell things other people don't smell, we all didn't have to hear, smell, and see things the same way. This was never the case in the history of humanity. The ordinary human might, when depressed, see the sky become dark or the sun cloud over. The whole world was once part of man's psyche. But no longer. Everything now has got to be experienced all the time in the same way as everyone else. Experience has become homogenized.

R.D. Laing

On all sides God surrounds you, staring out upon you from the mountains and from the face of the rocks, and of men, and of animals. Will you rush past forever insensate and blindfold, hurrying breathless from one unfinished task to another, and to catch your ever-departing trains, . . . flying from His face?

Edward Carpenter

Anyone who imagines that bliss is normal in life is going to waste a lot of time running around shouting that he's been robbed. The fact is that most putts don't drop, most beef is tough, most children grow up to be just people, most successful marriages require a high degree of mutual toleration, and most jobs are more often dull than otherwise. Life is like an old-time rail journey — delays, sidetracks, smoke, dust, cinders, and jolts, interspersed only occasionally with beautiful vistas and thrilling bursts of speed. The trick is to thank God for letting you have the ride.

Jenkins Lloyd Jones

Every morning and every evening, and whenever anything happens to you, keep on saying, "Thanks for everything. I have no complaint whatsoever."

Sono

The important thing is not to stop questioning. Curiosity has its own reason for existence. One cannot help but be in awe when one contemplates the mysteries of eternity, of life, of the marvelous structures of reality. It is enough if one tries merely to comprehend a little of this mystery each day. Never lose a holy curiosity.

Albert Einstein

I never saw a wild thing / Sorry for itself.

D. H. Lawrence

ဢ

All things are God's grace . . . everything in the world and the very world itself.

Philo of Alexandria

He had vowed long ago, and renewed his vow frequently, that if holding hands in a circle and singing hymns . . . was what it took to make life endurable, he would rather die.

Annie Dillard, *The Living*

Beware of the man whose God is in the skies.

George Bernard Shaw

Here's the thing with me and the religious thing. This is the flat-out truth: I find the religiosity and philosophy in the music. I don't find it anywhere else. Songs like "Let Me Rest on a Peaceful Mountain" or "I Saw the Light" — that's my religion. I don't adhere to rabbis, preachers, evangelists, all of that. . . . The songs are my lexicon. I believe the songs.

Bob Dylan

I do not believe in God. I believe in cashmere.

Fran Lebowitz

God is no white knight who charges into the world to pluck us like distressed damsels from the jaws of dragons, or diseases. God chooses to become present to and through us. It is up to us to rescue one another.

Nancy Mairs

The peculiar grace of a Shaker chair is due to the fact that it was made by someone capable of believing that an angel might come and sit on it.

Thomas Merton

All the beautiful sentiments in the world weigh less than a single lovely action.

James Russell Lowell

Christianity is good news, not good advice.

Dean Inge

You think religion is what's inside a little building filled with pretty lights from stained-glass windows. But it's not. It's wings! Wings!

Dorothy Canfield Fisher

At the next meal — I was head server — tears were pouring down my face as I served . . . and afterwards, when I went out to the zendo, . . . there was a tree there, and looking at the tree, I didn't feel I was the tree; it went deeper than that. I felt the wind on me, I felt the birds on me, all separation was gone.

Bernard Tetsugen Glassman

In the evening of life we shall be judged on love, and not one of us is going to come off very well, and were it not for my absolute faith in the loving forgiveness of my Lord, I could not call on Him to come.

Madeleine L'Engle

[Writer and Trappist monk Thomas Merton] wasn't a dour monk at all. . . . I often went down to visit him at the monastery in Kentucky. The abbott would give him a day off, and I'd rent a car. . . . We would stop in the woods and he'd change into his farmworker's bluejeans and a beret to hide his tonsure. Then we'd hit the bars across Kentucky. He loved beer, and he loved that smoked ham they have down there. He was a wonderful person. He wanted to read contemporary writers, but the books were often confiscated, so we had a secret system. I sent the books he wanted to the monastery psychiatrist in Louisville, who would get them to Merton. . . . Once I asked him, "Tom, why do you stay here? You could get out and be a tremendous success in the world." He answered that the monastery was where God wanted him to be.

James Laughlin

For the wonderful thing about saints is that they were human. They lost their tempers, got hungry, scolded God, were egotistical or testy or impatient in their turns, made mistakes and regretted them. Still, they went on doggedly blundering toward heaven.

Phyllis McGinley

Prayer gives a man the opportunity of getting to know a gentleman he hardly ever meets. I do not mean his maker, but himself.

Dean Inge

Once you accept the existence of God — however you define Him, however you explain your relationship to Him — then you are caught forever with His presence in the center of all things.

Morris West

He thought God surrounded Himself with paradox to keep us from approaching Him in any way but by faith.

Sibyl Johnston

God is infinite, and his shadow is also infinite.

Meher Baba

☞

Christmas reminds us that it is not enough to bring God into our hearts. When God comes, God never comes alone. Jesus asks us to take in his strange friends, his dispossessed and uprooted children, his unpopular causes and projects.

Doris Donnelly

Going to church doesn't make you a Christian any more than going to the garage makes you a car.

Laurence J. Peter

No matter how many Christmas presents you give your child, there's always that terrible moment when he's opened the very last one. That's when he expects you to say, "Oh yes, I almost forgot," and take him out and show him the pony.

Mignon McLaughlin

I was in love with the whole world and all that lived in its rainy arms.

Louise Erdrich, *Love Medicine*

Sometimes it happens that love is sweetly awakened in the soul and joyfully arises and stirs itself in the heart without any help from human acts.

Beatrice of Nazareth

There is nothing heavier than compassion. Not even one's pain weighs so heavy as the pain one feels with someone, for someone, a pain intensified by the imagination and prolonged by a hundred echoes.

Milan Kundera

If they can get you asking the wrong questions, they don't have to worry about answers.

Thomas Pynchon

When I speak of darkness, I am referring to a lack of knowing. It is a lack of knowing that includes everything you do not know or else that you have forgotten, whatever is altogether dark for you because you do not see it with your spiritual eye. And for this reason it is not called a cloud of the air, but rather a cloud of unknowing that is between you and your God.

The Cloud of Unknowing

He who wishes to teach us a truth should not tell it to us, but simply suggest it with a brief gesture, a gesture which starts an ideal trajectory in the air along which we glide until we find ourselves at the feet of the new truth.

José Ortega y Gasset

God, the sky is blue, and the air is shot with gold. A moment ago, we passed a farmyard where a girl about twelve, wearing a blue-and-white dress, stood waving, dwarfed by a lilac bush whose blossoms were already rusted. She seemed to beckon, but of course she was just waving at the world — us — passing by. She would have been alarmed if we'd stopped. But the impression remains that she was inviting us in.

Patricia Hampl and Steven Sorman

Students achieving oneness will move ahead to twoness.

Woody Allen

A door opens to me. I go in and am faced with a hundred closed doors.

Antonio Porchia

He prayed as he breathed, forming no words and making no specific requests, only holding in his heart, like broken birds in cupped hands, all those people who were in stress or grief.

Ellis Peters,
A Morbid Taste for Bones

Prayer does not change God, but it changes him who prays.

Søren Kierkegaard

Everything praises God. Darkness, privations, defects, evil too praise God and bless God.

Meister Eckhart

If you talk to God, you are praying; if God talks to you, you have schizophrenia.

Thomas Szasz

᠗

This kind of split makes me crazy, this territorializing of the holy. Here God may dwell. Here God may not dwell. It contradicts everything in my experience, which says: God dwells where I dwell. Period.

Nancy Mairs

The physicist Leo Szilard once announced to his friend Hans Bethe that he was thinking of keeping a diary. "I don't intend to publish it. I am merely going to record the facts for the information of God." "Don't you think God knows the facts?" Bethe asked. "Yes," said Szilard. "He knows the facts, but he does not know this version of the facts."

Richard Kehl

I recently invented a new theory: ambitheism. This is the doctrine that God both does and doesn't exist. I have noticed that when I try to believe in God, I am filled with sudden moments of despair that God is absent, but when I try to be an atheist, I slowly come to believe in a divine will. Thus, I have concluded that both ideas are true. God simultaneously is and isn't.

Michael Gorelick

Both faith and faithlessness have destroyed men.

Hesiod

Faith is not simply a patience which passively suffers until the storm is passed. It is rather a spirit which bears things — with resignation, yes, but above all with blazing, serene hope.

Corazon Aquino

Who are those who will eventually be damned? Oh, the others, the others, the others!

Elbert Hubbard

A group of people gathered on the edge of a flooding stream want to go to the far shore but are afraid. They don't know what to do until one wise person comes along, assesses the situation, takes a running leap, and jumps to the other side. Seeing the example of that person, the others say, "Yes, it can be done." Then they also jump. In this story the near shore is our usual confused condition, and the far shore is the awakened mind. Inspired by witnessing another, we say, "Yes, it can be done." That is one level of faith. After we have jumped ourselves, when we say, "Yes, it can be done," that is quite another level of faith.

Sharon Salzberg

The aim of life is to live, and to live means to be awake, joyously, drunkenly, serenely, divinely awake.

Henry Miller

A man who is eating, or lying with his wife, or preparing to go to sleep in humility, thankfulness, and temperance is, by Christian standards, in an infinitely higher state than one who is listening to Bach or reading Plato in a state of pride.

C.S. Lewis

Faith is not a series of gilt-edged propositions that you sit down to figure out — and if you follow all the logic, and accept all the conclusions, then you have it. [Faith] is crumpling and throwing away everything, proposition by proposition, until nothing is left, and then writing a new proposition, your very own, to throw in the teeth of despair.

Mary Jean Irion

The life of faith is the untiring pursuit of God through all that disguises and disfigures him and, as it were, destroys and annihilates him.

Jean-Pierre de Caussade

Life's a tough proposition, and the first hundred years are the hardest.

Wilson Mizner

My grandfather always said that living is like licking honey off a thorn.

Louis Adamic

You find out that the universe is a system that creeps up on itself and says, "Boo!" and then laughs at itself for jumping.

Alan Watts

If there were no other proof of the infinite patience of God with men, a very good one could be found in His toleration of the pictures that are painted of Him and of the noise that proceeds from musical instruments under the pretext of being in His "honor."

Thomas Merton

I did not ask for success, I asked for wonder. And you gave it to me.

Abraham Joshua Heschel

An idea isn't responsible for the people who believe in it.

Don Marquis

The way we define and delimit the self is arbitrary. We can place it between our ears and have it looking out from our eyes, or we can widen it to include the air we breathe, or at other moments we can cast its boundaries farther to include the oxygen-giving trees and plankton, our external lungs, and beyond them the web of life in which they are sustained.

Joanna Macy

A priest friend of mine has cautioned me away from the standard God of our childhoods, who loves and guides you and then, if you are bad, roasts you: God as high-school principal in a gray suit who never remembers your name but is always leafing unhappily through your files.

Anne Lamott

God is a concept by which we measure our pain.

John Lennon

God made everything out of nothing, but the nothingness shows through.

Paul Valéry

Metaphysics is not reality. . . . Metaphysics is a restaurant where they give you a thirty-thousand-page menu and no food.

Robert M. Pirsig

Some people think that they will practice the dharma once they have finished with their worldly business. This is a mistaken attitude, because our work in the world never finishes. . . . The busywork with which we fill our lives is completed only at the time of our death.

Geshe Kelsang Gyatso

Saint John of the Cross, alone in his room in profound prayer, experienced a rapturous vision of Mary. At the same moment, he heard a beggar rattling at his door for alms. He wrenched himself away and saw to the beggar's needs. When he returned, the vision returned again, saying that at the very moment he had heard the door rattle on its hinges, his soul had hung in perilous balance. Had he not gone to the beggar's aid, she could never have appeared to him again.

David Whyte

One of the annoying things about believing in free will and individual responsibility is the difficulty of finding somebody to blame your troubles on. And when you do find somebody, it's remarkable how often his picture turns up on your driver's license.

P.J. O'Rourke

Would you make obeisance to your guru, O my heart? He is there at every step, on all sides of the path, for numberless are your gurus. To how many of them would you make your obeisance? The welcome offered to you is your guru, the agony inflicted on you is your guru. Every wrench at the heartstrings that makes the tears to flow is your guru.

Bauls verse

Imagine walking along a sidewalk with your arms full of groceries, and someone roughly bumps into you so that you fall and your groceries are strewn over the ground. As you rise up from the puddle of broken eggs and tomato juice, you are ready to shout out, "You idiot! What's wrong with you? Are you blind?" But just before you can catch your breath to speak, you see that the person who bumped into you actually is blind. He, too, is sprawled in the spilled groceries, and your anger vanishes in an instant, to be replaced by sympathetic concern: "Are you hurt? Can I help you up?" Our situation is like that. When we clearly realize that the source of disharmony and misery in the world is ignorance, we can open the door of wisdom and compassion.

B. Alan Wallace

If an Arab in the desert were suddenly to discover a spring in his tent, and so would always be able to have water in abundance, how fortunate he would consider himself — so, too, when a man, who as a physical being is always turned toward the outside, thinking that his happiness lies outside him, finally turns inward and discovers that the source

is within him; not to mention his discovery that the source is his relation to God.

Søren Kierkegaard

That which hinders your task is your task.

Sanford Meisner

PAPER LANTERNS

In This Very Breath

In this very breath that we take now lies the secret that all great teachers try to tell us.

Peter Matthiessen

Tomorrow is an old deceiver, and his cheat never grows stale.

Samuel Johnson

The old futures have a way of hanging around. . . . Everyone sort of knows that the real future is going to be cluttered with all the same junk we have today, except it will be old and beat up and there will be more of it.

William Gibson

I would sum up my fear about the future in one word: boring. And that's my one fear: that everything has happened; nothing exciting or new or interesting is ever going to happen again. . . . The future is just going to be a vast, conforming suburb of the soul.

J.G. Ballard

If we can recognize that change and uncertainty are basic principles, we can greet the future and the transformation we are undergoing with the understanding that we do not know enough to be pessimistic.

Hazel Henderson

I've developed a new philosophy. I only dread one day at a time.

Charlie Brown, in Charles Schulz's *Peanuts*

It is only possible to live happily ever after on a day-to-day basis.

Margaret Bonnano

In order to be utterly happy the only thing necessary is to refrain from comparing this moment with other moments of the past, which I often did not fully enjoy because I was comparing them with other moments of the future.

André Gide

The man who sees two or three generations is like one who sits in the conjuror's booth at a fair and sees the tricks two or three times. They are meant to be seen only once.

Arthur Schopenhauer

Jane's gift of an apple. The sweet apple I didn't eat that day became the even sweeter apple I wouldn't eat any day. A year later, it has shrunk to half its original size, the red skin now pinched up all about it, its color the brown of milk chocolate. A whiskey smell up close. An intoxicating idea at a distance: to keep something beyond its time is somehow to have kept it forever. No way now to throw it out. The shrunken, fermented apple is not a version of the apple it was. It is another thing, to another purpose. I myself am a version of all that I could never, not in a million years, have imagined I would become.

Marvin Bell

What we call evil is only a necessary moment in our endless development.

Franz Kafka

Ferris glimpsed the disorder of his life: the succession of cities, of transitory loves; and time, the sinister glissando of the years, time always.

Carson McCullers, *The Sojourner*

The word *now* is like a bomb through the window, and it ticks.

Arthur Miller

Stress is an ignorant state. It believes that everything is an emergency. Nothing is that important. Just lie down.

Natalie Goldberg

He was caught in a rare moment of contentment that did not depend on the moment that would follow.

Anne Roiphe

However fashionable despair about the world and about people may be at present, and however powerful despair may become in the future, not everybody, or even most people, thinks and lives fashionably; virtue and honor will not be banished from the world, however many popular moralists and panicky journalists say so. Sacrifice will not cease to be because psychiatrists have popularized the idea that there is often some concealed self-serving element in it; theologians always knew that. Nor do I think love as a high condition of honor will be lost; it is a pattern in the spirit, and people long to make the pattern a reality in their own lives, whatever means they take to do so.

Robertson Davies, *The Manticore*

In this very breath that we take now lies the secret that all great teachers try to tell us.

Peter Matthiessen

O, how incomprehensible everything was, and actually sad, although it was also beautiful. One knew nothing. One lived and ran about the earth and rode through forests, and certain things looked so challenging and promising and nostalgic: a star in the evening, a blue harebell, a reed-green pond, the eye of a person or a cow. And sometimes it seemed that something never seen yet long desired was about to happen, that a veil would drop from it all; but then it passed, nothing happened, the riddle remained unsolved, the secret spell unbroken, and in the end one grew old and looked cunning . . . or wise . . . and still one knew nothing perhaps, was still waiting and listening.

Hermann Hesse,
Narcissus and Goldmund

In fact, I've come to the conclusion that I never did know anything about it.

Thomas Edison, on electricity

The present is like a doomed princess, elegant and inexpressibly beautiful.

Robert Grudin

By being both here and beyond / I am becoming a horizon.

Mark Strand

I am only one, but still I am one. I cannot do everything, but I can do something, and because I cannot do everything, I will not refuse to do the one thing I can do.

Edward Everett Hale

Thoroughly unprepared, we take the step into the afternoon of life; worse still, we take this step with the false assumption that our truths and ideals will serve us as hitherto. But we cannot live the afternoon of life according to the program of life's morning; for what was great in the morning will be little at evening, and what in the morning was true will at evening have become a lie.

Carl Jung

Not a runner knows where the light was lighted, not a runner knows where it carries fire to, / Hand kisses hand in the dark, the torch passes, the man / Falls, and the torch passes.

Robinson Jeffers

The world is full of hundreds of beautiful things we can never possibly have time to discover, and there is no time to be unkind or envious or ungenerous, and no sense in enslaving the mind to the trivialities of the moment. For you can be equal to the greatness of life only by marching with it; not by seeking love but by giving it, nor seeking to be understood but learning to understand. And when it is all over, there will be an agony of remorse because one spared the effort and did not make more of that little span of opportunity; and knowing reality at last, who knows but that one will look back with unassuageable regret upon one's pitiful little faith.

Vivienne de Watteville

Life is not lost by dying; life is lost minute by minute, day by dragging day, in all the thousand small uncaring ways.

Stephen Vincent Benét

As if you could kill time without injuring eternity.

Henry David Thoreau

Where does discontent start? You are warm enough, but you shiver. You are fed, yet hunger gnaws at you. You have been loved, but your yearning wanders in new fields. And to prod all these there's time, the Bastard Time.

John Steinbeck

Work as if you were to live a hundred years. Pray as if you were to die tomorrow.

Benjamin Franklin

Man is the only animal who has to be encouraged to live.

Friedrich Nietzsche

The fundamental delusion of humanity is to suppose that I am here and you are out there.

Yasutani Roshi

The divine will is an abyss of which the present moment is the entrance; plunge fearlessly therein and you will find it more boundless than your desires.

Jean-Pierre de Caussade

Exhaust the little moment. Soon it dies.

Gwendolyn Brooks

I tell you the past is a bucket of ashes.

Carl Sandburg

To be a warrior is to learn to be genuine in every moment of your life.

Chögyam Trungpa Rinpoche

Either I exist or I do not exist, and no amount of pap which I happen to be lapping can dull me to the loss.

William Carlos Williams

It is not hard to live through a day, if you can live through a moment. What creates despair is the imagination, which pretends there is a future, and insists on predicting millions of moments, thousands of days, and so drains you that you cannot live the moment at hand.

Andre Dubus

The only difference between me and a madman is that I'm not mad.

Salvador Dali

The ultimate destiny of the human spirit is a condition in which all identification with the . . . finite self will disappear. . . . As an inconsequential dream vanishes completely on awakening, as the stars go out in deference to the morning sun, so individual awareness will be eclipsed in the blazing light of total awareness. Some say, "The dewdrop slips into the shining sea." Others prefer to think of the dew-drop as opening to receive the sea itself.

Huston Smith

The young student said to his master, "Am I in possession of Buddha consciousness?" The master said, "No." The student said, "Well, I've been told that all things are in the possession of Buddha consciousness: the rocks, the trees, the butterflies, the birds, the animals, all beings." The master said, "You are correct. All things are in possession of Buddha consciousness: the rocks, the trees, the butterflies, the bees, the birds, the animals, all beings — but not you." "Not me? Why not?" "Because you are asking this question."

D.T. Suzuki

The question is asked, if life's journey be endless, where is its goal? The answer is, it is everywhere. We are in a palace which has no end, but which we have reached.

Rabindranath Tagore

One day we were born, one day we shall die, the same day, the same second, is that not enough for you?

Samuel Beckett,
Waiting for Godot

And now I have to confess the unpardonable and the scandalous in an age which scorns happiness. I am a happy man. And I am going to tell you the secret of my happiness. It is quite simple. I love mankind. I love love. I hate hate. I try to understand and accept.

Jean Cocteau

There it is. I don't believe in anything, but I'm always glad to wake up in the morning. It doesn't depress me. I'm never depressed. My basic nervous system is filled with this optimism. It's mad, I know, because it's optimism about nothing. I think of life as meaningless and yet it excites me. I always think something marvelous is about to happen.

Francis Bacon

Nonattachment is not the elimination of desire. It is the spaciousness to allow any quality of mind, any thought or feeling, to arise without closing around it, without eliminating the pure witness of being. It is an active receptivity to life.

Stephen Levine

So many gods, so many creeds, / So many paths that wind and wind, / While just the art of being kind, / Is all the sad world needs.

Ella Wheeler Wilcox

Before, I always lived in anticipation . . . that it was all a preparation for something else, something "greater," more "genuine." But that feeling has dropped away from me completely. I live here and now, this minute, this day, to the full, and the life is worth living.

Etty Hillesum

We should tackle reality in a slightly jokey way, otherwise we miss its point.

Lawrence Durrell

The greatest mystery is in unsheathed reality itself.

Eudora Welty

Things falling apart is a kind of testing and also a kind of healing. We think that the point is to pass the test or to overcome the problem, but the truth is that things don't really get solved. They come together and they fall apart. Then they come together again and fall apart again. It's just like that. The healing comes from letting there be room for all of this to happen: room for grief, for relief, for misery, for joy.

Pema Chödrön

"My feet are cold," one says, and the legless man replies: "So are mine. So are mine."

Kentucky folklore

The future is made of the same stuff as the present.

Simone Weil

One must be deeply aware of the impermanence of the world. . . . We are born in the morning and die in the evening; the man we saw yesterday is no longer with us today. . . . Think of what might happen today, this very moment. . . . Perhaps tonight, perhaps tomorrow, you will fall seriously ill; find your body racked with unendurable pain; die suddenly, cursed by some unknown demons; meet misfortune at the hands of robbers; or be slain by someone seeking vengeance. Life is indeed an uncertain thing. . . . It is absurd to plan your life, intrigue maliciously against others, and spend your time in fruitless pursuits.

Dōgen

Reb Bunam said, "You must imagine the evil spirit as a thug hovering over you with a raised hatchet to chop off your head." "What if I can't imagine it?" asked a Hasid. "That's a sure sign that he has already chopped it off."

Abraham Joseph Heschel

What a wonderful life I've had! I only wish I'd realized it sooner.

Colette

The highest art is the art of living an ordinary life in an extraordinary manner.

Tibetan proverb

The amelioration of the world cannot be achieved by sacrifices in moments of crisis; it depends on the efforts made and constantly repeated during the humdrum, uninspiring periods, which separate one crisis from another, and of which normal lives mainly consist.

Aldous Huxley

To allow oneself to be carried away by a multitude of conflicting concerns, to surrender to too many demands, to commit oneself to too many projects, to want to help everyone in everything is to succumb to violence.

Thomas Merton

I long to accomplish a great and noble task, but it is my chief duty and joy to accomplish humble tasks as though they were great and noble.

Helen Keller

I did not go to the Maggid of Mezeritch to learn Torah from him, but to watch him tie his boot laces.

A Hasidic rabbi

We have no art; we do everything as well as we can.

Balinese saying

One is always seeking the touchstone that will dissolve one's deficiencies as a person and as a craftsman. And one is always bumping up against the fact that there is none except hard work, concentration, and continued application.

Paul William Gallico

Anyone who can handle a needle convincingly can make us see a thread which is not there.

E.H. Gombrich

Strangely enough, the profound and the transcendental are to be found in the factory. It may not fill you with bliss to look at it, it may not sound as good as the spiritual experiences that we have read about, but somehow reality is to be found there, in the way in which we relate to everyday problems.

Chögyam Trungpa Rinpoche

Rabbi Moshe Leib of Sassov said: How to love men is something I learned from a peasant. He was sitting in an inn along with other peasants, drinking. For a long time he was silent as all the rest, but when he was moved by the wine, he asked one of the men seated beside him: "Tell me, do you love me or don't you love me?" The other replied: "I love you very much." But the first peasant replied: "You say that you love me, but you do not know what I need. If you really loved me you would know." The other had not a word to say to this, and the peasant who had put the question fell silent again. But I understood. To know the needs of men and to bear the burden of their sorrow — that is the true love of men.

Martin Buber

It may be that true happiness lies in the conviction that one has irremediably lost happiness. Then we can begin to move through life without hope or fear, capable of finally enjoying all the small pleasures, which are the most lasting.

María Luisa Bombal

If you imagine that once you have accomplished your ambitions you will have time to turn to the Way, you will discover that your ambitions never come to an end.

Yoshida Kenko

By memorable events are understood, in the murky bell jar of prison, things like getting potato soup instead of bean soup for the midday meal, a few privately exchanged words with the warder or the orderly, a cigarette given one by the warder, a spider in the window, or a bug in the bed. These are breathtaking experiences; they employ and stimulate the free-running mechanism of thought for hours at a time. They are substitutes for visits to the movies, making love, reading the newspapers, and the cares of daily life. Storms in teacups are, for those whose horizon extends no farther than the rim of the cup, quite as real as storms at sea.

Arthur Koestler

A spiritual truth, an object of our faith, which doesn't hold up in a prison cell or during an earthquake isn't a big enough truth.

Bo Lozoff

The little things? The little moments? They aren't little.

Jon Kabat-Zinn

☺

Sylvie, on her side, inhabited a millennial present. To her, the deteriorations of things were always a fresh surprise, a disappointment not to be dwelt on.

Marilynne Robinson,
Housekeeping

At the funeral of a great Hasidic master, a disciple was asked what was most important to his teacher. He responded, "Whatever he happened to be doing at the moment."

Hasidic story

One of the best means for arousing the wish to work on yourself is to realize that you may die at any moment. But first you must learn how to keep it in mind.

G.I. Gurdjieff

The present moment is a powerful goddess.

Johann Wolfgang von Goethe

Disciple: Is there no afterlife? What about punishment for our sins?
Lama Thubten Yeshe: Why not enjoy your chocolate? Your life is here and now. Birth is not a beginning; death is not an end.

Lama Thubten Yeshe

Each act is virgin, even the repeated one.
René Char

Even a stopped clock is right twice every day. After some years, it can boast of a long series of successes.

Marie von Ebner-Eschenbach

If we get used to life, that is the crime.
Jean Garrigue

Nothing ever gets anywhere. The earth keeps turning round and gets nowhere. The moment is the only thing that counts.

Jean Cocteau

Spring comes: the flowers learn their colored shapes.

Maria Konopnicka

You are sitting on the earth, and you realize that this earth deserves you and you deserve this earth. You are there fully, personally, genuinely.

Chögyam Trungpa Rinpoche

And the stars come down so close, and sadness and pleasure so close together, really the same thing. Like to stay drunk all the time. Who says it's bad? Who dares to say it's bad? Preachers — but they got their own kinda drunkenness. Thin, barren women, but they're too miserable to know. Reformers — but they don't bite deep enough into living to know. No — the stars are close and dear and I have joined the brotherhood of the worlds. And everything's holy — everything, even me.

John Steinbeck, *The Grapes of Wrath*

It appears that even the different parts of the same person do not converse among themselves, do not succeed in learning from each other what are their desires and their intentions.

Rebecca West

There are four legs to stand on. The first, be romantic. The second, be passionate. The third, be imaginative. And the fourth, never be rushed.

Charles Olson

It's a hard, sad life for most people. Don't scorn the simple things that give them pleasure.

D. Sutten

My goal in life is never to have a moment when I could not say, "This is how I want to die."

Mark DeBolt

☉

Life is like playing a violin solo in public and learning the instrument as one goes on.

Samuel Butler

You will never be happy if you continue to search for what happiness consists of. You will never live if you are looking for the meaning of life.

Albert Camus

A single day is enough to make us a little larger or, another time, a little smaller.

Paul Klee

I once saw in a cemetery in India an old woman just sobbing away at the grave of her son who had been tortured by Tamil terrorists. She spread herself over the whole grave and sobbed. And I . . . said to my companion, "I don't want to love if that is what love is." And he said, "Are you crazy? What she feels is so immeasurably beautiful because she grieves that much, she loves that much, and love lives on in her." Love's glory was in her weeping, love's glory was in her sobbing, love's glory was in her abandonment to her grief. That is love's glory, and love's glory has blood all over it.

Andrew Harvey

We become persons through dangerous experiences of darkness; we can survive these difficult initiations. Any real initiation is always a movement from death to new life.

Thomas Moore

It is the dread of something happening, something unknown and awful, that makes us do anything to keep the flicker of talk from dying out.

Logan Pearsall Smith

We are well-advised to keep on nodding terms with the people we used to be, whether we find them attractive company or not. Otherwise, they turn up unannounced and surprise us, come hammering on the mind's door at 4 A.M. of a bad night and demand to know why we deserted them, who betrayed them, who is going to make amends. We forget all too soon the things we thought we could never forget.

Joan Didion

To live several lives, you have to die several deaths.

Françoise Giroud

I remember Rudi [a friend and teacher] saying once that all life is about transcendence. If you're ugly you have to transcend your ugliness; if you're beautiful you have to transcend your beauty; if you're poor you have to transcend your poverty; if you're rich you have to transcend your wealth. . . . You get nothing at birth except things to transcend.

Milton Glaser

Your life feels different to you, once you greet death and understand your heart's position. You wear your life like a garment from the mission bundle sale ever after — lightly because you realize you never paid nothing for it, cherishing because you know you won't ever come by such a bargain again.

Louise Erdrich, *Love Medicine*

In a sense, we are all crashing to our death from the top story of our birth to the flat stones of the churchyard and wondering with an immortal Alice in Wonderland at the patterns of the passing wall.

Vladimir Nabokov

The event of creation did not take place so many aeons ago, astronomically or biologically speaking. Creation is taking place every moment of our lives.

D.T. Suzuki

Life has no meaning until one lives it with a will, at least to the limit of one's will. Virtue, good, evil are nothing but words, unless one takes them apart in order to build something with them; they do not win their true meaning until one knows how to apply them.

Paul Gauguin

I do believe it is possible to create, even without ever writing a word or painting a picture, by simply molding one's inner life. And that, too, is a deed.

Etty Hillesum

I have always known that at last I would take this road, but yesterday I did not know that it would be today.

Narihara

When one is young one doesn't feel a part of it yet, the human condition. One does things, because they are not for good, everything is a rehearsal . . . to be put right when the curtain goes up in earnest. One day you know that the curtain was up all the time. That was the performance.

Sybille Bedford

Life is that which — pressingly, persistently, unfailingly, imperially — interrupts.

Cynthia Ozick

When you eventually see through the veils / to how things really are, / you will keep saying, again and again, / "This is certainly not like we thought it was!"

Rumi

There is a woman who swam around Manhattan, and I asked her, "Why?" She said, "It hadn't ever been done before." Well, she didn't have to do that. If she wanted to do something no one had ever done before, all she had to do was vacuum my apartment.

Rita Rudner

All of life is a foreign country.

Jack Kerouac

There's an old joke: Two elderly women are at a Catskill Mountain resort and one of them says, "Boy, the food at this place is really terrible." The other one says, "Yeah, I know, and such small portions." Well, that's essentially how I feel about life.

Woody Allen

Life is short, but it's wide.

Spanish proverb

You are destined to fly, but that cocoon has to go.

Nelle Morton

The universe was not made in jest but in solemn incomprehensible earnest. By a power that is unfathomably secret, and holy, and fleet. There is nothing to be done about it but ignore it, or see. And then you walk fearlessly, eating what you must, growing wherever you can.

Annie Dillard

In many cases, people who've become aware of their mortality find that they've gained the freedom to live. They are seized with an appreciation for the present: every day is my best day; this is my life; I'm not going to have this moment again. They spend more time with the things and people they love and less time on people and pastimes that don't offer love or joy. This seems like such a simple thought — shouldn't we all spend our lives that way? But we tend not to make those kinds of choices until somebody says, "You have twelve months to live."

Bernie Siegel

❍

Reality is not protected or defended by laws, proclamations, ukases, cannons, and armadas. Reality is that which is sprouting all the time out of death and disintegration.

Henry Miller

You've never seen death? Look in the mirror every day and you will see it like bees working in a glass hive.

Jean Cocteau

When you don't have any money, the problem is food. When you have money, it's sex. When you have both, it's health. . . . If everything is simply jake, then you're frightened of death.

J.P. Donleavy

Every parting gives a foretaste of death, every reunion a hint of the Resurrection.

Arthur Schopenhauer

Draw your chair up close to the edge of the precipice and I'll tell you a story.

F. Scott Fitzgerald

It is written that when a man is hanged, he ejaculates. Is this ultimate proof that something good always comes from a stressful experience?

Jim Lewis

The irony of man's condition is that the deepest need is to be free of the anxiety of death and annihilation; but it is life itself which awakens it, and so we must shrink from being fully alive.

Ernest Becker

I know something about dread myself, and appreciate the elaborate systems with which some people manage to fill the void, appreciate all the opiates of the people.

Joan Didion

I'm for anything that gets you through the night, be it booze or religion.

Frank Sinatra

Carrying / a medicine for which no one had found / the disease and hoping / I would make it in time.

Richard Shelton

In the cellars of the night, when the mind starts moving around old trunks of bad times, the pain of this and the shame of that, the memory of a small boldness is a hand to hold.

John Leonard

I look back on my life like a good day's work. It was done and I feel satisfied with it.

Grandma Moses

The fact that our task is exactly as large as our life makes it appear infinite.

Franz Kafka

Love the moment, and the energy of that moment will spread beyond all boundaries.

Corita Kent

In God's economy, nothing is wasted. Through failure, we learn a lesson in humility which is probably needed, painful though it is.

Bill Wilson

Sure we're all one, but — shh — don't spread it around.

Jay Lynch

Although it takes us many years and many tears to discover it, life is only another name for death; they cannot exist independently.

Kathleen Norris

Life is like Sanskrit read to a pony.

Lou Reed

Guns are always the best method for a private suicide. They are more stylish looking than single-edged razor blades, and natural gas has gotten so expensive. Drugs are too chancy. You might miscalculate the dosage and just have a good time.

P.J. O'Rourke

The birth of a man is the birth of his sorrow. The longer he lives, the more stupid he becomes, because his anxiety to avoid unavoidable death becomes more and more acute. What bitterness! He lives for what is always out of reach! His thirst for survival in the future makes him incapable of living in the present.

Chuang Tzu

I've stopped thinking all the time of what happened yesterday. And stopped asking myself what's going to happen tomorrow. What's happening today, this minute, is what I care about. I say: What are you doing at this moment, Zorba? . . . I'm kissing a woman. Well, kiss her well, Zorba. And forget all the rest while you're doing it; there's nothing else on earth, only you and her!

Nikos Kazantzakis,
Zorba the Greek

From the cowardice that shrinks from new truth, / From the laziness that is content with half-truths, / From the arrogance that thinks it knows all truth, / O God of Truth, deliver us.

Ancient prayer

The coming to consciousness is not a discovery of some new thing; it is a long and painful return to that which has always been. . . . It is when we admit our powerlessness that the guide appears.

Helen Luke

A primary cause of suffering is delusion: our inability . . . to see things the way they truly are. . . . The world is in fact a seamless and dynamic unity: a single living organism that is constantly undergoing change. Our minds, however, chop it up into separate, static bits and pieces, which we then try mentally and physically to manipulate. One of the mind's most dear creations is the idea of the person and, closest to home, of a very special person which each one of us calls "I": a separate, enduring ego or self. In a moment, then, the seamless universe is cut in two. There is "I" — and there is all the rest.

John Snelling

Once again, as in the sixties, many of us sense the door of collective awareness opening, albeit slightly, allowing for the possibility that our lives together, as a society, could be lived with more consciousness and compassion.

Ram Dass

It may be that we are doomed, that there is no hope for us, any of us, but if that is so then let us set up a last agonizing, bloodcurdling howl, a screech of defiance, a war whoop! Away with lamentation! Away with elegies and dirges! Away with biographies and histories, and libraries and museums! Let the dead eat the dead. Let us living ones dance about the rim of the crater, a last expiring dance. But a dance!

Henry Miller

Maybe the things I perceive, the animals, plants, men, hills, / shining and flowing waters, / The skies of day and night, colors, densities, forms, / maybe these are (as doubtless they are) only apparitions, / and the real something has yet to be known.

Walt Whitman

Our black cat lay on the windowsill, against the black night outside. When his eyes were open, his body was visible, dimly outlined; but as soon as he closed them, the whole cat vanished, leaving only the unbroken darkness of the window.

Rudolf Arnheim

Because consciousness must involve both pleasure and pain, to strive for pleasure to the exclusion of pain is, in effect, to strive for the loss of consciousness.

Alan Watts

Like it or not, we are slaves of the hour and its colors and forms, subjects of the sky and the earth. Even that part of us that burrows deepest into itself, dis-

daining its surroundings, does not burrow along the same paths when it rains as when the sky is clear.

Fernando Pessoa

One bright, moonlit night a messenger thrust a note into the anteroom where I was staying. On a sheet of magnificent scarlet paper, I read the words, "There is nothing." It was the moonlight that made this so delightful; I wonder whether I would have enjoyed it at all on a rainy night.

The Pillow Book of Sei Shonagon

Be very careful about locating good or God, right or wrong, legal or illegal, at your favorite level of consciousness.

Timothy Leary

Country people do not behave as if they think life is short; they live on the principle that it is long, and savor variations of the kind best appreciated if most days are the same.

Edward Hoagland

We imagine that our mind is a mirror, that it is more or less accurately reflecting what is happening outside us. On the contrary, our mind itself is the principal element of creation.

Rabindranath Tagore

Never in any case say, "I have lost such a thing," but, "I have returned it." Is your child dead? It is a return. Is your wife dead? It is a return. Are you deprived of your estate? Is this not also a return?

Epictetus

The Great Way is obvious to all my friends. They point it out quite readily on request, sometimes without request. Their words are painful because they threaten my character. I have to choose between the Great Way and me. An easy choice on paper — a hard one in fact.

Robert Aitken

[J.] Krishnamurti was in a car with three friends who were heatedly discussing "awareness." There was a jolt to the car but no one paid any attention as they were all intent upon the arguments. Krishnamurti turned to them and asked what everyone was discussing. "Awareness" came the reply and they all wanted him to join. He asked, "Did any of you notice what happened just now?" "No." "We knocked down a goat. Did you not see it?" "No." "And you were discussing awareness?"

Pupul Jayakar

All shall be well, and all shall be well, and all manner of thing shall be well.

Julian of Norwich

I saw that the universe is not composed of dead matter, but is, on the contrary, a living Presence; I became conscious in myself of eternal life. It was not a conviction that I would have eternal life, but a consciousness that I possessed eternal life then; I saw that all men are immortal; that the cosmic order is such that without any peradventure all things work together for the good of each and all; that the foundation principle of the world, of all the worlds, is what we call love, and that the happiness of each and all is in the long run absolutely certain.

The vision lasted a few seconds and was gone, but the memory of it and the sense of the reality of what it taught has remained during the quarter of a century which has since elapsed.

R.M. Bucke

The hunger of the spirit for eternity — as fierce as a starving man's for bread — is much less a craving to go on living than a craving for redemption. Oh, and a protest against absurdity.

Storm Jameson

If logic tells you that life is a meaningless accident, don't give up on life. Give up on logic.

Shira Milgrom

ℭ

The Buddhist Sutra of Mindfulness speaks about the meditation on the corpse: meditate on the decomposition of the body, how the body bloats and turns violet, how it is eaten by worms until only bits of blood and flesh still cling to the bones. Meditate up to the point where only white bones remain, which in turn are slowly worn away and turn to dust. Meditate like that, knowing that your own body will undergo the same process. Meditate on the corpse until you are calm and at peace, until your mind and heart are light and tranquil and a smile appears on your face. Thus, by overcoming revulsion and fear, life will be seen as infinitely precious, every second of it worth living.

Thich Nhat Hanh

I've never been very good at feasting on the daily newspaper. It turns bitter in my mouth. And yet, this is my world. This face of suffering I must embrace as a part of my responsibility. Part of the feast is becoming aware of the world that is mine. Part of the feast is owning this broken world as my own brokenness.

Macrina Wiederkehr

Those who are awake all live in the same world. Those who are asleep live in their own worlds.

Heraclitus

We all hope for a . . . recipe; we all believe, however much we know we shouldn't, that maybe somebody's got that recipe and can show how not to be sick, suffer, and die.

Nan Shin

Nature has no mercy at all. Nature says, "I'm going to snow. If you have on a bikini and no snowshoes, that's tough. I am going to snow anyway."

Maya Angelou

They gave him a seashell: "So you'll learn to love the water." They opened a cage and let a bird go free: "So you'll learn to love the air." They gave him a geranium: "So you'll learn to love the earth." And they gave him a little bottle sealed up tight. "Don't ever, ever open it. So you'll learn to love mystery."

Eduardo Galeano

It is good that fire should burn, even if it consumes your house; it is good that force should crush, even if it crushes you; it is good that rain should fall, even if it destroys your crops and floods your land. Plagues and pestilences attest to the constancy of natural law. They set us to cleaning our streets and houses and to readjusting our relations to outward nature. Only in a live universe could disease and death prevail. Death is a phase of life, a redistribution of the type. Decay is another kind of growth.

John Burroughs

I knew nothing of reality until Mummy died. She shielded us from everything. And then suddenly I was having to deal with the butler, the two chauffeurs, the cook, and everything else.

Charlotte Brown (nee de Rothschild)

I've a strong impression our world is about to go under. Our political systems are deeply compromised and have no further uses. Our social behavior patterns, interior and exterior, have proved a fiasco. The tragic thing is, we neither can nor want, nor have the strength, to alter our course. It's too late for revolutions, and deep down inside ourselves we no longer even believe in their positive effects. Just around the corner an insect world is waiting — and one day it's going to roll over our ultra-individualized existence. Otherwise, I'm a respectable Social Democrat.

Ingmar Bergman

Like a harp / burning on an island / nobody knows about.

James Tate

If, every day, I dare to remember that I am here on loan, that this house, this hillside, these minutes, are all leased to me, not given, I will never despair. Despair is for those who expect to live forever. I no longer do.

Erica Jong

Despair, surely the least aggressive of sins, is dangerous to the totalitarian temperament because it is a state of intense inwardness, thus independence. The despairing soul is a rebel.

Joyce Carol Oates

The stabbing horror of life is not contained in calamities and disasters, because these things wake one up and one gets very familiar and intimate with them and finally they become tame again. . . . No, it is more like being in a hotel room in Hoboken, let us say, and just enough money in one's pocket for another meal.

Henry Miller

No one has the right to sit down and feel hopeless. There's too much work to do.

Dorothy Day

Noble deeds and hot baths are the best cures for depression.

Dodie Smith

The village had no rain for a long time. All the prayers and processions had been in vain; the skies remained shut tight. In the hour of its greatest need, the village turned to the great rainmaker. He came and asked for a hut on the edge of the village and for a five-day supply of bread and water. Then he sent the people off to their daily work. On the fourth day it rained. The people . . . gathered in front of the rainmaker's hut to congratulate him and ask him about the mystery of rainmaking. He answered them, "I can't make it rain." "But it is raining," the people said. The rainmaker explained: "When I came to your village, I saw the inner and outer disorder. I went into the hut and got myself in order. When I was in order, you, too, got in order; and when you were in order, nature got in order; and when nature got in order, it rained."

Willigis Jager

☉

The whole secret lies in arbitrariness. . . . You go to see the middle of a play, you read the third part of a book. By this means you ensure yourself a very different kind of enjoyment from that which the author has been so kind as to plan for you. You enjoy something entirely accidental; you consider the whole of existence from this standpoint.

Søren Kierkegaard

His vocation was orderliness, which is the basis of creation. Accordingly, when a letter came, he would turn it over in his hands for a long time, gazing at it meditatively; then he would put it away in a file without opening it, because everything had its own time.

Salvatore Satta,
The Day of Judgment

There is no human problem which could not be solved if people would simply do as I advise.

Gore Vidal

The miracle is not to walk on water. The miracle is to walk on the green earth in the present moment, to appreciate the peace and beauty that are available now. . . . It is not a matter of faith; it is a matter of practice.

Thich Nhat Hanh

One cannot weep for the entire world. It is beyond human strength. One must choose.

Jean Anouilh

Nothing in life is trivial. Life is whole wherever and whenever we touch it, and one moment or event is not less sacred than another.

Vimala Thakar

If someone comes to you asking for help, do not say in refusal, "Trust in God. God will help you." Rather, act as if there is no God, and no one to help except you.

Hasidic teaching

There are too many distractions. You should enter a ballpark as you would enter a church.

Bill Lee

Who were the mad and who the sane? . . . People sold themselves for jobs, for the paycheck, and if they only received a high enough price, they were honored. If their cheating, their theft, their lie were of colossal proportions, if it were successful, they met with praise, not blame.

Dorothy Day

If you would convince a man that he does wrong, do right. But do not care to convince him. Men will believe what they see. Let them see.

Henry David Thoreau

Be careful how you live. You may be the only Bible some person ever reads.

William J. Toms

I didn't make myself, and you didn't make yourself. I didn't do all those things myself. It was done for me. We don't choose to draw air into our own lungs. God does it for us. He's using me for a vessel.

Muhammad Ali

Look at every path closely and deliberately. Try it as many times as you think necessary. Then ask yourself, and yourself alone, one question. Does the path have a heart? The trouble is nobody asks the question; and when a man finally realizes that he has taken a path without a heart, the path is ready to kill him. At that point, very few men can stop to deliberate and leave the path.

Carlos Castaneda

Many of us have no long-range vision in much of our struggle. We think only of the moment, this time, this place, this circumstance. But think of the ten generations of children that inherit love, and their children, and theirs. . . . Anyone can count the seeds of an apple. Who can count the apples in a seed?

Stephen Covey

Life always gets harder toward the summit — the cold increases, responsibility increases.

Friedrich Nietzsche

Life is an onion which one peels crying.

French proverb

The world breaks everyone and afterward many are strong at the broken places.

Ernest Hemingway

A friend's son was in the first grade. His teacher asked the class, "What is the color of apples?" Most of the children answered red. A few said green. Kevin, my friend's son, raised his hand and said white. The teacher tried to explain that apples could be red, green, or sometimes golden, but never white. Kevin was quite insistent and finally said, "Look inside."

Joseph Goldstein

☉

How easily we slide into thinking of our prayers as the "real" prayer. What is the "real" prayer — the grace we say at the table, or the meal that follows it? ... And if we pray at all times, as we should, our eating and drinking will be real prayer. ... Gratefulness will turn the whole meal into prayer, for after we pray our prayers, we will pray our soup, salad and dessert, and then pray another set prayer at the end as a reminder to continue to pray even after the meal. ... It is not prayers that count, but prayerfulness.

David Steindl-Rast

How easy it is to misunderstand. How innocently we find ourselves believing that our pain and loneliness are something other than a version of a deep longing to know and to feel God's presence within. ... When we finally know our problems to be prayers and are willing to look away from distraction, then we will know from within the presence of One who cares.

Stephen R. Schwartz

Opening the window, I open myself.

Natalya Gorbanevskaya

There's a phrase in West Africa called "deep talk." When a person is informed about a situation, an older person will often use a parable, an axiom, and then add to the end of the axiom, "Take that as deep talk." Meaning that you will never find the answer. You can continue to go down deeper and deeper.

Maya Angelou

It is a long baptism into the seas of humankind, my daughter. Better immersion than to live untouched.

Tillie Olsen,
from the short story "O Yes"

Observe things as they are and don't pay attention to other people.

Huang Po

The world is quite right. It does not have to be consistent.

Charlotte Perkins Gilman

There is no reality except the one contained within us. That is why so many people live such an unreal life. They take the images outside them for reality and never allow the world within to assert itself.

Hermann Hesse

I like reality. It tastes of bread.

Jean Anouilh

While Georgia Lloyd-Jones and her family were dashing about their leaking living room with pots and pans during a downpour in Tulsa, Oklahoma, she made a wry observation about the house her husband's cousin, Frank Lloyd Wright, had designed for them in 1929. "Well," she said, "this is what we get for leaving a work of art out in the rain." Her less equable husband later called his architect long distance. "Damn it, Frank," he shouted, "it's leaking on my desk!" Wright calmly replied, "Richard, why don't you move your desk?"

Thomas S. Hines

There is a bird in a poem by T.S. Eliot who says that mankind cannot bear very much reality; but the bird is mistaken. A man can endure the entire weight of the universe for eighty years. It is unreality that he cannot bear.

Ursula K. Le Guin

We always affirm with conditions. I affirm the world on condition that it gets to be the way Santa Claus told me it ought to be. But affirming it the way it is — that's the hard thing.

Joseph Campbell

Conduct your blooming in the noise and whip of the whirlwind.

Gwendolyn Brooks

Life is better than death, I believe, if only because it is less boring, and because it has fresh peaches in it.

Alice Walker

If you wish to drown, do not torture yourself with shallow water.

Bulgarian proverb

Fate is not an eagle; it creeps like a rat.

Elizabeth Bowen

If you can't change your fate, change your attitude.

Amy Tan

If you don't change your beliefs, your life will be like this forever. Is this good news?

Robert Anthony

Look, we're all the same; a man is a fourteen-room house — in the bedroom he's asleep with his intelligent wife, in the living room he's rolling around with some bare-assed girl, in the library he's paying his taxes, in the yard he's raising tomatoes, and in the cellar he's making a bomb to blow it all up.

Arthur Miller,
Ride Down Mount Morgan

She felt again that small shiver that occurred to her when events hinted at a destiny being played out, of unseen forces intervening.

Dorothy Gilman,
Mrs. Pollifax and the Whirling Dervish

However intense my experience, I am conscious of the presence and criticism of a part of me which, as it were, is not a part of me, but a spectator, sharing no experience, but taking note of it, and that is no more I than it is you. When the play — it may be the tragedy — of life is over, the spectator goes his way. It was a kind of fiction, a work of the imagination only, so far as he was concerned.

Henry David Thoreau

Darkness was upon the face of the deep, and God said, "Let there be light." Darkness laps at my sleeping face like a tide, and God says, "Let there be Buechner." Why not? Out of the primeval chaos of sleep he calls me to life again. . . . He calls me to be this rather than that; he calls me to be here rather than there; he calls me to be now rather than then.

Frederick Buechner

A name is a road.

Iris Murdoch

We are the protagonists and the authors of our own drama. It is up to us; there is no one left to blame. Neither the "system," nor our leaders, nor our parents. We can't go out and hang the first amoeba.

Rebecca McClen Novick

Every damn thing is your own fault, if you're any good.

Ernest Hemingway

Take your life in your own hands and what happens? A terrible thing: no one to blame.

Erica Jong

There is a luxury in self-reproach. When we blame ourselves, we feel that no one else has a right to blame us.

Oscar Wilde

Some people once brought a blind man to Jesus and asked him, "Rabbi, who sinned, this man or his parents, that he was born blind?" They all wanted to know why this terrible curse had fallen on this man. And Jesus answered, "It was not that this man sinned, or his parents, but that the works of God might be made manifest in him." He told them not to look for why the suffering came but to listen for what the suffering could teach them. Jesus taught that our pain is not punishment; it is no one's fault. When we seek to blame, we distract ourselves from an exquisite opportunity to pay attention, to see even in this pain a place of grace, a moment of spiritual promise and healing.

Wayne Muller

I am not afraid. . . . I was born to do this.

Joan of Arc

☾

Nor is it certain how long you will live. . . . Your life is like the flame of a butter lamp in a hurricane, a bubble on water, or a drop of dew on a blade of grass.

Kalu Rinpoche

Millions long for immortality who don't know what to do with themselves on a rainy Sunday afternoon.

Susan Ertz

Time is the only true purgatory.

Samuel Butler

Time and space are fragments of the infinite for the use of finite creatures.

Henri Frederic Amiel

The today that never comes on time.

Octavio Paz

Trying to control thoughts with thoughts is like trying to bite your own teeth.

Alan Watts

The fact that we are totally unable to imagine a form of existence without space and time by no means proves that such an existence is itself impossible.

Carl Jung

Everything that has a beginning has an ending. Make your peace with that and all will be well.

The Buddha

Reality is a staircase going neither up nor down. We don't move, today is today, always is today.

Octavio Paz

The rules are simple — start on dry land, finish on dry land.

Mike Read, on swimming the English Channel

He has learned to touch his way across the bedroom in the pitch dark, touching the glass top of the bedside table and then with an outreached arm after a few blind steps the slick varnished edge of the high bureau, and from there to the knob of the bathroom door. Each touch, it occurs to him every night, leaves a little deposit of sweat and oil from the skin of his fingertips; eventually it will darken the varnished bureau edge . . . and that accumulated deposit of his groping touch, he sometimes thinks when the safety of the bathroom and its luminescent light switch has been attained, will still be there, a shadow on the varnish, a microscopic cloud of his body oils, when he is gone.

John Updike, *Rabbit at Rest*

Set out from any point. They are all alike. They all lead to a point of departure.

Antonio Porchia

Time, when it is left to itself and no definite demands are made on it, cannot be trusted to move at any recognized pace. Usually, it loiters; but just when one has come to count upon its slowness, it may suddenly break into a wild, irrational gallop.

Edith Wharton

One must be deeply aware of the impermanence of the world. This realization is not achieved by some temporary method of contemplation. It is not creating something out of nothing and then thinking about it. Impermanence is a fact before our eyes. Do not wait for the teachings from others, the words of the scriptures, and for the principles of enlightenment. We are born in the morning and we die in the evening; the man we saw yesterday is no longer with us today.

Bodhin Kjolhede

The supreme value is not the future but the present. The future is a deceitful time that always says to us, "Not yet," and thus denies us. The future is not the time of love: what man truly wants he wants now. Whoever builds a house for future happiness builds a prison for the present.

Octavio Paz

[The famous French soldier Marshal Lyautey] asked his gardener to plant a row of trees of a certain rare variety in his garden the next morning. The gardener said he would be glad to do so, but he cautioned the marshal that trees of this type take a century to grow to full size. "In that case," replied Lyautey, "plant them this afternoon."

Douglas R. Hofstadter

You lose an umbrella. You can also lose time.

Gabriella Roepke

Time pulses from the afternoon like blood from a serious wound.

Hilma Wolitzer

Any time that is not spent on love is wasted.

Torquato Tasso

The disease of Tomorrow.

G.I. Gurdjieff

You phone the Time Lady and listen to her tell the minutes and seconds. . . . She distinctly names the present moment, never slipping into the past or sliding into the future.

Maxine Hong Kingston

I wish I could have known earlier that you have all the time you need right up to the day you die.

William Wiley

I have always liked the story about Johnny Kerr, the pro basketball player with bad legs who set a record for consecutive games. Clearly, he played in pain. After he had set the record, he was asked how he could play hurt night after night. His answer: "I tell my legs lies."

Richard Kehl

The danger is not lest the soul should doubt whether there is any bread, but lest, by a lie, it should persuade itself that it is not hungry.

Simone Weil

I hate it when people pray on the screen. It's not because I hate praying, but whenever I see an actor fold his hands and look up in the spotlight, I'm lost. There's only one thing in the movies I hate as much, and that's sex. You just can't get in bed or pray to God and convince me on the screen.

Orson Welles

You pray in your distress and in your need; would that you might pray also in the fullness of your joy and in your days of abundance.

Khalil Gibran

Prayer does not use any artificial energy, it doesn't burn up any fossil fuel, it doesn't pollute.

Margaret Mead

Does God have a set way of prayer, a way that he expects each of us to follow? I doubt it. I believe some people — lots of people — pray through the witness of their lives, through the work they do, the friendships they have, the love they offer people and receive from people. Since when are words the only acceptable form of prayer?

Dorothy Day

I throw myself down in my chamber . . . and invite God and his Angels thither, and when they are there, I neglect God and his Angels for the noise of a fly, for the rattling of a coach, for the whining of a door.

John Donne

Don't pray when it rains if you don't pray when the sun shines.

Satchel Paige

If prayers worked, Hitler would have been stopped at the border of Poland by angels with swords of fire.

Nancy Willard

Life is God's novel. Let him write it.

Isaac Bashevis Singer

Bill Moyers, [Lyndon] Johnson's press secretary, was saying grace when Johnson bellowed: "Speak up, Bill. I can't hear a damn thing."

Moyers looked up and said quietly,

"I wasn't addressing you, Mr. President."

Paul F. Boller

⟲

Flowers are without hope. Because hope is tomorrow and flowers have no tomorrow.

Antonio Porchia

You see I thought love got easier over the years so it didn't hurt so bad when it hurt, or feel so good when it felt good. I thought it smoothed out and old people hardly noticed it. I thought it curled up and died, I guess. Now I saw it rear up like a whip and lash.

Louise Erdrich, *Love Medicine*

One must stop before one has finished.

Barbara Tuchman

The great thing is to last and get your work done and see and hear and learn and understand and write when there is something that you know; and not before; and not too damned much after.

Ernest Hemingway

The only thing one can be proud of is of having worked in such a way that an official reward for your labor cannot be envisaged by anyone.

Jean Cocteau

Everyone has a talent at twenty-five. The difficulty is to have it at fifty.

Edgar Degas

All human life has its seasons, and no one's personal chaos can be permanent: winter, after all, does not last forever, does it? There is summer, too, and spring, though sometimes when branches stay dark and the earth cracks with ice, one thinks they will never come, that spring, that summer, but they do, and always.

Truman Capote

It takes a long time to understand nothing.

Edward Dahlberg

Life does not accommodate you, it shatters you. It is meant to, and it couldn't do it better. Every seed destroys its container or else there would be no fruition.

Florida Scott-Maxwell

My book is the man I am, the confused man, the negligent man, the reckless man, the lusty, obscene, boisterous, thoughtful, scrupulous, lying, diabolically truthful man that I am.

Henry Miller

Memory, the priestess, kills the present / and offers its heart to the shrine of the dead past.

Rabindranath Tagore

The late F.W.H. Meyers used to tell how he asked a man at a dinner table what he thought would happen to him when he died. The man tried to ignore the question, but on being pressed, replied: "Oh well, I suppose I shall inherit eternal bliss, but I wish you wouldn't talk about such unpleasant subjects."

Bertrand Russell

Die in your thoughts every morning and you will no longer fear death.

Hagakure

In this world we live in a mixture of time and eternity. Hell would be pure time.

Simone Weil

A person who cannot move and live a somewhat normal life because he is pinned under a boulder has more time to think about his hopes than someone who is not trapped that way.

Václav Havel

Time is the substance from which I am made. Time is a river which carries me along, but I am the river; it is a tiger that devours me, but I am the tiger; it is a fire that consumes me, but I am the fire.

Jorge Luis Borges

Life is not long, and too much of it must not pass in idle deliberation of how it shall be spent.

Samuel Johnson

Eat chocolate now. After you're dead there isn't any.

Jean Powell

The present is the only thing that has no end.

Erwin Schrödinger

Sundays are terrible because it is clear that there is no one in charge of the world. And this knowledge leaves you drifting around, grappling with unfulfilled expectations and vague yearnings.

Sheila Ballantyne

Coming late, as always, / I try to remember what I almost heard.

W.S. Merwin

Time . . . is not a great healer. It is an indifferent and perfunctory one. Sometimes it does not heal at all. And sometimes when it seems to, no healing has been necessary.

Ivy Compton-Burnett

Time is a great traitor who teaches us to accept loss.

Elizabeth Borton de Treviño

The day I was imprisoned, / I had a small pencil / which I used up within a week. / If you ask the pencil, it will say, / "My whole lifetime." / If you ask me, I'll say, / "So what? Only a week."

Nazim Hikmet

৬

Into The Darkness They Go

Into the darkness they go, the wise and the lovely.

Edna St. Vincent Millay

I acknowledge the cold truth of her death for perhaps the first time. She is truly gone, forever out of reach, and I have become my own judge.

Sheila Ballantyne

I'm OK. So thankful to God. Had him sixty-six years and now I'm glad to give him back to God.

Rubye Stronger, on the death of her eighty-nine-year-old husband, Bill

The length of our life is less important than its depth.

Mary David Fisher

If I had my life over again I should form the habit of nightly composing myself to thoughts of death. I would practice, as it were, the remembrance of death. There is no other practice which so intensifies life. Death, when it approaches, ought not to take one by surprise. It should be part of the full expectancy of life. Without an ever-present sense of death, life is insipid. You might as well live on the whites of eggs.

Muriel Spark, *Memento Mori*

Oh God! May I be alive when I die.

D.W. Winnicott

Mystery on all sides! And faith the only star in this darkness and uncertainty.

Henri Amiel

Alas, the world is full of enormous lights and mysteries, and man shuts them from himself with one small hand!

Baal Shem Tov

Births and deaths don't confine your life; there have been many births and many deaths. Births and deaths are just small episodes in the eternity of your life, and the moment you become aware of this eternity — another name for now, this timelessness — all fear, all anxiety about death immediately evaporates.

Bhagwan Shree Rajneesh

It is hard to have patience with people who say, "There is no death," or "Death doesn't matter." There is death. And whatever is, matters. And whatever happens has consequences, and it and they are irrevocable and irreversible. You might as well say that birth doesn't matter.

C.S. Lewis

I'm trying to die correctly, but it's very difficult, you know.

Lawrence Durrell

Let nothing disturb you. Let nothing frighten you. Everything passes away except God.

Saint Teresa of Avila

Danger past, God is forgotten.

Thomas Fuller

By daily dying I have come to be.

Theodore Roethke

Oscar Wilde, on his deathbed, was drifting in and out of consciousness. Once, when he opened his eyes, he was heard to murmur, "This wallpaper is killing me; one of us has got to go."

Richard Kehl

Human beings are afraid of dying. They are always running after something: money, honor, pleasure. But if you had to die now, what would you want?

Taisen Deshimaru

When death, the great reconciler, has come, it is never our tenderness we repent of, but our severity.

George Eliot

The dead carry with them to the grave in their clutched hands only that which they have given away.

DeWitt Wallace

I think that the dying pray at the last not please but thank you, as a guest thanks his host at the door. Falling from airplanes the people are crying thank you, thank you, all down the air; and the cold carriages draw up for them on the rocks.

Annie Dillard

On his deathbed he had asked, still insatiable, to be lifted up in order that he could catch through the window a glimpse of one more spring.

**Loren Eiseley, on
Henry David Thoreau**

It was typical of him that he lacked the taste to make a final exit. He spent too long at his farewells, chatting in the doorway, letting in the cold.

**Anne Tyler,
Dinner at the Homesick Restaurant**

We die, and we do not die.

Shunryu Suzuki

Rachmaninoff . . . was laid low in the middle of a concert tour. It was cancer. He was put into a hospital in Los Angeles, and he knew his end was near. He looked at his hands. "My dear hands. Farewell, my poor hands."

Harold Schonberg

It's never been my experience that men part with life any more readily at eighty than they do at eighteen.

Anthony Gilbert

Noon one may keep as one will, but evening sets in on its own account.

Swedish proverb

Toulouse-Lautrec was lying on his bed, dying, when his father, an old eccentric, came to see him and began catching flies. Lautrec said, "Old fool!" and died.

Jules Reynard

Live as you will wish to have lived when you are dying.

Christian Gellert

We do survive every moment, after all, except the last one.

John Updike

What is hardest to accept about the passage of time is that the people who once mattered the most to us are wrapped up in parentheses.

John Irving

Into the darkness they go, the wise and the lovely.

Edna St. Vincent Millay

Dante says that the journey begins right here. In the middle of the road. Right beneath your feet. This is the place. There is no other place and no other time. Even if you are successful and follow the road you have set yourself, you can never leave here. Despite everything you have achieved, life refuses to grant you immunity from its difficulties. Becoming aware of this after a lifetime of accepting success as the ultimate healing balm is, declares Dante, like waking up in a dark wood.

David Whyte

It is only when we realize that life is taking us nowhere that it begins to have meaning.

P.D. Ouspensky

The most important thing I learned on Tralfamadore was that when a person dies he only appears to die. He is still very much alive in the past, so it is very silly for people to cry at his funeral. All moments, past, present, and future, always have existed, always will exist. The Tralfamadorians can look at all the different moments just the way we can look at a stretch of the Rocky Mountains, for instance. They can see how permanent all the moments are, and they can look at any moment that interests them. It is just an illusion we have here on earth that one moment follows another one, like beads on a string, and that once a moment is gone it is gone forever.

Kurt Vonnegut,
Slaughterhouse-Five

Wishing to be known only for what one really is is like putting on an old, easy, comfortable garment. You are no longer afraid of anybody or anything. You say to yourself, "Here I am — just so ugly, dull, poor, beautiful, rich, interesting, amusing, ridiculous. Take me or leave me. . . ." It is like a great burden rolled off a man's back when he comes to want to appear nothing that he is not, to take out of life only what is truly his own, and to wait for something strong and deep within him or behind him to work through him.

David Grayson

For some strange reason, we believe that anyone who lived before we were born was in some peculiar way a different kind of human being from any we have come in contact with in our own lifetime. This concept must be changed; we must realize in our bones that almost everything in time and history has changed except the human being.

Uta Hagen

Do not cherish the unworthy desire that the changeable might become the unchanging.

The Buddha

If it is hard to believe in God, it is no easier to believe in man.

Margot Asquith

Do you think that the same power that gave you radiance in the womb would abandon you now? It is you who have turned away and walked alone into the dark.

Kabir

Death destroys the body, as the scaffolding is destroyed after the building is up and finished. And he whose building is up rejoices at the destruction of the scaffolding and of the body.

Leo Tolstoy

The only way into truth is through one's own annihilation; through dwelling a long time in a state of extreme and total humiliation.

Simone Weil

Surprise will be my last emotion, not fear.

Storm Jameson

Death is patiently making my mask as I sleep. Each morning I awake to discover in the corners of my eyes the small tears of his wax.

Philip Dow

Death transfigured her. In a matter of minutes I saw the beauty of her young days reassert itself on her blurred care-worn face. It was like something in music, the reestablishment of the original key, the return of the theme.

Sylvia Townsend Warner

*

When Pablo Casals reached ninety-five, a young reporter asked him a question: "Mr. Casals, you are ninety-five and the greatest cellist who ever lived. Why do you still practice six hours a day?" Casals answered, "Because I think I'm making progress."

Source unknown

No one will ever get out of this world alive. Resolve therefore to maintain a reasonable perspective and sense of values.

Lloyd Shearer

Everything is a little bit of darkness, even the light.

Antonio Porchia

When my grandmother was dying of cancer, she wanted to live to see the roses in her garden in June. When they came, it was as if she was seeing the fullness and glory of the world for the first time: Christ's blood flowing through the rose.

Andrew Harvey

It was gorgeous traffic, it was beautiful traffic — that's what was not usual. It was a beauty to see, to hear, to smell, even to be part of. It was so dazzlingly alive it all but took my breath away. It rattled and honked and chattered with life — the people, the colors of their clothes, the marvelous hodgepodge of their faces, all of it; the taxis, the shops, the blinding sidewalks. The spring day made everybody a celebrity — blacks, whites, Hispanics, every last one of them. It made even the litter and clamor and turmoil of it a kind of miracle.

Frederick Buechner

I have nothing new to teach the world. Truth and nonviolence are as old as the hills. All I have done is to try experiments in both on as vast a scale as I could.

Mohandas K. Gandhi

While you have a thing it can be taken from you . . . but when you give it, you have given it. No robber can take it from you. It is yours then forever when you have given it. It will be yours always.

James Joyce

Experience, which destroys innocence, also leads one back to it.

James Baldwin

Whether people are beautiful or plain, friendly or cruel, ultimately they are human beings, just like oneself. Like oneself, they want happiness and do not want suffering. Furthermore, their right to overcome suffering and be happy is equal to one's own. Now, when you recognize that . . . you automatically feel empathy and closeness for them. Through accustoming your mind to this sense of universal altruism, you develop a feeling of responsibility for others: the wish to help them actively overcome their problems. This wish is not selective; it applies equally to all.

The Dalai Lama

I still believe that standing up for the truth of God is the greatest thing in the world. This is the end of life. The end of life is not to be happy. The end of life is not to achieve pleasure and avoid pain. The end of life is to do the will of God, come what may.

Martin Luther King Jr.

Our lives don't really belong to us, you see — they belong to the world, and in spite of our efforts to make sense of it, the world is a place beyond our understanding.

Paul Auster

There is another world, but it is in this one.

Paul Éluard

And did you get what / you wanted from this life, even so? / I did. / And what did you want? / To call myself beloved, to feel myself / beloved on the earth.

Raymond Carver

By the time you read this, it is dark on the next page.

W.S. Merwin

Death twitches my ear. "Live," he says. "I am coming."

Virgil

☙

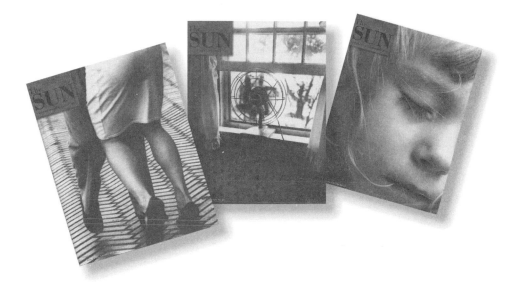

Subscribe To *The Sun*

In the publishing world *The Sun* is a rare exception: an independent, ad-free magazine sustained by loyal readers who appreciate its honest and compassionate approach to the human condition. *The Sun* isn't strictly a literary magazine, though each issue includes memoirs, fiction, and poetry. It isn't self-consciously spiritual, though its contributors celebrate the mystery at the heart of our existence. Nor is it overtly political, though each issue features an in-depth interview with a provocative thinker who challenges the status quo. On presenting *The Sun* its Independent Press Award for Best Writing, *Utne* described the magazine as "an intimate forum where some of the finest contemporary writers share their most polished and provocative prose." For more information or to order a subscription, please visit **www.thesunmagazine.org**.

Also Available

The Mysterious Life Of The Heart
WRITING FROM *THE SUN* ABOUT PASSION, LONGING, AND LOVE

SOFTCOVER: $18.95

In fifty personal essays, short stories, and poems that originally appeared in *The Sun*, some of the magazine's most talented writers explore the enigma of love.

Stubborn Light
THE BEST OF *THE SUN*, VOLUME III

SOFTCOVER: $22.95

The most compelling works from *The Sun*'s second decade.

A Bell Ringing In The Empty Sky
THE BEST OF *THE SUN*, VOLS. I & II

SOFTCOVER; EACH: $15.95

This two-volume set includes the finest interviews, short stories, essays, photos, and poems from the first decade of *The Sun*.

Sunbeams
A BOOK OF QUOTATIONS

SOFTCOVER: $15.95

Our first collection of memorable Sunbeams from the magazine's back page.

Four In The Morning
ESSAYS BY SY SAFRANSKY

SOFTCOVER: $13.95

Thirty of editor Sy Safransky's best essays.

To order books or subscribe to *The Sun*,
please visit www.thesunmagazine.org.